SO-BNA-177

QUALITATIVE AND QUANTITATIVE RESEARCH METHODS READER

A CANADIAN ORIENTATION

DISCARD

Humber College Library
3199 Lakeshore Blvd. West
Toronto, ON   M8V 1K8

QUALITATIVE AND QUANTITATIVE RESEARCH METHODS READER

A CANADIAN ORIENTATION

edited by

JOHN A. WINTERDYK
Mount Royal College

LINDA COATES
University of Lethbridge

SCOTT BRODIE
Simon Fraser University

PEARSON

Prentice Hall

Toronto

Library and Archives Canada Cataloguing in Publication

Qualitative and quantitative research methods reader : a Canadian orientation / edited by John A. Winterdyk, Linda Coates, Scott Brodie.

ISBN 0-13-126818-X

1. Social sciences—Research—Methodology—Textbooks. I. Winterdyk, John, 1953– II. Coates, Linda Jane, 1966– III. Brodie, Scott, 1973–

H62.Q35 2006   300'.72   C2005-900219-0

Copyright © 2006 Pearson Education Canada, a division of Pearson Canada Inc., Toronto, Ontario.

Pearson Prentice Hall. All rights reserved. This publication is protected by copyright and permission should be obtained from the publisher prior to any prohibited reproduction, storage in a retrieval system, or transmission in any form or by any means, electronic, mechanical, photocopying, recording, or likewise. For information regarding permission, write to the Permissions Department.

This edition is authorized for sale only in Canada.

ISBN 0-13-126818-X

Vice President, Editorial Director: Michael J. Young
Acquisitions Editor: Patty Riediger
Signing Representative: Lise Mills
Executive Marketing Manager: Judith Allen
Associate Editor: Paula Drużga
Production Editor: Söğüt Y. Güleç
Copy Editor: Lenore Latta
Proofreader: Susan McNish
Production Coordinator: Janis Raisen
Manufacturing Coordinator: Susan Johnson
Composition: Phyllis Seto
Art Director: Julia Hall
Cover and Interior Design: Anthony Leung
Cover Image: Digital Vision (left, middle); Comstock (right)

Statistics Canada information is used with the permission of the Minister of Industry, as Minister responsible for Statistics Canada. Information on the availability of the wide range of data from Statistics Canada can be obtained from Statistics Canada's Regional Offices, its World Wide Web site at http://www.statcan.ca, and its toll-free access number 1-800-263-1136.

2 3 4 DPC 09 08 07

Printed and bound in Canada.

The underlying picture of the world is always capable of identification in the form of a set of premises. These premises are constituted by the nature given either explicitly or implicitly to the key objects that comprise the picture.

—Herbert Blumer

(1969:25) *Symbolic Interactionism,*
Englewood Cliffs, NJ: Prentice-Hall.

Contents

PART 3

Preface

With each passing year, the number of research methods books in respective disciplines seems to grow. For those of us who (co)author and/or teach methods courses, it has become a difficult task to find those elusive articles which help students overcome their anxiety surrounding the subject. While different disciplines might favour certain methods over others, the "tools" of the trade are intrinsically universal.

Most textbooks endeavour to integrate relevant examples to illustrate key concepts, major methods, and related subject matter. However, it has been our experience that even if an integrated textbook performs an admirable job of helping students grasp the subject matter, we often have to draw on external material, from a range of sources, to provide more detailed and concrete examples. Therefore, the purpose of this reader is threefold:

- To offer a cross-section of original social science articles to help students understand the nuances of what they are reading and studying in the text.
- To present the articles in a single reader, rather than requiring students or instructors to provide a list of recommended readings— a daunting task to construct.

- To include Canadian-authored articles to illustrate the diversity of research being conducted in Canada, as well as to stimulate future research.

To our knowledge, this is the first methods reader of its type. We have endeavoured to select articles from a wide range of social sciences. We have intentionally tried not to follow the format of any one methods text so as to allow adaptation across disciplines without bias toward any one text. In the Introduction we have included a Cross-Referencing Chart that summarizes the key elements of research methods that can be found in the various articles. At the end of each chapter we have identified a series of questions for each article in an effort to facilitate the reading of these pieces. Our main objective is to provide a Canadian-oriented methods reader that can be readily used in virtually all social science research methods courses without prejudice.

We have carefully selected the articles based on key subject areas and on feedback from various anonymous reviewers. And while we are ultimately responsible for the content and selection, we hope that instructors and students will find this text an invaluable aid when studying research methods.

ACKNOWLEDGMENTS

I would like to thank all the people at Pearson Education Canada who were involved in the process of developing this reader. The folks at Pearson have been most supportive of my various projects over the years, and it has been a true pleasure to work with them. I would particularly like to acknowledge the support of Jennifer Murray in guiding us through various hurdles and of Liz Fritz who pitched in when Jennifer went off to an important event.

I am particularly pleased to acknowledge the support of one of my former students and now co-editor and friend, Scott Brodie, who embraced like a "pro" the opportunity to assist with the reader. I hope that this project is just the beginning of what he will be involved in and/or will produce in the years to come. His talent and skills are inspiring.

Thanks also to Linda, whom I met while a Visiting Endowed Chair at St. Thomas University in Fredericton—her passion for research and willingness to assist in the project, in spite of her hectic schedule and the (then) pending arrival of her first newborn, is greatly appreciated.

And thanks to all my students who, throughout the years, planted the seed for this project. It has always been a joy to watch how many of them did a "180-degree turn" from fearing methods to whole-heartedly embracing them.

Finally, I am indebted to my partner, Rose, and our two boys, Alex and Michael, for their understanding and support. Trying to find balance seems to be a perpetual challenge for me, but their collective strength and wisdom and generous manner have benefited us all. THANK YOU from the bottom of my heart.

John Winterdyk

I would like to thank the reviewers of this reader for taking the time to examine the reader and offer helpful comments. I thank John Winterdyk for all of his work in getting this project going,

and Scott Brodie for making time for this project even while attending graduate school. I also thank the students who persevere through methods and statistics courses with hard work and unfailing determination. You inspire my teaching. It is particularly gratifying for me to have the privilege of teaching students who use the information in these courses to help them critically seek knowledge rather than isolated "facts." Finally, I thank my partner, Blair, whose critical analysis always benefits my work. His help, support, and love of knowledge replenishes and rejuvenates my spirit.

Linda Coates

I have the utmost gratitude for all the writers and editors who, without complaint, dropped everything to assist in building this reader; your attentiveness, wisdom, and patience were greatly appreciated. I would like to thank Dr. John Winterdyk—a mentor, friend, and colleague—for his undying support and confidence in me, a fact that cannot be underscored enough. Finally, thank you to my family and friends for putting up with my constant rambling about the world of science; you have taught me well.

Scott Brodie

We thank all those who provided articles for inclusion in this reader. We would have liked to include many more articles, but we had to be mindful of space. We are grateful for all the support and assistance provided by Paula Drużga at Pearson as she helped us navigate through the logistics of dealing with copyright articles, and for her patience as we searched for representative articles. Finally, we acknowledge our students, whose feedback over the years has played a significant role in our desire to provide such a resource for future research methods students.

QUALITATIVE AND QUANTITATIVE RESEARCH METHODS READER

A CANADIAN ORIENTATION

- What ethical and/or methodological issues required specific attention?

- Did the author(s) draw conclusions that were tightly related to what they studied and how they studied it?

- What inferences were not directly supported by the data?

- How does the article contribute to the field of study?

Finally, as we have already mentioned, with the privilege of becoming educated comes the burden of responsibility. Students who enter into professions where they have power (either directly or indirectly) over others, especially those who have not had the privilege of higher education, must meet their professional obligations and responsibilities to society. As professionals, they may be asked to develop policies or practices, or apply research. If they cannot actively critique research, they greatly increase their chances of failing their societal responsibilities and obligations. The people they serve may even be harmed by their inability to critically evaluate the information or practices they are being asked to apply.

ARTICLE SELECTION

We solicited and/or identified a considerable number of prospective articles for this reader. However, given the objective of the text and recognizing that most articles, because of the nature of engaging in research, address or cover more than one theme, we reduced the number. Therefore, we have endeavoured to provide a cross-section of articles that, in addition to being relatively recent, are readily understandable, and collectively cover all the main themes. As noted below, the chart is intended to facilitate understanding as students learn the concepts and general meaning of research methodology.

USING THE CROSS-REFERENCING CHART

In order to facilitate an instructor's or student's choice of which of the 16 articles to read and when to read them, we have included a chart that lists the features of each article. Under the column heading "Type of Article," we note whenever the publication is not an actual study but an article that raises important issues for the field (e.g., discussion or review articles). Under "Research Design" we list the design of the study (e.g., survey, experiment). A variety of qualitative and quantitative designs is included in this reader. Under "Sample" we record the sampling method used (e.g., convenience, random), while under "Analysis" we list the statistics used (e.g., descriptive, *t*-test, multiple regression). Under "Other Features" we catalogue other noteworthy features of the articles (e.g., discussion of construct validity, response rates). Finally, under "Ethics" we record whether ethical concerns were highlighted in the article. Collectively, these columns cover a majority of the themes and topics covered in most research methods texts.

STUDY QUESTIONS

To help students actively engage with the material they are reading, we have put study questions at the end of each chapter. These questions are designed to alert the student to particular issues that appear in the article. The questions are not intended to cover all of the relevant issues in an article, but to highlight a few. For example, why did the authors use a particular sampling method, and what are the strengths or weaknesses of that method?

FINAL NOTE

In undertaking this project, we are well aware that it would not be possible (within reasonable limits) to provide an article for every key theme, method, ethical situation, or statistical technique. Therefore, we have endeavoured to provide a sufficiently broad selection of Canadian studies which illustrate the main themes found in most research methods textbooks. We have also endeavoured to offer a selection of fairly recent articles from across the social sciences to reach a wider audience as well as to promote an appreciation for how research methods and the associated issues are generic to all the disciplines.

Cross-Referencing Chart

Article	Type of Article	Research Design	Sample	Analysis	Other Features	Ethics
PART I: ISSUES RELATED TO RESEARCH METHODS						
Chapter 1: Andrey, J. (2000). The automobile imperative.	Presentation of theory	n/a	n/a	Descriptive statistics	n/a	n/a
Chapter 2: Brannigan, A., & Gibbs Van Brunschot, E. (1997). Youthful prostitution and child sexual trauma.	Review article	n/a	n/a	n/a	n/a	n/a
Chapter 3: Joseph, J. (2003) on Benton, T., & Craib, I. *Philosophy of Social Science.*	Review of philosophical foundations of knowledge	n/a	n/a	n/a	n/a	n/a
Chapter 4: Lowman, J., & Palys, T. (2001). Limited confidentiality, academic freedom, and matters of conscience: Where does CPA stand?	Discussion; limited confidentiality in inmate research	n/a	n/a	n/a	Balancing professional ethics with statutory obligations (Law)	Confidentiality, public safety & validity

continued

Article	Type of Article	Research Design	Sample	Analysis	Other Features	Ethics
Chapter 5: Procter, S., et al. (2000). The development of an applied whole-systems research methodology in health and social service research.	Presentation of research framework	Surveys from previous research	n/a	n/a	n/a	
Chapter 6: van den Hoonaard, W. C. (2001). Is research-ethics review a moral panic?	Exposition & discussion	n/a	n/a	n/a	Law, morality & ethics; the Wigmore test and erosion of confidentiality	Tri-Council research ethics policy: appropriate for qualitative research?
PART II: QUALITATIVE						
Chapter 7: Agbo, S. A. (2003). Changing school-community relations through participatory research	Primary source research article	Participant-observation; action research	Convenience/purposive; non-probability; available school teachers, community members, executive	Thematic	Various types of member validation; triangulation; face validity; catalytic validity	
Chapter 8: Cleary, J., et al. (2002). Discussing sexual health with a partner.	Primary source research article	Semi-structured interviews	Convenience; non-probability	Grounded theory analysis; open, axial, and selective coding	Grounded theory	
Chapter 9: Downe-Wamboldt, B., & Tamlyn, D. (1997). An international survey of death education trends in faculties of nursing and medicine.	Descriptive exploratory study of "death education" in Canadian and United Kingdom nursing and medicine faculties	Survey Questionnaire	Self-selected respondents from complete population; non-probability	Descriptive statistics	Dealing with low response rates; sampling frame	

continued

Article	Type of Article	Research Design	Sample	Analysis	Other Features	Ethics
Chapter 10: Kidd, S. A., & Kral, M. J. (2002). Suicide and prostitution among street youth.	Primary source research article	1. Qualitative content analysis; analysis of themes; 2. Interview: Semi-structured, open-ended questions; qualitative validation techniques (e.g., transparency)	Convenience/purposive; non-probability; available and willing Toronto youth outreach agency clients, less than 24 yrs old, homeless longer than 1 week; paid $10 in food coupons; non-probability	Descriptive statistics; Fisher's Exact Test	Reactive	
Chapter 11: Risdon, C, Cook, D., & Willms, D. (2000). Gay and lesbian physicians in training.	Primary source research article; inductive article of discrimination against gay and lesbian students in Canadian medical schools; qualitative	Pilot study and study; semi-structured interviews, focus groups, and posting on listserv	Pilot: how obtained not stated. Study: snowball sample and responses to posting on listserv over 3 months; non-probability	Thematic	Triangulation of data, methods, and investigator used; member validation of results	Highlights confidential issues and institute ethics committee approval

PART III: QUANTITATIVE

Article	Type of Article	Research Design	Sample	Analysis	Other Features	Ethics
Chapter 12: Ogborne, A. C., & Smart, R. G. (2001). Public opinion on the health benefits of moderate drinking.	Primary source research article	Secondary analysis of survey data		Descriptive statistics; χ^2; logistic regression; weighted sample	Mentions response rate	
Chapter 13: Pfeifer, J. E., & Ogloff, J. R. P. (2003). Mock juror ratings of guilt in Canada.	Primary source research article	Experiment	Convenience; non-probability	ANOVA; 7-point bipolar scale; dichotomous ratings	Random assignment	
Chapter 14: Sanders, T., & Roberts, J. V. (2000). Public attitudes towards conditional sentencing.	Primary source research article	Telephone surveys and experiment	Representative sample; multistage sampling frame; probability	Descriptive statistics; χ^2	Random assignment (experiment); response rate; random digit dialing	

continued

Article	Type of Article	Research Design	Sample	Analysis	Other Features	Ethics
Chapter 15: Streiner, D. L. (2002). Breaking up is hard to do.	Discussion of statistical practice; theoretical and practical implications	n/a	n/a	Dichotomizing continuous data; correlation; Fisher's Exact Test	n/a	n/a
Chapter 16: Verberg, N., et al. (2000). Gender differences in survey respondents' written definitions of date rape.	Primary source research article; qualitative & quantitative analysis of written definitions of "date rape"	Survey	Self-selected members of a mid-sized Canadian city; non-probability	Descriptive statistics; χ^2; thematic content analysis		

PART 1

Issues Related to Research Methods

Chapter 1

The Automobile Imperative:
Risks of Mobility and Mobility-Related Risks

Jean Andrey

Source: Reprinted from *The Canadian Geographer*, Vol. 44:4, 2000, article by Andrey, J.

INTRODUCTION

Transportation is important to both the Canadian economy and the Canadian way of life. Transport industries (including air, rail, shipping, for-hire trucking and buses) account for 3.9 percent ($27.8 billion) of Canada's gross domestic product and approximately 6.4 percent (730,000) of all jobs in Canada (Transport Canada 1999a). The overall importance of transportation activities is much higher, however, due to the large volume of private transportation, especially by automobiles and trucks. The 1992 Royal Commission on National Passenger Transportation estimated that $103 billion was spent on transportation in 1989; in 1997, the amount was closer to $125 billion (Transport Canada 1998a).

Of the total expenditures, approximately four-fifths is devoted to road transport. The road network itself (over 900,000 kilometres of two-lane equivalent) has an asset value approaching $100 billion (Richardson 1996), with annual expenditures (including construction, maintenance, traffic control and policing) of approximately $11 billion (Nix 1995). A much larger sum, however, is spent by individuals on personal vehicles. In 1998, the average Canadian household spent $6,848 (15% of its budget) on transportation, more than was spent on food; 87 percent of this was used to purchase/lease, maintain, and operate private automobiles (Transport Canada 1999a).

Despite the many advantages of a well-developed transport system and mobile society, increased attention is being focused on the negative impacts of transportation. These impacts—environmental pollution (from emissions and the production and transport of oil), noise, congestive delay and roadway collisions—amount to billions of dollars each year (Litman 1995). Costs associated with accidents are particularly striking. In Canada, over the past decade, approximately 8 million transportation accidents and 40,000 related deaths were reported (Transport Canada 1998b, 1999a), the true costs of which are estimated to be in the order of $200 to $300 billion (based on the costs reported in Miller 1993; Ontario Ministry of Transportation 1994; Bordeleau 1997). The vast majority of these occurred on roads.

In this paper, I focus on the nature of road transportation risks in Canada—on the magnitude of the problem and reasons for its persistence. Based on literature and the analysis of secondary data, I argue that the ultimate root of this problem is the dominance of mobility over safety, both in transportation planning and in individual decision making. I advocate a mobility-based approach to road safety research because of its ability to both improve understanding and contribute to long-term solutions. Links between a mobility-based approach and the geography of road safety are also outlined.

TRANSPORTATION SAFETY OVERVIEW

The Magnitude of the Problem

Over the past century, global auto use has resulted in 30 million deaths and more than 100 million seriously injured people (Navin *et al.* 1997). In Canada, there were 600,000 transportation accidents last year, more than one every minute (Transport Canada 1999a). The word accident is a general term for describing a variety of events, including motor vehicle collisions, airplane engine failures, train derailments, boat groundings and pipeline ruptures. Although many of the most publicized events are associated with modes other than roads, for example the wreck of the Edmund Fitzgerald (1975, 29 killed), the Mississauga derailment (1979, one-half million residents evacuated) and the Dryden plane crash (1989, 24 killed) (Liverman and Wilson 1981; Jones 1992; Halliday 1997), most transportation accidents occur on roads. In fact, 99 percent of all transportation accidents and approximately 93 per-

cent of all related deaths are due to road crashes (Transport Canada 1999a) (Table 1.1). Most victims are occupants of motor vehicles, but a significant number are pedestrians and cyclists (Table 1.2)—citizens who pose little threat to other road users but are themselves exposed to disproportionately high risk levels (e.g., Pucher 1997; Aultman-Hall and Hall 1998).

The seriousness of the road safety problem is underscored by two additional facts. First, because of the young age of many transportation accident victims (Table 1.3), the human toll is more extreme than suggested by absolute tallies. For example, analysis of U.S. data indicates that more pre-retirement years of life are lost in road crashes than from either

Table 1.1 Transportation Accidents in Canada

	Air[1]	Marine[2]	Pipe-line[3]	Road[4]
# Accidents				
Most Recenet Yar[a]	384	487	27	635412
Previous 5 Years[b]	378	668	23	682287
# Fatalities				
Most Recent Year[c]	83	47	0	3064
Previous 5 Years[d]	87	33	0	3361

1 Canadian-registered aircraft, excluding ultralights
2 Canadian and foreign-flag vessels, excluding leisure craft, in Canadian waters
3 Operations in Canada
4 Motor vehicle collisions on roads in Canada
a 1996 for road; 1997 for pipeline; 1998 for other modes
b 1991 to 1995 for road; 1992 to 1996 for pipeline; 1993 to 1997 for other modes
c 1997 for road and pipeline; 1998 for other modes
d 1992 to 1996 for road and pipeline; 1993 to 1997 for other modes

Sources: Transport Canada 1999a; 1999b

Table 1.2 Fatalities by Categories of Road Users

Year	Drivers	Pass-engers	Motor-cyclists	Bi-cyclists	Pedes-trians	Other
1997	1569	822	120	67	403	83
Av. (1992–96)	1682	912	171	73	445	77

Source: Transport Canada 1999b, 42

Table 1.3 Casualties from Motor Vehicle Collisions by Age Group, Canada, 1995

Age Group	# Killed	# Injured	% of All Deaths Due to Motor Vehicle Collisions
0 to 4	70	3997	2.5
5 to 14	149	16830	20.6
15 to 19	419	32689	36.9
20 to 24	431	32726	30.4
25 to 34	634	53004	15.2
34 to 44	500	40334	7.0
45 to 54	333	25943	2.8
55 to 64	243	14618	1.1
65 +	544	15573	0.3
Not stated	24	6086	
Total	3347	241800	1.6

Sources: Transport Canada 1997; Statistics Canada 1997a

heart disease or cancer (Evans 1991). In addition, incident rates are typically higher for road travel than for competing motorized modes, such as air (Evans *et al.* 1990) or rail (Smith 1981).

Notwithstanding the seriousness of today's road accident problem, significant safety gains have been achieved over the past two decades. In the early 1970s there were approximately 8 million passenger automobiles and nearly 11 million licensed drivers in Canada (Statistics Canada various years). The annual number of fatalities (i.e., number of people killed) was approximately 6,000; in fact an all time high of 6,706 deaths was reported for 1973 (Transport Canada 1998b). By the mid-1990s, the number of vehicles and drivers had increased by approximately 65 percent and 75 percent, respectively, and the amount of auto travel per person had increased by almost 40 percent. Nevertheless, the number of fatalities declined to 2,927 in 1998 (Transport Canada 1999b) and the number of injured persons (all levels of injury severity) had more or less stabilized at one-quarter million victims per year (Figure 1.1), which translates into much lower

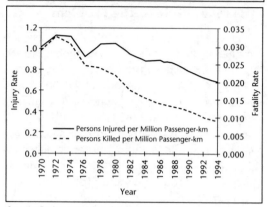

Figure 1.2   Road Traffic Casualty Rates in Canada, 1970 to 1994

Sources: Environment Canada 1995; Transport Canada 1998b

risk rates per unit of travel (Figure 1.2). These reductions are more than just a statistical aberration. In fact, the same general trend has been observed in most developed nations (Hutchinson 1987; Evans 1991).

To what can this safety improvement be attributed? Most attribute the reduced rate of serious collisions to a number of factors that collectively reflect a maturation of the highway system—better vehicle and roadway engineering, a "broad evolution in social norms related to driving" (Oppe 1989; Evans 1991, 345; also see Shinar *et al.* 1999) and improved medicine. Some of the most significant initiatives are listed in Table 1.4. These initiatives are organized in a nine-cell 'Haddon' matrix, based on whether the safety intervention focuses on the road user, vehicle or road environment and whether the measure is intended to prevent crashes or ameliorate harm either during or after the crash. Although it is conceivable that further improvements in casualty rates (i.e., fatal plus non-fatal injuries divided by travel) can be achieved through further refinement of the driver-vehicle-road system (e.g., Sanderson 1996), some road safety experts believe that we have reached the point

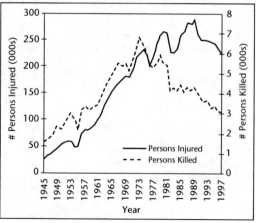

Figure 1.1   Road Traffic Casualties in Canada, 1945 to 1997

Sources: Transport Canada 1998b, 1999b

Table 1.4 Measures That Have Been Taken to Improve Road Safety		
	Road User	**Vehicle**	**Road Environment**
Pre-Crash	• Impaired driving programs • Novice driver training/licensing • Technology-aided law enforcement (e.g., speed photo radar, red light camera)	• Improved brakes • Daytime running and high tail lights • Improved vehicle handling • Vehicle inspections	• Upgrading roads • Median barriers • Remediation of accident-prone sites • Reflective lines
Crash	• Seat belt legislation • Child restraints • Helmet legislation for motorcyclists and cyclists	• Energy-absorbing steering column • Instrument panel changes and padded dash • Side door beams • Roof crush resistance • Windshield glazing • Air bags • Head restraints	• Safer highways furniture (e.g., breakaway poles) • Removal of roadside obstacles
Post-Crash		• Fuel system integrity • Non-flammable materials in occupant compartment	• Improved emergency medicine • Guard rails

Sources: Evans 1991; Myers 1997; Navin et al. 1997; Transport Canada 1999b

of diminishing returns (Whitelegg 1987; Ranney and Simmons 1993). Regardless of whether this is true, the absolute toll remains high, with nearly one percent of Canadians being injured each year in traffic accidents. It is thus important to consider why the problem persists.

Crash Etiology

Up until quite recently, the dominant view in the international road safety community was that driver errors, such as alcohol impairment and inappropriate actions, were the main cause of 80 to 90 percent of crashes. The phrase that was coined was 'the nut behind the wheel' (Polanis 1992). This conclusion was based primarily on police reports of collisions, i.e., on a reporting protocol that is intended to provide information that satisfies legal requirements and documents any violations of the safety code. These data necessarily define crashes in terms of human culpability and proximate

cause: they are, however, insufficient for a complete understanding of driving risk. Indeed, traditional road safety analysis is similar to the dominant view of natural hazards as discussed in Hewitt (1983, 15), where the problem is defined " . . . in the language and apparatus of the accident", where accident implies that outcomes are unexpected and that human error is largely responsible for negative consequences.

Beginning in the 1960s with Ralph Nader's (1965) safety crusade, and accelerating in the 1980s, the driver-centred approach began to be replaced by a philosophy of 'over-engineering' and concepts such as the 'forgiving highway'. The rationale behind this change was that greater reductions in the frequency and consequences of crashes could be more promptly attained by improving the engineered components of the system rather than by modifying driver behaviour. As noted by Waller (1980, 15), while associate director for driver studies at the Highway Safety Research Center at the University of North Carolina,

. . . it is a serious error to consider the vehicle and the environment as noncontributing simply because they meet the currently established standards. Most drivers also meet the currently established standards. After all, driver licensing programs exist precisely to see that this is the case . . . The fact that the "human error" identified in accident causation studies is frequently related to information failure (including recognition errors) strongly suggests that the demands of the driving situation may be more than the driver can handle.

As part of this movement to go beyond the legalistic interpretation of crash etiology, the word accident has been replaced with terms such as crash or collision, and risk levels and contributing factors are discussed instead of primary cause. But in many respects, the dominant approach to road safety research has not changed all that much in the past 40 years: the focus continues to be on individual components of the operating system and on the '3 e' approach for solutions—engineering, enforcement and education. Even today, the road safety community seldom looks beyond the time and place of the collision, or beyond technocratic and legalistic solutions. Indeed, some of the most critical commentaries on road safety research (Hauer 1989; Sabey 1991; Evans 1993) fail to challenge the traditional emphases on behavioural and engineering solutions.

There is an emerging view that the problem is more fundamental than this, that the traditional emphasis on proximate causal factors provides a naive or circumscribed view of the problem—an opportunity to incrementally improve individual components of the system but no opportunity to alter the structure of the problem. Rather, explanation seems to be embedded in ordinary life, in the choices that society has made with respect to transport and land use, and in the tradeoffs that are made between mobility and other social goals including safety. Again, this is consistent with some of the recent thinking in geographical

hazards research that argues that risk is continuously and socially constructed (Hewitt 1997).

RISKS OF MOBILITY

Some of those who argue for a reconceptualization of the road safety problem are geographers. For example, Whitelegg (1983, 153) writes that the current approach

. . . is locked into a fundamental misconception in so far as it assumes that blame, responsibility or engineering inadequacies can explain road traffic accidents. The whole system of motorized transport, mobility patterns, land uses, governmental intervention and large company support has deprived society of realistic alternatives to the motor car and bequeathed a deficient technology with several societal disbenefits. Long term solutions to the problem of road traffic accidents involve basic change to this system's design. Anything less will continue to reinforce the present trajectory.

The argument by Whitelegg is consistent with ideas presented by critics of the traditional natural hazards research paradigm (Torry 1979; Hewitt 1983), i.e., the hazardous event cannot be understood or solved if one removes it from the political, social, economic and natural context from which it arises. The context within which automobile collisions arise is the automobile culture. One could therefore argue that the ultimate cause is the auto-mobility imperative.

If auto-mobility is at the core of the problem, then a mobility-based approach is needed in research and accident countermeasure design. In the mobility-based approach, the focus is on both the travel characteristics of society in general as well as the specific travel environments that expose people to elevated levels of risk. The former deals mainly with the quantity of exposure, whereas the latter focuses on quality of exposure. The mobility-based approach is different than either the driver-centred model or the engineering solution because it challenges the tenet that travel of any amount under any condition is acceptable. Furthermore, the mobility perspective is both inherently geographical and practical, as suggested by Tolley and Turton (1995, 321–322) in their recent textbook entitled *Transport Systems, Policy and Planning*

... it is evident that the 'three Es' have, to date, collectively failed to remove the scourge of RTAs [road traffic accidents] from society. We are left with the prevailing view that 'accidents are accidents', an inevitable, inescapable consequence of human frailty in a complex world, a regrettable but acceptable tragedy (as long as it does not happen to you). But accidents are 'space-time events', collisions between vehicles and people going to various destinations at various times in order to meet some need that could not be satisfied at the places where the journeys started. In other words, accidents are a result of movement which is spatially and temporally explicable. These factors are ignored in the traditional view—yet they can actually be influenced much more by policy than can human error or behaviour (Tolley and Turton, 1995, 321–322).

Linkages between Quantity of Exposure and Safety

The association between mobility and safety has been recognized for at least 50 years (Smeed 1949). In simplest terms, without mobility there would be no accidents; as mobility increases, accident involvements increase, and, as mobility decreases, incidents decrease. For example, the number of fishing vessels involved in shipping incidents in Atlantic Canada decreased by more than one-half from 1994 to 1997 as fishing activity declined (Transportation Safety Board of Canada 1998). Also, decreased highway casualties have been associated with both the energy crisis in the 1970s (Agent *et al.* 1976; Haight 1994) and high unemployment in the 1980s (Mercer 1987), both of which reduced travel.

The relationship between mobility and collisions is positive and typically non-linear at both the societal and individual level.

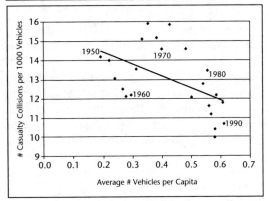

Figure 1.3 Motor Vehicle Ownership versus Collision Rate in Canada, 1950 to 1994

Sources: Statistics Canada Catalogue 53-219 various years; Transport Canada 1998b

Countries with low levels of mobility tend to have low numbers of collisions but high rates per unit of travel (e.g., Jacobs and Sayer 1983; Vasconcellos 1999). As the degree of motorization increases, collisions also increase, but at a slower rate than travel. This results in decreased casualty rates, as shown for Canada in Figures 1.3 and 1.4. Similarly, individuals who drive more tend to be involved in more

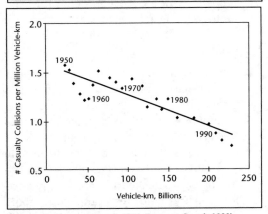

Figure 1.4 Auto Travel versus Casualty Rate in Canada, 1950 to 1994

Sources: Environment Canada 1995; Transport Canada 1998b

collisions but have lower crash rates per kilo-metre travelled than those who drive less (e.g., Janke 1991). Put another way, we could say that the marginal risks associated with motorized travel are quite low.

At some point, however, it is important to ask whether marginal risks and rates based on travel are appropriate indicators of societal safety. Although they are crucial for understanding the various risk factors that affect safety and are useful for documenting the relative safety of different transport modes, they ignore the direct link between mobility and safety and thus create an illusion that safer travel per kilometre translates into less risk for citizens. It is necessary, therefore, to consider not just whether rates are too high but whether the total cost to society is acceptable. Unfortunately, there is little evidence that society is doing this. Indeed there is evidence of the opposite. Consider the following three trends:

1. Instead of reaping the safety benefits of improved vehicles and highways, people travel more. This produces what is, in effect, a societal-level risk homeostatic response. Figure 1.5 compares casualty rates in Canada per kilometre of travel versus per capita. While the former has dropped substantially over the past two decades, the latter has changed much less. In fact, the probability of a Canadian being hurt in a motor vehicle accident today is similar to what it was in the 1970s and is higher than what it was in the 1950s.

2. Choice has been removed or at least made very difficult. In many places and circumstances, there is no viable alternative to the automobile; the freedom once offered by the discretionary use of automobiles has been transformed into an automobile imperative. The positive feedback loop that has been established between segregated, low-density land uses and automobile dependence continues to erode the viability

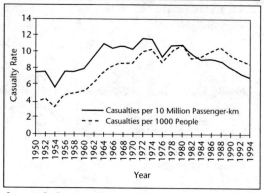

Figure 1.5   Canadian Road Casualty Trends per Unit of Travel versus per Capita, 1950 to 1994

Sources: Environment Canada 1995; Statistics Canada 1996b; Transport Canada 1998b

of alternate modes. As shown in Figure 1.6, Canadians are becoming increasingly auto-focused. Nationally, auto travel accounts for approximately 93 percent of all passenger movements (Statistics Canada 1994) and 81 percent of all kilometres travelled (Environment Canada 1998). In 1996, each Canadian took an average of only 46 trips on some form of urban transit, the lowest level in the past 25 years (Statistics Canada 1997b; also see Pucher 1998). Despite all the rhetoric about sustainable transportation and transportation demand management, there is little evidence that automobile alternatives are being seriously considered in Canada, or indeed in most other developed nations of the world.

3. Transport systems continue to be planned with mobility in mind and safety as an add-on. We do not work to solve the problem but merely to manage it. As noted by Haight (1985), safety considerations are not fully integrated into transportation planning. This is because the transport engineers' assignment is normally to promote mobility, and then to attempt to maximize safety for what-

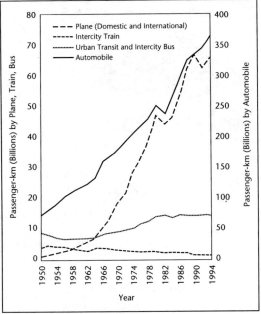

Figure 1.6 Estimates of How Canadians Travel, 1950 to 1994

Source: Environment Canada 1995

mobility are in conflict and some tradeoff is required, safety is typically the loser, because it is difficult to implement regulations and strategies that call for increasing safety at the expense of mobility. This point is also made in a study by Koltzow (1993) in which in-depth interviews were conducted with top-level decision makers in the road sector in Norway. Results suggest that impediments to safety intervention are tied to the perception that road mobility is of primary importance because it brings economic productivity and a preferred lifestyle. As a consequence there is more lobbying for mobility than for safety, and, since the same officials are responsible for both, mobility concerns normally take precedence. As a result, few safety initiatives seek to manage mobility. The obvious exceptions are drunk driving laws and speed limits.

MOBILITY-RELATED RISKS

Linkages between Quality of Exposure and Safety

A mobility perspective is useful for considering not only how the quantity of exposure contributes to health risks, but also how the quality of exposure defines risk patterns over time and space for different driver groups. Young drivers' accident patterns provide an interesting example. Prior to graduated licensing the aggregate accident-involvement rate of Ontario drivers aged 16–19 was 3.6 times higher than the rate for 25–59 year old drivers (Doherty and Andrey 1998) (Table 1.5). It is tempting to interpret the results as meaning that young drivers are three and one-half times as likely to crash as middle-aged drivers, given the same trip. But this interpretation would be flawed because drivers of different ages do not have the same composite driving patterns; a greater proportion of youth driving is done in cities, on weekends and at night, all of which are associated with higher accident-involvement rates for all driver groups.

ever engineering facilities are needed (Haight 1994). Interestingly, sometimes road safety is used as a proxy argument for interests promoting mobility, even if the safety implications have not been estimated or are unknown (e.g., Koltzow 1993; I experienced this first-hand when I met with Ontario Ministry of Transport officials in January, 2000, to discuss the proposed re-alignment of Highway 7); this is because of the broad public appeal of the concept of safe transportation.

This preeminence of mobility over other societal goals is also evident in the safety initiatives that are adopted. Safety measures tend to be either mobility-enhancing (e.g., upgraded roads; improved tires, brakes and headlights; better road signs) or mobility-neutral (e.g., improved crashworthiness of vehicles, seat belt legislation) (Evans 1991). When safety and

Empirical analysis shows that young drivers as a group are at much greater risk than middle-aged drivers in some circumstances but have similar involvement rates for other situations, as shown in Table 1.5. Of course, these rates are only estimates because they were derived from government data bases, which are characterized by two classic problems: under-reporting of accidents and limited exposure data. Still, they highlight how risk varies from one situation to another even for the same driver group.

Aggregate accident rates for different communities or regions are also of interest, but are difficult to estimate and problematic to compare. In addition to methodological problems (e.g., lack of travel data or through-flow traffic inflating per capita rates), there are locational differences in several variables that affect either accident propensity or accident severity (e.g., roadway design and geometrics, traffic

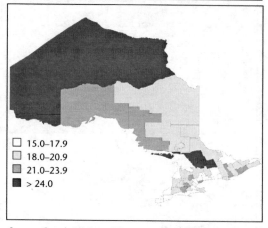

Figure 1.7   Number of Traffic Collisions (All Severities) per 1000 People in 1995

☐ 15.0–17.9
☐ 18.0–20.9
▨ 21.0–23.9
■ > 24.0

Sources: Ontario Ministry of Transportation 1995; Statistics Canada 1995

conditions, driver demographics, vehicle fleet composition). As an illustration, Figure 1.7 provides per capita road collision rates for the various counties and regional municipalities of Ontario in 1995. The relatively high rates in parts of northern Ontario and the more moderate rates in the most southerly jurisdictions could reflect differences in the quantity of exposure, but this is likely to be a minor factor. Although county-level travel data are not available, a 1988 Ontario travel survey suggests that travel quantity is similar for northern parts of Ontario and urban areas in the southern part of the province (Chipman *et al.* 1991). Therefore, differences are more likely due to variations in the nature of travel, for example road types and traffic characteristics. In other words, quality of exposure can be just as important as quantity of exposure in understanding accident patterns.

Weather Hazards

The aspect of exposure that fits best with traditional geographic hazards research is weather,

Table 1.5	Casualty Collision Involvement Rates, Ontario Drivers, 1988		
	Rate per Million Driver-km		**Young Drivers' Relative Risk**
	16–19 Yr Olds	**25–59 Yr Olds**	
Aggregate Data	4.4	1.2	3.6
Speed Limit Time of Day			
60 kph 0500–0959	3.5	1.0	3.5
1000–1459	7.1	1.9	3.8
1500–1959	7.0	1.9	3.7
2000–2359	7.9	2.0	4.0
0000–0459	15.7	6.9	2.3
70 to 90 kph 0500–0959	2.7	0.8	3.4
1000–1459	2.6	0.6	4.2
1500–1959	2.9	0.7	4.2
2000–2359	2.7	1.1	2.4
0000–0459	9.7	7.1	1.4
100 kph 0500–0959	1.4	0.6	2.5
1000–1459	1.1	0.6	1.7
1500–1959	1.4	0.8	1.7
2000–2359	0.9	1.0	0.9
0000–0459	2.8	1.6	1.8

Source: Doherty and Andrey 1998, 239

and not surprisingly, geographers have contributed more to this area of traffic safety research than any other. In fact, most of the early investigations of weather-related traffic risk were conducted under the rubric of the natural hazards research paradigm and focused on the disruptive impact of extreme snowfall events (Rooney 1967; Earney and Knowles 1974; de Freitas 1975; Changnon 1979). More recently the emphasis has been on routine weather conditions, but the focus on precipitation continues. The interest in precipitation stems in large part from the fact that rain and snow are tangible hazards, and the associated physical changes in visibility and road friction are reasonably well understood. What is not well understood, however, are driver responses to inclement weather and the degree to which these are able to compensate for the added risk.

While various methodological approaches have been used (Andrey and Olley 1990), most studies attempt to estimate the crash risk during precipitation relative to dry conditions through the comparison of crash data for matched time periods. Results from such studies in the United Kingdom (Haghigh-Talab 1973; Codling 1974; Smith 1982), the United States (Satterthwaite 1976; Sherretz and Farhar 1978; Bertness 1980) and Canada (Mende 1982; Andrey 1989; Andrey and Yagar 1993; Suggett 1998) all indicate that the collision rates increase substantially during precipitation. Risk estimates vary from study to study, but it is difficult to know what exactly these variations mean, since there are differences not only in storm types and local geography, but also in accident reporting systems and the spatial and temporal scale of analysis. Overall, however, the results suggest that property damage rates typically double and injury rates increase by approximately 50 percent during precipitation events.

These results indicate that weather is an important risk factor in road travel and that driver compensation is insufficient to offset the dangers associated with reduced visibility and friction. Interestingly, a study by Andrey and Knapper (1993) established that Ontario drivers are aware of the added risk associated with travel during inclement weather but make only minimal adjustments in their driving. For example, only a small minority alter travel plans. The majority of drivers indicate that they drive more slowly during inclement weather, but a separate survey by Doherty *et al.* (1993) indicates that, while travel speeds are reduced, the reduced speeds still tend to be higher than the posted speed limits. The resulting conclusion is that the mobility imperative is stronger than people's concerns about safety when faced with less than ideal driving conditions.

Nighttime and Young Drivers

A second example of research on situational risks has quite a different ending. This time the focus is on the elevated risks of young drivers at night. Several studies have documented risk levels by time of day, and it is clear that, on a mileage basis, nighttime driving, especially after midnight, is more risky than daytime travel for drivers in general (Stewart and Sanderson 1984; Schwing and Kamerud 1988; Massie *et al.* 1995), mainly because of reduced visibility and the higher incidence of alcohol impairment at night. For young drivers, however, the problem is particularly acute, with casualty-involvement rates (per million kilometres of driving) rising to double digits as shown in Table 1.5. It is partially on this basis that a number of jurisdictions have introduced laws that restrict the nighttime driving of young people.

In many U.S. jurisdictions, driving restrictions are a byproduct of city ordinances that impose a general curfew on young people, typically those aged under 18. A 1996 U.S. Justice Department survey found curfews in 73 percent of the 200 largest U.S. cities (Holewa 1997). These curfews are intended to keep young people off the street during specified hours (e.g., 11 p.m. to 6 a.m.) mainly because of crime concerns, but they also have been associated with decreases in road crash involvement (Preusser *et al*. 1984; Levy 1988).

In other jurisdictions, a different approach is being taken—one that specifically targets driving. Graduated driver licensing programs are being introduced. These programs are designed to curtail driving that is particularly challenging or high risk so as to give new drivers the opportunity to develop skills (and maturity) in low risk situations. The gradual extension of driving privileges occurs as experience is gained and tests are passed, thus the term graduated licensing. Jurisdictions that have implemented graduated licensing programs include New Zealand in 1987; Victoria, Australia, in 1987; four Canadian provinces— Ontario and Nova Scotia in 1994 and New Brunswick and British Columbia in 1998; and some American states; as of 1999, 11 states had matched or exceeded all components of a model Graduated Driver Licensing law drafted by the National Committee on Uniform Traffic Law (NHTSA 1999). Each jurisdiction has somewhat different driving restrictions. They may relate to the type of vehicle that can be driven, the type of roads that can be driven on, the number and seating position of passengers, and the blood alcohol limit of the driver. A common element, however, is a total ban on 'nighttime' driving. For example, Ontario novice drivers with a G1 license must not drive between midnight and 5 a.m.

As would be expected, evaluations of graduated licensing indicate substantial reductions in crash rates for novice/young drivers, both overall and more specifically for nighttime driving (Langley *et al*. 1997; Ontario Government 1998; NHTSA 1999). Perhaps more important, however, is the fact that graduated licensing systems are the first serious attempt to manage mobility for safety reasons since drunk driving legislation. This is a major break with tradition. Some might argue that these programs are not all that bold in that they target young people, who have little political clout. Interestingly, however, some experts and policy makers are now discussing the potential merit of driving restrictions or graduated de-licensing programs for older drivers (Hildebrand and Wilson 1989; Transportation Research Board Committee on Operator Education and Regulation 1994).

THE RISK OF GEOGRAPHY VERSUS THE GEOGRAPHY OF RISK

Virtually all of the discussion to this point has focused on the links between travel patterns and road safety. In large part this is a discussion of the risk of geography, i.e., the risk of being Canadian—of adopting a highly mobile lifestyle, of being almost totally dependent on automobile travel, and of driving in less than ideal circumstances. It does not, however, provide insight into the geography of risk per se, i.e., place differences either within Canada or between nations. This is not because the mobility approach that is being advocated cannot inform this type of study. Quite the opposite, I would argue that a mobility-based approach, which is founded on the concepts of quantity and quality of exposure, is necessary for understanding place differences. Rather, data limitations restrict what can currently be said about the geography of road safety.

It is possible to compile information on accident frequencies for different jurisdictions and to map the results. Several such studies have been completed over the past decade, indicating that there are substantial locational differences in accident experience both in Canada and in other countries (Baker *et al*. 1987; Whitelegg 1987; Baker *et al*. 1991; Joly *et al*. 1992; Pouliot *et al*. 1994; Edwards 1996). In a similar vein, Figure 1.8 provides accident data for the various provinces and territories of Canada, and Table 1.6 indicates

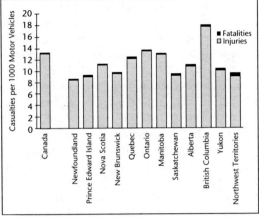

Figure 1.8 Casualty Rates by Province, 1996

Casualties per 1000 Motor Vehicles

■ Fatalities
□ Injuries

Canada, Newfoundland, Prince Edward Island, Nova Scotia, New Brunswick, Quebec, Ontario, Manitoba, Saskatchewan, Alberta, British Columbia, Yukon, Northwest Territories

Source: Transport Canada 1998b

how Canada compares with selected other countries. But the rates that are reported do not incorporate quantity and quality of exposure, largely because such data do not exist or are not comparable between locations. As a result, it is impossible to know whether accident variations are the result of differences in the extent and nature of travel or, indeed, are related to other factors such as regional socio-demographics. Without detailed, disaggregate travel data, studies of the geography of risk stop at the hypothesis stage; an argument is made that there are

Table 1.6 Fatality Rates, 1993–1995, OECD Countries

	# Deaths per 10,000 Motor Vehicles
Sweden	1.31
Norway	1.32
United Kingdom	1.46
Switzerland	1.68
Japan	1.76
Australia	1.84
Canada	**1.96**
Germany	1.99
Netherlands	2.00
United States	2.17

Source: Transport Canada 1998b

spatial differences, but the importance of place in understanding these differences cannot be fully explored.

It is encouraging to note that, at a 1997 meeting of the Canadian Council of Motor Vehicle Administrators, there was unanimous support for the collection of exposure to risk data so that analysts can determine the relative risk of collisions for various factors in the road system. Such data would enable the further development of a mobility-based approach in road safety research, and could lay the foundation for more insightful studies of the geography of road safety risk in Canada.

CONCLUDING COMMENTS: TOWARD A MOBILITY-BASED APPROACH

Road accidents represent a significant technological hazard in Canada, accounting for approximately one-quarter of a million injured persons and 3,000 deaths each year. Trend data indicate that, while accident rates per unit of travel have declined over the past 25 years, largely due to improved engineering, education and enforcement, casualty levels and monetary costs remain high largely because of the automobility imperative. In this paper, I have attempted to demonstrate that the ultimate root of this problem is the dominance of mobility over safety, both in transportation planning and in individual decision making, and I have argued for a mobility-based approach to road safety research. What might such an approach look like? Are there examples of this type of analysis in current literature? In the remainder of the paper, I will attempt to provide a partial answer to these questions.

The defining characteristic of a mobility-based approach to road safety research is an emphasis on understanding how travel patterns affect risk patterns, i.e., a recognition that traffic accidents are time-space events that are embedded in human activity patterns. Conceptually, the main advantage of this approach is that it encourages people to consider safety as something that is doubly derived, whereby accidents are a product of travel, and travel is derived from spatial complementarity, i.e., the physical separation of supply and demand. A mobility-based approach would engender research that looks beyond the accident scene and considers factors that affect travel patterns—land use and related policies; pricing of transport options; and external influences such as demographics, economic cycles and climate variability. It would provide a much needed complement to driver-centred and engineering-based programs, because it would encourage safety analysts, planners and policy makers to more fully integrate safety considerations in transportation and land use decisions.

Although the term, 'a mobility-based approach', has not been widely used, selected studies in the literature are consistent with this approach. An exemplary illustration is the work of Forsstrom (1984), who developed and implemented a model describing the time-space of commuting risk for public transit users in Stockholm. In terms of understanding historical trends in highway fatalities, a recent study by Chu (1999) underscores the importance of considering changes in travel patterns including shifts from rural to urban driving environments, from peak hour periods to more early morning and mid-day driving, and from mostly male drivers to a more even gender mix. In terms of urban design, studies by Arlinghaus and Nystuen (1991) and Henning-Hager (1986) considered the effects of street geometrics and neighbourhood design on traffic conflicts and road safety in residential areas. From a policy perspective, Allsop and Robertson (1994) demonstrated that fare increases for public transport in London resulted in increased auto use, which increased road casualties; while

Meyerhoff (1978) showed that daylight saving time policies reduce accidents because of decreased exposure to darkness. Another recent example is the apparent link between international trade agreements, the volume of truck traffic on Ontario highways, and traffic fatalities (e.g., Boyle 2000). Finally, from an enforcement perspective, Hodgson *et al.* (1995) used location-allocation models to identify ideal locations for vehicle inspection, and Arthur and Waters (1997) used a geographic information system to evaluate photo radar as a safety intervention. In each of these studies the amount and nature of travel were central to the analysis.

It is especially important that future research carefully examine the implications of a wide range of policy, investment and technology issues that are likely to change the nature of mobility over the next few decades. These include such things as transportation demand management options, infrastructure programs, telework and intelligent vehicle technology. Related to this, it is crucial that the safety community help to identify options that would not only improve safety but would have other benefits as well. A useful starting point would be an examination of the myriad of strategies that have been proposed as congestion relief measures. Some of the proposed measures would appear to have safety benefits, e.g., distance-based vehicle insurance premiums (as discussed by Litman 1997) and separating truck traffic from lighter vehicles (as discussed by Samuel 1999). In most cases, however, the safety implications are not firmly established. A mobility-based approach would encourage safety analysts to first consider the mobility implications of these policies/measures and then estimate how these mobility changes would affect traffic conflicts and road casualties. In this way it would be possible to work toward a more sustainable and safer transportation future.

STUDY QUESTIONS

1. Why did Andrey report the fatality rates as deaths per 10 000?

2. What are the limitations, if any, with the type of data used in Andrey's article?

3. What kind of statistical analysis does Andrey use? Discuss its limitations.

4. How effective is the title in conveying the theme of the article? Explain.

REFERENCES

Agent, K.R., Herd, D.R. and Rizenbergs, R.L. 1976 'First-year effects of the energy crisis on rural highway traffic in Kentucky' *Transportation Research Record 567*, 70–81.

Allsop, R.E. and Robertson, S.A. 1994 'Road casualties in London in relation to public transport policy' *Journal of Transport Economics and Policy 28*, 61–82.

Andrey, J. 1989 'Relationships between weather and traffic safety' unpublished PHD dissertation, Department of Geography, University of Waterloo.

Andrey, J. and Knapper, C.K. 1993 *Weather Hazards: Driver Attitudes and Driver Education, Final Report to the Ontario Coordinator of Highway Safety Research Grant Program* (Downsview: Ministry of Transportation, Ontario, Safety Planning and Policy Branch).

Andrey, J., and Olley, R. 1990 'Relationships between weather and road safety: past and future research directions' *Climatological Bulletin 24*, 123–137.

Andrey, J. and Yagar, S. 1993 'A temporal analysis of rain-related crash risk' *Accident Analysis and Prevention 25*, 465–472.

Arlinghaus, S.L. and Nystuen, J.D. 1991 'Street geometry and flows' *The Geographical Review 22*, 206–214.

Arthur, R.M. and Waters, N.M. 1997 'Formal scientific research of traffic collision data utilizing GIS' *Transportation Planning and Technology 21*, 121–137.

Aultmann-Hall, L. and Hall, F. 1998 'Ottawa-Carleton commuter cyclist on- and off-road incident rates' *Accident Analysis and Prevention 30*, 29–43.

Baker, S.P., Waller, A. and Langlois, J. 1991 'Motor vehicle deaths in children: geographic variations' *Accident Analysis and Prevention 23*, 19–28.

Baker, S., Whitefield, R.A. and O'Neill, B. 1987 'Geographic variations in mortality from motor vehicle crashes' *New England Journal of Medicine 316*, 1384–1387.

Bertness, J. 1980 'Rain related impacts on selected transportation activities and utility services in the Chicago area' *Journal of Applied Meteorology 19*, 545–556.

Bordeleau, B. 1997 'Évaluation et évolution de 1985 à 1994 des couts de l'insécurité routière du Québec' *Proceedings of the Canadian Multidisciplinary Conference X* (Toronto, Ryerson Polytechnic University, June 9–11) 36–46.

Boyle, T. 2000 'Killer road a moving 'warehouse of goods'' *The Toronto Star* 5 September, 2000, A7.

Canadian Council of Motor Transport Administrators 1997 *Proceedings of the Workshop on Road Safety Data and Research Needs* (Ottawa) 19–21.

Changnon, S.A. 1979 'How a severe winter impacts on individuals' *Bulletin of the American Meteorological Society 60*, 110–114.

Chipman. M.L., Macgregor, C., Smiley, A. and Lee-Gosselin, M. 1991 'The role of exposure in comparisons of crash risk among different drivers and driving environments' *Proceedings of the 35th Conference of the Association for the Advancement of Automotive Medicine Toronto* (Des Plaines, IL: Association for the Advancement of Automotive Medicine) 439–450.

Chu, X. 1999 'Effects of changes in travel patterns on highway fatalities' *Accident Analysis and Prevention 31*, 221–227.

Codling, P.J. 1974 'Weather and road accidents' in ed. J.A. Taylor *Climatic Resources and Economic Activity* (Newton Abbot: David and Charles Holdings) 205–222.

De Freitas, C.R. 1975 'Estimation of the disruptive impact of snowfalls in urban areas' *Journal of Applied Meteorology 14*, 1166–1173.

Doherty, S.T. and Andrey, J. 1998 'Young drivers and graduated licensing: the Ontario case' *Transportation 24*, 227–251.

Doherty, S.T., Andrey, J. and Marquis, J.C. 1993 'Driver adjustments to wet weather hazards' *Climatological Bulletin 27*, 154–164.

Earney, F.C. and Knowles, B.A. 1974 'Urban snow hazard: Marquette, Michigan' in ed. G.F. White *Natural Hazards: Local, National, Global* (New York: Oxford University Press) 167–174.

Edwards, J.B. 1996 'Weather-related road accidents in England and Wales: a spatial analysis' *Journal of Transport Geography 4*, 201–212.

Environment Canada. 1995 'Canadian Passenger Transportation Technical Supplement' http://www1.ec.gc.ca/~ind/English/Transpo/Tech_Sup/ Accessed Jan 27, 1998.

——. 1998 'Canadian Passenger Transportation' *State of the Environment Reporting Program* Bulletin No. 98-5 (Ottawa: Environment Canada).

Evans, L. 1991 *Traffic Safety and the Driver.* (New York: Van Nostrand Reinhold).

——. 1993 'Future predictions and traffic safety research' *Transportation Quarterly 47*, 3–18.

Evans, L., Frick, M.C. and Schwing, R.C. 1990 'Is it safer to fly or drive?' *Risk Analysis 10*, 239–246.

Forsstrom, A. 1984 'Methodological approach to the study of commuting accidents' *Geografiska Annaler 66B*, 59–50.

Haghigh-Talab, D. 1973 'An investigation into the relationship between rainfall and road accident frequencies in two cities' *Accident Analysis and Prevention 5*, 343–349.

Haight, F.A. 1985 'Road safety: a perspective and a new strategy' *Journal of Safety Research 16*, 91–98.

——.1994 'Problems in estimating comparative costs of safety and mobility' *Journal of Transport Economics and Policy 28*, 7–29.

Halliday, H.A. 1997 *Wreck! Canada's Worst Railway Accidents* (Toronto: Robin Brass).

Hauer, E. 1989 'The reign of ignorance in road safety: a case for separating evaluation from implementation' in eds. L.N. Moses and I. Savage *Transportation Safety in an Age of Deregulation* (Oxford: Oxford University Press) 56–69.

Henning-Hager, U. 1986 'Urban development and road safety' *Accident Analysis and Prevention 18*, 135–145.

Hewitt, K. 1983 'The idea of calamity in a technocratic age' in *Interpretations of Calamity: From the Viewpoint of Human Ecology*, Hewitt, K. ed. (Boston: Allen & Unwin Inc.) 3–32.

——. 1997 *Regions of Risk: A Geographical Introduction to Disasters* (Harlow, Essex: Longman).

Hildebrand, E. and Wilson, F.R. 1989 'An assessment of elderly driver accident patterns' *Transportation Research Board Annual Meeting Pre-print* (Washington, D.C.).

Hodgson, M.J., Rosing, E. and Zhang, J. 1995 'Location-allocation models for vehicle inspection in transportation networks' *Canadian Association of Geographers Annual Meeting Abstracts* (Montréal: Université du Québec à Montréal, May 31 to June 4) 168.

Holewa, L. 1997 'Curfew laws for kids prove popular' *Toronto Star* Oct. 28th.

Hutchinson, T.P. 1987 *Road Accident Statistics* (Adelaide: Rumsby Scientific Publishing).

Jacobs, G.D. and Sayer, I. 1983 'Road accidents in developing countries' *Accident Analysis Prevention 15*, 337–353.

Janke, M.K. 1991 'Accidents, mileage, and the exaggeration of risk' *Accident Analysis and Prevention 23*, 183–188.

Joly, M.F., Thouez, J.P., Bourbeau, R., Bussière, Y. and Rannou, A. 1992 'Geographical variation in traffic-related mortality and morbidity among pedestrians in Quebec, 1983–1988' *Journal of Advanced Transportation 26*, 61–77.

Jones, R.L. 1992 'Canadian disasters: an historical survey' *Natural Hazards 5*, 43–51.

Koltzow, K. 1993 'Road safety rhetoric versus road safety politics' *Accident Analysis and Prevention 25*, 647–657.

Langley, J.D., Wagenaar, A.C., and Begg, D.J. 1997 'An evaluation of the New Zealand graduated driver licensing system' *Accident Analysis and Prevention 28*, 139–146.

Levy, D.T. 1988 'The effects of driving age, driver education, and curfew laws on traffic fatalities of 15–17 year olds' *Risk Analysis 8*, 569–574.

Litman, T. 1995 *Transportation Cost Analysis: Techniques, Estimates and Implications* (Victoria: Victoria Transport Policy Institute).

——. 1997 'Distance-based vehicle insurance as a TDM strategy' *Transportation Quarterly 51*, 119–131.

Liverman, D. and Wilson, J.P. 1981 'The Mississauga train derailment and evacuation, 10–16 November, 1979' *The Canadian Geographer 25*, 365–375.

Massie, D.L, Campbell, K.L. and Williams, A.F. 1995 'Traffic accident involvement rates by driver age and gender' *Accident Analysis and Prevention 27*, 73–78.

Mende, J.I. 1982 'An analysis of snowstorm related accidents in Metropolitan Toronto' MENG dissertation, Civil Engineering Department, University of Toronto.

Mercier, G.W. 1987 'Influences on passenger vehicle casualty accident frequency and severity: unemployment, driver gender, driver age, drinking driving and restraint device use' *Accident Analysis and Prevention 19*, 231–236.

Meyerhoff, N.J. 1978 'The influence of daylight saving time on motor vehicle fatal traffic accidents' *Accident Analysis and Prevention 10*, 207–221.

Miller, T. 1993. 'Costs and functional consequences of U.S. roadway crashes' *Accident Analysis and Prevention 25*, 593–607.

Myers, R. 1997 'Canada motor vehicle safety standards: a description' *Proceedings of the Canadian Multidisciplinary Conference X* (Toronto: Ryerson Polytechnic University, June 9–11) 323–351.

Nader, R. 1965 *Unsafe At Any Speed.* (New York: Grossman Publishing).

Navin, F., Ho, E. and Johnson, M. 1997 'A model for road safety planning: the theory' *Proceedings of the Canadian Multidisciplinary Conference X* (Toronto: Ryerson Polytechnic University, June 9–11) 47–56.

NHTSA (National Highway Traffic Safety Administration), U.S. Department of Transportation 1999 *State Legislative Fact Sheet: Graduated driver licensing system* http://www.nhtsa.dot.gov/people/outreach/safesobr/19qp/factsheets/graduated.html Accessed August 12, 1999.

Nix, F. 1995 *Transportation in Canada: A Statistical Overview* (Ottawa: Transportation Association of Canada).

Ontario Government 1998 'Government of Ontario Press Releases' http://www.newswire.ca/government/ontario/english/releases/May1998/15/C3754.htm/ Accessed May 21, 1998.

Ontario, Ministry of Transportation 1994 *The Social Cost of Motor Vehicle Crashes in* Ontario (Downsview: Ministry of Transportation, Ontario).

——. 1995 *Ontario Road Safety Annual Report* (Downsview: Ministry of Transportation, Ontario, Safety Research Office).

Oppe, S. 1989 'Macroscopic models for traffic and traffic safety' *Accident Analysis and Prevention 21*, 225–232

Polanis, S.F. 1992 'Reducing traffic accidents through traffic engineering' *Transportation Quarterly 46*, 235–242.

Pouliot, M., Morin, D. et Vandersmissen, M-H. 1994 'Les accidents de la route et les contraventions routière au Québec: analyse géographique' *Le Géographe canadien 38*, 229–239.

Preusser, D.F., Williams, A.F., Zador, P.L. and Blomberg, R.D. 1984 'The effect of curfew laws on motor vehicle crashes' *Law and Policy 6*, 115–128.

Pucher, J. 1997 'Bicycling boom in Germany: a revival engineered by public policy' *Transportation Quarterly 51*, 31–46.

——. 1998 'Back on track' *Alternatives Journal 24*, 26–34.

Ranney, T.A. and Simmons, L.A. 1993 'Emerging trends in roadway transport and their impact on highway safety' *Transportation Quarterly* October, 565–582.

Richardson, S. 1996 *Valuation of the Canadian Road and Highway System*, TP 1279E (Ottawa: Transport Canada).

Rooney, J.R. Jr. 1967 'The urban snow hazard in the United States' *Geographical Review 57*, 538–559.

Sabey, B.E. 1991 'Road safety: research and reality' *Transportation 18*, 111–130.

Samuel, P. 1999 'Traffic congestion: a solvable problem' *Issues in Science and Technology* Spring, 49–56.

Sanderson, R. 1996 *Canadian Road Safety and Public Highway Infrastructure* TP12801E (Ottawa: Transport Canada).

Satterthwaite, S.P. 1976 'An assessment of seasonal and weather effects on the frequency of road accidents in California' *Accident Analysis and Prevention 8*, 87–96.

Schwing, R.C. and Kamerud, D.B. 1988 'The distribution of risks: vehicle occupant fatalities and time of the week' *Risk Analysis 8*, 127–133.

Sherretz, L.A. and Farhar, B.C. 1978. An analysis of the relationship between rainfall and the occurrence of traffic accidents. *Journal of Applied Meteorology 17*, 711–715.

Shinar, D., Schechtman, E. and Compton, R. 1999 'Trends in safe driving behaviors and in relation to trends in health maintenance behaviors in the USA: 1985–1995' *Accident Analysis and Prevention 31*, 497–503.

Smeed, R.J. 1949 'Some statistical aspects of road safety research' *Journal of Royal Statistical Society* CXII(Part 1), 1–23.

Smith, T. 1981 'Death on the road' *New Scientist 92*, 1276, 260–261.

Smith, K. 1982 'How seasonal and weather conditions influence road accidents in Glasgow' *Scottish Geographical Magazine 98*, 103–114.

Statistics Canada 1994 Catalogue 53-215 *Passenger Bus and Urban Transit Statistics* (Ottawa).

——.1995 Catalogue 91-213 *Annual Demographic Statistics* (Ottawa).

——. 1996a Catalogue 15-001 *Gross Domestic Product by Industry* (Ottawa).

——. 1996b *CANSIM* D31248 (Ottawa).

——. 1997a Catalogue 84-208 *Causes of Death* (Ottawa).

——. 1997b Catalogue 50-002 *Surface and Marine Transport* (Ottawa).

——. various years Catalogue no. 53-219 *Road Motor Vehicles—Registrations* (Ottawa).

Stewart, D.E. and Sanderson, R.W. 1984 'The measurement of risk on Canada's roads and highways' in *Transport Risk Assessment: Proceedings of a Symposium on Risk in Transport. 3rd Symposium of Institute for Risk Research*, ed. S. Yagar (Waterloo: University of Waterloo Press) 1–21.

Suggett, J. 1998 'The effects of precipitation on traffic safety' MSC thesis, Department of Geography, University of Regina.

Tolley, R. and Turton, B. 1995 *Transport Systems, Policy and Planning: A Geographical Approach*. (Essex: Longman Scientific and Technical).

Torry, W.I. 1979 'Hazards, hazes and holes: a critique of 'The environment as hazard' and general reflections on disaster research' *The Canadian Geographer 23*, 368–383.

Transport Canada 1997 *Canadian Motor Vehicle Collision Statistics* 1995 TP 3322 (Ottawa: Transport Canada).

——. 1998a *Transportation in Canada 1997 Annual Report* TP13198E. http://www.tc.gc.ca/t-facts/t.facts2e/ Accessed June 15, 1998.

——. 1998b *Safety Road Collisions and Casualties* http://www.tc.gc.ca/roadsafety/rsindx_e.htm Accessed June I5, 1998.

——. 1999a *Transportation in Canada 1998 Annual Report* TP13198E. http://www.tc.gc.ca/t-facts/t-facts2e/ Accessed July 13, 1999.

——. 1999b *Road Safety Statistics* http://www.tc.gc.ca/roadsafety/rsindx_e.htm Accessed April 10, 2000.

Transport Safety Board of Canada 1998 *Annual Report of Parliament 1997* (Ottawa: Minister of Public Works and Government Services).

Transportation Research Board Committee on Operator Education and Regulation 1994 'The licensing of older drivers' *Transportation Research Circular* #429 ISSN 0097-8515 (Washington, DC: National Research Council).

Vasconcellos, E.A. 1999 'Urban development and traffic accidents in Brazil' *Accident Analysis and Prevention 31*, 319–328.

Waller, P. 1980 'In traffic crashes—is human error the only culprit?' *Traffic Safety 80*, 14–16.

Whitelegg, J. 1983 'Road safety: defeat, complicity and the bankruptcy of science' *Accident Analysis and Prevention 15*, 153–160.

——. 1987 'A geography of road traffic accidents' *Transactions, Institute of British Geographers 12*, 161–176.

Chapter 2

Youthful Prostitution and Child Sexual Trauma

Augustine Brannigan and Erin Gibbs Van Brunschot

Source: Reprinted from the *International Journal of Law and Psychiatry*, Vol. 20, Brannigan et al., "Youthful prostitution and child sexual trauma." pp. 337–354 (1997), with permission from Elsevier.

INTRODUCTION

Over the past two decades, research has established the centrality of the family as an institutional crucible in the formation of delinquent conduct and attitudes (Loeber & Stouthamer-Loeber, 1986; McCord, 1979; Riley & Shaw, 1985; West & Farrington, 1977). Effective family functioning involving positive psychosocial attachments appears more important than family structure (Laub & Sampson, 1988; Van Voorhis et al., 1988). These observations are also consistent with the first systematic studies of delinquents from the 1920s and 1930s (Glueck & Glueck, 1934).

PROSTITUTION: A CONTINUITY IN VICTIMIZATION OVER THE LIFE CYCLE?

In the case of prostitution, the family's influence has been examined in the context of childhood abuse and subsequent trauma. A recurring thesis in recent work is that childhood victimization, and sexual victimization in particular, leads to prostitution, a role itself characterized by sexual exploitation. But is it generally true that specific childhood traumas preordain the nature of the adult delinquency? By contrast, in the case of the robber, thief or shoplifter, few analysts would attribute larcenous misconduct in later life to the child's earlier material deprivation, as though the adult crime was fixated on the childhood experience. "Today, it is not reasonable to assume that offenders tend to specialize in particular types of crime; research shows that they do not" (Gottfredson & Hirschi, 1990, p. 266). The typical robber is just as likely to deal drugs, to steal, to drink and drive, and to commit assault or murder.

Likewise, in the case of maltreated children, Zingraff et al. (1993, p. 173) report that "specific forms of maltreatment are not especially predictive of any offense type." But in the case of prostitutes, many experts suggest that incest and precocious exposure to sexual behaviour are linked to careers in the sex trade, i.e., that childhood sexual abuse leads to delinquent sexual specialization in prostitution. A typical illustration is offered by Newton-Ruddy and Handelsman (1986, p. 815), who suggest that "up to 95 percent" of adolescent prostitutes are the victims of childhood incest or sexual abuse and become prostitutes as a consequence of this.

Newton-Ruddy and Handelsman advocate a Jungian feminist psychology for examining the links between childhood sexual victimization (incest) and subsequent sexual delinquency (prostitution). They argue that in incestuous families, the mother is frequently absent from home, ill and/or depressed, and that her role is taken over by the daughter, who "in being sexually abused has found a way to get what she needs (parental affection)" (p. 817)—as though the victim were the author of the incest in a process arising from maternal (but not paternal) failure. Surprisingly little agency is attributed to the father. In this account, the incest victims and young prostitutes fail to develop a strong personal identity in the absence of maternal bonds and become "little mothers" and "daddy's girls." Whether Newton-Ruddy and Handelsman have identified the precise psychodynamic process that connects incest and prostitution, they share with other commentators a presupposition that the process begins in dysfunctional family development.

Most authorities appear to follow a form of social learning or socialization theory (Akers et al., 1979). In the social learning perspective, childhood sexual exploitation teaches the victim to view herself as sexually degraded—as "loose," "dirty," and/or "damaged goods." In this approach, the victim acquires attitudes in childhood that condition her for both later adolescent and young adult misconduct and exploitation. In principle, social learning theories suggest that human nature is relatively plastic and that such negative socialization processes ought to be reversible by changing the patterns of subsequent reinforcement.

This contrasts with the prevailing understanding of delinquency suggested in Hirschi's social control theory (1969) and Gottfredson and Hirschi's *General Theory of Crime* (1990)— also developmental theories. The social control perspective suggests that the acquisition of delinquent lifestyles will follow from a range of breaches in the family bond that undermine emotional attachment to parents, commitment to a normative lifestyle, involvement in conventional activities, and subscription to conventional beliefs. The theory suggests that failures in the social bond, which may arise from many sources, including incest, will make adolescents vulnerable to the attractions of different types of delinquent opportunities. The general theory stresses that learning patterns are age-sensitive and that failures of family

bonding result in a generalized impulsiveness, which is evident before the ages of 8 or 10 and which persists for decades. No specific proclivity for prostitution is necessary, nor is a degraded sexual self-conception implicated.

Sampson and Laub's re-analysis (1993) of the classic Glueck and Glueck delinquency study (1950, 1964), which followed a matched sample of 500 male delinquents with 500 non-delinquents over a 25-year period, provides compelling evidence for this stability. They showed that background factors like poverty contributed to the demise of parental control structures and positive attachment to school. Failures in supervision and discipline produced youth vulnerable to delinquency and peer influence. Once delinquent, even allowing for all the previous variability, the boys were prone to a host of other interpersonal and employment failures and further brushes with the law, right through until middle age. The discovery of such long-term conduct disorders is unparalleled in social science investigations.

From the perspective of control theories, childhood trauma may be only one of several predictors of prostitution, and prostitution may be only one of several delinquent outcomes. Also, the choice of deviant alternatives may simply reflect environmental opportunities—with delinquent attractions in street prostitution being greater for girls than for boys given the sexual preferences of most male buyers. The reason for clarifying these explanatory differences is that they have implications for alternative social interventions. If female prostitution is symptomatic of child sexual trauma, a psychiatric response would appear more appropriate than a criminal law approach based on a rational choice theory. Indeed, Raine (1993) adopts just such an outlook on crime generally, promising to treat it as "a clinical disorder" as though all crimes would one day be DSM-IV diagnosable, and psychiatrically treatable. The case has not been made effectively for "ordinary crime." Is female prostitution an exception? And are remedies needed that are designed to deal with the peculiarities of involvement in prostitution? We turn first to a review of the contemporary research linking childhood abuse and prostitution.

EARLY WORK ON PRIOR CHILDHOOD ABUSE AND PROSTITUTION

Gray (1973) concluded in one of the first studies of its kind that for most teenage prostitutes, promiscuity—as opposed to incest or sexual abuse—began at the same time as starting to prostitute, and therefore these "initial sexual experiences do not seem to set them apart from adolescent females . . . who do not prostitute" (1973, p. 409). In addition, she noted that "incestual relationships were not reported by the girls in the study" (p. 409) and there was no evidence that they were traumatized by their first sexual experiences. However, the age of first coitus was relatively young—12.9 years on average for the White respondents and 2 years earlier on average for the Black respondents—10.9. The Black girls typically had sex with a boyfriend "within about five years of her own age"—i.e., almost 16. Gray's research was based on interviews with 21 incarcerated females in Seattle who ranged in age from 13 to 21 (mean age = 16.9 years).

James and Meyerding examined the early exposure to sexual advances by adults through an interview question: "Prior to your first intercourse, did any older person—more than ten years older—attempt sexual play or intercourse with you?" (1977, p. 35). They interviewed two samples of female prostitutes—92 prostitutes in 1970–71 (72 adults, 20 adolescents) and 136 in 1974–75. They discovered that 52% of the 136 subjects in the second sample responded in the affirmative. The respondents were described as 70 prostitutes and 66 addict-

prostitutes contacted through the local jail (26%), treatment programs (7%), and the street (67%). They also reported that the plurality of the subjects (57%) in the second sample had been victims of rape. Given what Gray determined about the prior sexual experiences of these subjects, this appears to be a sequela of exposure to prostitution.

James and Meyerding concluded that they wished to "emphasize the effects of certain sexual patterns and experiences on the life of the individual. . . . [E]arly, traumatic sexual self-objectification may be one factor influencing some women toward entrance into prostitution" (1977, p. 40). However, they did not give the levels of prior abuse for the first sample. They did report that "the incidence of rape experiences among our study populations . . . and especially among the adolescents in the 1970–71 study is so high that these samples present the characteristic of an especially victimized group" (p. 38). Indeed, they had specifically targeted the adolescents initially to throw light on delinquency onset. "Questions on early sexual history were directed primarily at the latter group [adolescents] in an attempt to elicit and elucidate the dynamics of entrance into prostitution" (p. 33). However, this adolescent sample was the same group that had been interviewed by Gray and who were reportedly low in terms of their self-defined experiences of trauma.

By contrast, in James and Meyerding's account, "65% of the adolescent prostitutes had been the victims of coerced sexual activities" (p. 38). How can such stark disparities be reconciled? A clue is suggested in the following account (James & Meyerding, 1977, p. 36):

That the superficial, non-emotionally charged nature of the first sexual intercourse of many of these women initiated a series of such encounters is supported by the fact that the mean number of private (not-for-profit) sexual partners of subjects in our study was 23. Making this figure even more significant is the fact that the mean number of persons with whom these subjects felt they had developed a "significant relationship" was only five.

This passage raises more questions than it answers. If the initial sexual encounter was "superficial" and "non-emotional," then prostitution does not appear to arise from incestuous trauma at all. This does not preclude coercion in adolescent sexual encounters. However, if a young person has an average of 23 partners, what are the chances that these will all be fully consensual? Even if a small number are emotionally injurious, the chances that 65% of the girls would find themselves involved in any one such instance is not surprising given the mean number of partners.

The evidence of this study does not support an incest-prostitution link as much as a link through promiscuity and the lapse in parental supervision and control which this suggests. Also, if we accept the conclusion that the initial exploitation was *not* traumatic, why should an initial encounter of such little affect lead to a larger number of subsequent partners? As we move away from the image of an initial traumatic involvement as a cause of prostitution to the image of a series of nonemotional, casual attachments, the ability of the argument to explain the onset of promiscuous sex declines. Having a lot of casual attachments becomes the cause of having more. The strongest predictor of future behaviour is prior behaviour. The evidence suggests that the initial onset of coitus among this sample is relatively early, i.e., that girls who later become very active sexually are sexually precocious.

None of these studies examined control groups to compare the precocity and promiscuity of prostitutes versus non-prostitutes. The first comparative study was reported in 1981. Vitaliano, James, and Boyer (1981) examined the age of first coitus among 152 female prostitutes and 117 other female offenders contacted through correctional programs in Seattle. Vitaliano et al. found no differences in

whether the subjects had experienced advances from an older male prior to first intercourse in contrast to the earlier James and Meyerding study. However, this may have been because both prison samples were similarly exploited by older males. They did establish that the prostitutes were more likely to have experienced their first sexual intercourse prior to age 15, i.e., to have been sexually precocious (42% vs. 28%), and that they experienced higher levels of force or coercion during that event (28% vs. 12%) (Vitaliano et al., 1981, p. 470).

They suggest that the event was more likely to lead to negative labeling in the case of women who became prostitutes. This suggests that the stigma followed prostitution but did not cause it. Certainly the prostitutes were more likely to report that "individuals other than [the] partner knew about intercourse and trouble resulted because of it" (29.6% vs. 15.4%). However, the prostitutes were far less likely to receive grief from their parents than the other offenders (15.8% vs. 38.9%). This suggests diminished parental influence. They were also far more likely to be "called promiscuous or whore" (25.6% vs. 5.6%), suggesting that their sexual involvements were viewed as deviant. Notably, the prostitutes were no more likely than the comparison group to get into trouble as a result of "molestation or rape" (20.6% vs. 22.2%) (Vitaliano et al., 1981, p. 470). The early negative sexual experiences do not appear to suggest this. They appear to involve girls who are sexually precocious, less subject to parental supervision, and more likely to be stigmatized for their sexual conduct.

An obvious methodological question is whether young females are sexually exploited because they are younger and more vulnerable, or whether the girls are at a higher risk of exploitation because they become sexually active in advance of their peers, are active for longer periods, and are consequently exposed to more partners. Unfortunately, such questions were not addressed in subsequent research. In the 1980s there was an avalanche of new publications with a strong advocacy flavour and a rise in policy concerns vis-à-vis adolescent prostitutes. Most of these studies took the incest-prostitution link as a point of departure and virtually none of them explicitly tested the leading theories of delinquency.

RESEARCH IN THE 1980S AND 1990S

In San Francisco, the Delancey Street Foundation sponsored research by Mimi Silbert and Ayala Pines, which led to some eight publications based on interviews with a sample of 200 female prostitutes (Silbert & Pines, 1981a, b; 1982a, b; 1983; 1984; Silbert, 1984; Silbert, Pines & Lynch, 1982). Unlike previous studies, Silbert and Pines avoided recruitment of respondents from jails and social service organizations, and contacted subjects informally by word of mouth, public announcements, and circulation of leaflets. The sample subjects exhibited epidemic levels of victimization: some 96% were runaways, 78% had started prostitution as juveniles (indeed, 60% were 16 years and younger), and 73% had been raped in non-prostitution circumstances. In terms of childhood experiences, evidence of trauma was legion. Sixty-two percent were physically beaten while growing up; 60% were sexually exploited as juveniles by an average of two persons each on an average of two separate occasions. Sixty-seven percent were sexually abused by fathers or father figures (no breakdown was given), and over half were victims of both incest and child sexual abuse (Silbert & Pines, 1981a, b). The levels of victimization were surprisingly higher than even the addict-prostitute sample from Seattle. In fact, they have been unsurpassed in the literature, and the link between prior abuse and adolescent prostitution is, especially for social workers, associated with this work.

Where Silbert and Pines appear to attribute prostitution to traumatic childhood and adolescent abuse, Boyer and James reasoned that it was not the initial trauma that paved the road to prostitution as much as the societal reaction to the exploitation, as well as the victims' reaction to the label "promiscuous"; "female promiscuity, real or imputed, virtually guarantees loss of status in the majority culture" (1983, p. 115). Inciardi made a similar point in his study of "baby pros," females who worked as child prostitutes and pornography actresses. He found no evidence of trauma, a fact he attributed to *positive* labeling. Inciardi observed that "early and repeated observations of sexual activity combined with the guidance of a parent or other relative provided them with an easy transition into the worlds of pornography and prostitution" (1984, p. 76). Inciardi's informants were motivated to participate not out of prior abuse but "fear of rejection by a parent or guardian." Hence, promiscuity did not result in automatic stigma, because reference groups structured how the "baby pros" viewed themselves.

The labeling perspective assumes that serious personal dysfunctions occur as a consequence of stigma. However, few criminologists have measured these attitudinal changes accurately, and while psychiatrists may be able to measure attitudes with some reliability, the changes in attitude typically elude them. In 1988, Gibson-Ainyette, Templer, Brown, and Veaco (1988) compared 43 juvenile prostitutes with 44 non-prostitute delinquents and 43 normal female adolescents on standardized psychological tests (MMPI) to determine whether the prostitutes exhibited specific psychiatric dysfunctions. Prostitutes did show elevated levels of hypochondriasis, depression, hysteria, paranoia, psychathenia, schizophrenia, and hypomania over both comparison groups. The adolescent prostitutes "tend to be more disturbed" (1988, p. 437). Similarly, Dirk de Schampheliere (1990) reported results in another comparative study of 41 "professional prostitutes" in Belgium and a control group of 96 women "recruited from among employees of an international airline." Again, MMPI measures showed elevated fears, anxieties, low morale, resentment, depression, etc. In neither case is it evident whether the psychopathologies were antecedents to or sequelae of prostitution, or an interaction effect.

Price, Scanlon, and Janus (1984) did *not* report systematic levels of abuse in the family origins of 28 male prostitutes, but stressed the high levels of divorce and separation among the parents of the subjects—consistent with the general theory of crime (Gottfredson and Hirschi, 1990). Their work was an exploratory study of adolescents in an outreach program. Potterat et al. (1985) compared a group of 14 prostitutes attending an STD clinic with 15 other sexually active women and discovered no differences in prior physical or sexual abuse, number raped at first intercourse, or drug use. However, the prostitutes were involved in much more volatile interpersonal relationships and tended to be divorced at twice the rate as the comparison group; and a comparative study of juvenile prostitutes and other juvenile delinquents, which also tackled the issue of abuse, was reported by Bour, Young, and Henningsen in 1984. They investigated 25 female prostitutes and a comparison group of 25 female non-prostitute offenders in a detention centre in upstate New York. The prostitutes were found to have higher levels of parental absence during childhood, but no differences in parental abuse (1984, p. 97). However, the age of first intercourse remained an area of significant difference and appeared to be a factor in their respondents becoming prostitution-involved.

The issue of sexual abuse arose in reactions to the 1984 Report of the Committee on Sexual Offenses Against Children and Youths (Canada, 1984). The inquiry downplayed the link between prior sexual abuse and entry to a career of juvenile prostitution in a nationwide study of 229 youthful prostitutes. Among respondents, the strongest memory of life at home was continuous fighting and arguments (52.4%), alcohol abuse by a parent (34%), physical abuse (33%), followed by sexual abuse (21.4%) (Csapo, 1986). The conclusions of this inquiry were criticized by Lowman (1987), and by Bagley and Young (1987). Lowman reported that about half the respondents in his 1984 study were sexually abused as children, and the majority of these attributed their careers to this factor. Bagley and Young not only reported that the majority of their 45 "former prostitutes" were sexually (73%) and physically (62%) abused but that the sexual abuse was also the major predictor of mental health disturbances in respondents' subsequent careers. Their work suggested that incest trauma could foster long-term psychiatric dysfunction of which prostitution was symptomatic.

Clearly, the literature provides evidence, albeit highly inconsistent, of a link between early sexual experiences and subsequent involvement in prostitution, but the lack of consensus suggests that the matter is far from settled. One approach that has been used to throw light on this relationship has been to focus on runaways, as leaving home early often arises because of parent-child conflict and leaves the adolescent runaway with few legal resources. What does this literature suggest about the link between early childhood experience and prostitution?

ABUSE, RUNAWAY BEHAVIOUR AND ENGAGING IN PROSTITUTION

Hindelang, Gottfredson, and Garafalo (1978) explain victimization in terms of relative exposure to environmental hazards. In the case of prostitution, the decision to sell sex may be an artifact of runaway behaviour. This conclusion was drawn by Seng (1989), whose research was based on a comparison of 70 sexually abused children and 35 "prostitution-involved" children contacted in a treatment facility. "It is not so much that sexual abuse leads to prostitution as it is that running away leads to prostitution" (p. 665). Simons and Whitbeck (1991) similarly examined the links among abusive parenting, runaway behaviour, and prostitution in a comparative study of 40 female chronic runaways and 90 homeless women. They concluded that abuse fosters running-away behaviour, which in turn exposes adolescents to the hazards of the street. However, in their analysis they were able to show that even within the runaway and homeless populations, the resort to prostitution was most significant among victims of incest.

Earls and David (1990) found elevated levels of sexual contact with a family member during childhood, precocious sexual experience, and various measures of family disruption in their controlled study of 100 (50 male and 50 female) prostitutes in Montreal. "The exact nature of the living conditions within the family environment may be less important determinants of later prostitution than sexual abuse and factors that motivate the youth to leave home at an early age" (1990, p. 7). So far, so good. However, their examination of the *male* subjects in a separate article downplayed the role of family experience in the career of homosexual prostitutes. "Our findings suggest that factors related to family background may be less important as potential determinants for entry into prostitution than influences related to financial gain, sexual orientation (homosexuality) and early sexual experiences" (Earls & David, 1989, p. 401). Earls and David define "early sexual experiences" as nonfamily contacts.

McCarthy (1990) explored the relationship among "street life," prostitution, and other offenses, employing a sophisticated model of delinquency in a sample of nearly 400 street youth in Toronto. The relationship between prostitution and prior sexual abuse was significant at the .1 level (p. 253). Fisher (1989) reported significant levels of sexual abuse among a sample of 341 frequent runaways, but these did not appear to be the major determinants of running-away behaviour. Kufeldt and Nimmo (1987) also found significant levels of sexual abuse among Calgary runaways, but again this was not found to be as major a determinant of running-away behaviour as were other forms of abuse, conflict, and neglect. The level of Fisher's sample was 10% sexual abuse. Kufeldt and Nimmo reported 7% sexual and 28% physical abuse. McCarthy reported 2% sexual abuse for males and 14% sexual abuse for females. Only McCarthy examined the link from sexual abuse to prostitution mediated by running-away behaviour, and, as noted, he found that it was marginally significant.

What conclusions can be drawn from the runaway studies? Abuse certainly appears to be a major contributor to leaving home early, but the problems seem to arise from a host of conditions including, but hardly limited to, incest and/or sexual abuse. Family disruptions and sexual precocity are also implicated. In addition, the involvement in prostitution is largely opportunistic, with runaways just as likely to end up shoplifting or dealing drugs as going into prostitution, or doing all three. Certainly, little consensus exists among the reports about the strong link between child sexual abuse and becoming a prostitute later in life. However, it should also be noted that the studies differ very significantly in their approaches, and these differences may in part explain differences in the inferences they draw. In the following section we discuss four key areas in which these studies differ. They include issues of definition, sampling, appropriate controls, and theoretical foundations.

METHODOLOGICAL ISSUES IN STUDIES OF PROSTITUTION

Definitions

Though prostitution is the subject of all the previous citations, it is not clear that the studies are looking at the same behaviour—either in the outcome: involvement in prostitution, or the predictor: abuse (Seng, 1986). For example, John Potterat, an officer with the Public Health Office in Colorado Springs concerned with venereal diseases, classified 52.5% of those in his sample of prostitutes as "evanescent" (Potterat et al., 1990). In other words, the plurality of his sample were not seasoned professionals but young women who had merely a fleeting exposure to the street, and whose "master status" was probably not one of prostitute in the traditional sense. Glueck and Glueck (1934, p. 88) in their pioneering study of *500 Delinquent Women* distinguished "professional prostitute" from "occasional prostitute" from "one-man prostitute" (or mistress).

These differences may extend to adolescent versus adult prostitutes. The extent to which prostitution functions as a temporary vocational option for adolescents may depend on differences in the tolerance of the prostitutes for the work (Savitz & Rosen, 1988) or the short-term needs of the adolescent (Sullivan, 1985). For example, Hancock (1985) described adolescent prostitution as a continuum, with the legal perspective at one end in which prostitution is characterized as the provision of sexual activities for goods and services, such as food, shelter, or money, while the other end of the continuum is characterized by sexual activities for approval, attention, or affection. Although child-protection issues warrant the conflation of prostitution and promiscuity, the issues are not identical. Mathews (1993) refers to adolescent prostitution as "survival sex" pursued on a transitory short-term basis by runaways without immediate resources.

The activity of prostitution may be further differentiated when we compare male and female prostitutes. The literature suggests that male prostitution appears to be related to the development of a homosexual identity and the management of gay and bisexual contacts (Cates, 1989; Weisberg, 1985). Sexual identity is frequently associated with parental conflict and with leaving home early.

Also, some of the studies are designed in ways that conflate the target group with other artifacts. For example, Simons and Whitbeck (1991) examined 40 adolescent runaways and 95 homeless women. They did not sample working prostitutes, but people who at some time may have sold sexual favours on a temporary basis. James and Meyerding (1977) examined prostitutes and "prostitute addicts." It is not clear whether women turn to prostitution to maintain their drug habits—or whether they rely on narcotics to sustain their prostitution, or whether both are indications of their prior victimization. As a consequence, it is unclear what model is actually tested.

In terms of the predictor variable, James and Meyerding examined "attempted sexual play" involving an older person, while Silbert and Pines actually examined incest. Schaffer and De Blaissie (1984) cite a Minnesota study in which the most prevalent first sexual encounter of women who became prostitutes was rape. In the Glueck and Glueck study, 20.5% of their 500 female delinquents were raped at "first illicit sex experience" (1934, p. 431); 52% of the women were involved with prostitution prior to commitment. Earls and David (1990) examined the age differences between the sex partners of young persons who became prostitutes and adopted the statutory definition of sexual assault (more than 5 years difference in age involving an adolescent). Other researchers cited patterns of precocious sexual experiences and large numbers of partners, some of whom may have been aggressive or offensive. Clearly, these predictors vary dramatically in the amount of trauma associated with them and ought to vary significantly in the outcomes they produce. Certainly, this was what was suggested by Smith and Thornberry (1995, p. 470) in their study of childhood maltreatment and adolescent delinquency although "a direct causal link" was not implied by the correlation. Such maltreatment was likely to further general delinquency by contributing to aggressive coping, psychological withdrawal, and/or an inability to form prosocial school and peer relationships.

Sampling

The issues of sampling are a recurrent problem in the literature. Acquiring a random stratified sample representative of the population is difficult as this is a population with unknown boundaries and certainly no list of members (see Bloor et al., 1991). Prostitutes may, in fact, constitute several related but overlapping subpopulations. Most studies are based on samples of convenience—inhabitants of correctional facilities, contacts with ex-prostitutes through counselling or psychiatric services, an STD clinic, or prostitute-rights organizations. If the researcher employs networks of respondents who are undergoing psychiatric counselling, it should not be surprising that these prostitutes have elevated psychiatric problems compared with non-prostitutes, but this may have nothing to do with prostitution as much as sampling people who need therapy.

It is possible to bypass such designs and contact prostitutes directly on the city strolls, but the strolls also differ in characteristics (age, experience, narcotics involvement, etc.). In addition, there are differences between the street population and the off-street venues like massage parlours (Bryant & Palmer, 1975; Armstrong, 1978), escorts (Williams, 1992), and truck stops (Klein & Ingle, 1981; Luxenburg & Klein, 1984). In an ingenious approach, Earls and David (1989) recruited male prostitutes involved in "tea room" activities (i.e., public washrooms frequented by gay men), but it was not clear whether they were actually involved in the sale of sex as tea room encounters are often promiscuous but not commercial.

A problem with all these approaches is that they are retrospective and so they tend to capture only prostitution as an outcome—and miss cases in which the predictor (incest, abuse, neglect, promiscuity, etc.) had no such effect.

Some studies are based on small numbers of clinical cases—one in Coleman's study (1989), nine in Inciardi's (1984). Others are based on direct approaches to people actively working the strolls (i.e., streets frequented by prostitutes). Because refusal rates are reported only rarely, both comparison between studies and generalizations from them are difficult. Methods of subject recruitment both in the target population and, where given, the control group affect the representativeness of the sample and hence the generalizability of the results.

For example, Silbert and Pines (1981a, b) reported that 70% of their subjects were under age 21, and 60% were under age 16—suggesting that only 10% were between the ages of 16 to 20, the prime years for youthful prostitution. They also reported that the mean age was 22 years. This probably requires a bimodal age distribution in the sample with a vast majority of children and a smattering of older adults—a distribution that omits the preponderant age range of working prostitutes. Obviously, the relevance of findings from such studies is undermined by the characteristics of the samples. Although this is not a problem that is easily remedied, it is surprising how little attention is paid to it in the literature. A related matter concerns the definition of juvenile. The majority of the 229 "juvenile" prostitutes (56%) interviewed by the Badgley Committee

(Canada, 1984, p. 970) for the Canadian government were 18, 19, or 20 years of age. In other words, in this study most "juveniles" were the age of majority, but the research was used to develop policy on juveniles.

Control Groups

Another major issue of design involves the identification of appropriate control groups to determine whether the childhood hazards resulting from prostitution are experienced by practitioners of the sex trade at a rate different from the "normal" population. Some studies use delinquent non-prostitutes (Bour, Young, & Henningsenn, 1984; Vitaliano et al., 1981). Others use non-delinquents (Bagley & Young, 1987). Most early studies report no control groups at all. In their innovative study, Earls and David (1990) used controls from shopping malls "in an area close to a pinball arcade." Seng (1986) compared sexually abused and sexually exploited children in a Chicago treatment home with children "involved in prostitution but not sexually abused." Simons and Whitbeck (1991) compared female runaways and homeless women. It is impossible to find an investigation in which a representative sample of active prostitutes is compared with a control group matched for age and gender in which the refusal rate is known and where allowances can be made for this in terms of generalizations.

EXPLANATIONS

Because prostitution has attracted the attention of many disciplines, there is little coherence in the theoretical basis across the various studies noted here. Unlike the dominant theories in criminology, most researchers have followed a quasi-psychiatric line of thought. Silbert and Pines say that prostitutes exhibit "psychological paralysis," a form of learned helplessness that incapacitates the victims of childhood incest. Bagley and Young theorize in a similar vein:

"the girl who finally tries prostitution is one who is already degraded and demoralized, in a state of psychological bondage, with grossly diminished self-confidence" (Bagley & Young, 1987, p. 23)—someone who, were we to believe this improbable account, is already dysfunctional before she becomes a prostitute. Coleman (1989) argues that male prostitutes suffer from a "faulty psychosexual and psychosocial development"—a charge once made about homosexuality per se. Price, Scanlon, and Janus (1984) characterize their male prostitutes as suffering from "arrested development." Maiuro, Trupin, and James (1983) report androgynous personalities among prostitutes. Gibson-Ainyette et al. (1988), de Schampheleire (1990), and Ross et al. (1990) present different psychometric assessments suggesting that the prostitute exhibits various psychopathologies or pathological tendencies.

Most of these approaches seem to presuppose that the psychological paralysis, the bondage, and other signs of faulty development occur *before* prostitution. They seem to anticipate Raine's (1993) view of crime as psychopathology, but the "crime" in this case, sex for money or material considerations, is only a manifestation of a more deeply seated disorder. The real disorder, incest trauma or something comparable, is imagined more frequently than it is reliably identified. Our review has failed to establish that incest contributes uniquely to the onset of prostitution. In the work of James and Meyerding, the triggering event is "superficial, non-emotionally charged," and probably unrelated to incest at all. Likewise, our review of other research turns up a host of conditions that appear to be associated with entry into prostitution, including physical and sexual abuse, dysfunctional families, parental substance abuse, and sexual precocity.

The major problem with all the quasi-psychiatric constructs is that none of them constitute a definable mental illness or a distinct personality disorder, and most of them could just as easily be the outcomes of involvement with a hazardous and stigmatized activity, which is subject to routine police suppression and violent control by dates and pimps, and which is often conducted under the influence of drugs and alcohol. In that case, these constructs could amount to sequelae, not antecedents of prostitution.

DISCUSSION

In contrast to the pathological approaches, modern theories of delinquency put a premium on socialization in the acquisition of delinquent conduct, particularly learning in the context of family structures that contribute to, or undermine, social bonding, and the development of self-control. In our view, the decision to engage in prostitution should be examined theoretically in the context of factors that, in the first instance, weaken the social bond, and that subsequently develop in the context of opportunities and pressures in the non-conventional circumstances that arise when conventional attachments, commitments, involvements, and beliefs have failed.

The current literature has emphasized the impact of sexual trauma in the etiology of prostitution, but the evidence for this has been inconsistent and subject to alternative interpretations. The purported link between some sort of sexual trauma and prostitution seems to arise from failures of intergenerational attachments and/or inappropriate parenting behaviour deriving from any number of sources—including physical, verbal, and/or sexual abuse, substance abuse, spousal conflicts, and the like. Even in cases where child sexual abuse does occur, this situation is compounded by the fact that these families are overwhelmingly step-parented, suggesting that there has already been parental conflict and marital dissolution in the life of the children (Daly & Wilson, 1988, pp. 87–89).

There is a final area of some theoretical relevance that touches on the issue of sexual precocity among girls and young women involved in prostitution. The onset of sexual conduct in adolescence is related to age, hormonal changes, and pubertal development. Recent work by Udry (1988) shows that the effects of such hormonal changes are mediated by, among other things, social controls, including family structures. Udry reports that "for girls without fathers present in the household, there is a very strong effect of T[estosterone] on sexuality. This relationship is suppressed among girls with fathers, although it is still not zero" (p. 716). And it is only temporary. This suggests that so-called sexual precocity is normal sexuality which arises sooner than later in the absence of parental controls. This does not mean that female adolescents who become involved in prostitution are "sexually mature" by nature or become involved because of their earlier onset of menses. Glueck and Glueck suggested this in *500 Delinquent Women* when they explored "the extent to which [the women's] early sex indulgence is associated with sexual maturity or hypersexuality" (1934, p. 91). They reported that menses "among girls of the general population usually begins at fourteen years. In our group the mean is 13.94 years."

But this is *not* a substantial enough difference to explain the earlier initiation of sexual conduct reported among prostitutes, and it does not support the Victorian equivalence of female sexuality, danger, and delinquency (Chesney-Lind, 1989). If Udry's model is correct, the mechanism linking *early* sexual activity and youthful prostitution is, in part, parental control. Although all adolescents, male and female, experience biological signals that heighten interest in sexuality, in the absence of social control, adolescents will become more sexually active in response to such signals in advance of their age-peers from intact homes. There was a 2-year age difference at first coitus for prostitutes versus non-prostitutes reported by Gray (1973).

However, becoming sexually active is not the same thing as becoming a prostitute. Thus, onset and parental regulation are not the only important intervening factors. Instead, a cluster of conditions and hazards further mediate the link. First, there tends generally to be an age difference between heterosexual couples who date. Males typically date females 1 or 2 years younger than themselves although they often express short-term interest in much younger females (Buss, 1994, p. 78). In part this age gap results from the fact that male and female adolescents become sexually mature at different ages. In this scenario, the young adolescent females who become sexually active earlier than their female peers appear to become active with boys who are not just 1 or 2 years older than themselves—which is the norm—but who are substantially older than themselves. According to Gray, the average age difference at first sex between girls who became prostitutes and their mates was 5 years. That means that 12–14-year-old females were sexually active with 17–19-year-old males. Given the large social differences that mark adolescent age transitions, such relationships are not particularly stable and are peculiarly hazardous for the females.

Because males are under less parental supervision, and because more males as opposed to females are thought to have a short-term dating strategy based on the short-term benefits of sexual contact, a young, sexually active female is likely to experience far more sexual attention than a sexually active heterosexual male of the same age. Young females who have become prostitution-involved are likely to have already experienced a large number of short-term relationships, many of which were exploitative (5 in 26 are "meaningful" according to James and Meyerding), many of which involved significantly older, and probably more sexually experienced males, and some of which involved rape during the female's first heterosexual encounter.

A final factor puts such early sexual development into a larger focus. In adolescence, Udry (1988, p. 709) suggests "studies show that sexual behaviour belongs to a class of adolescent norm violations whose occurrence is both inter-correlated and predicted by the same models." Glueck and Glueck (1934, p. 90) report similarly: "A close relationship was found to exist between the age at the first illicit sex experience and the onset of other delinquent conduct, such as truancy, running away from home, lying, stealing." Both the Udry and the Glueck conclusions are highly consistent with the control perspective, and the general theory of crime in particular (Gottfredson and Hirschi, 1990), especially as it points to the non-specialization of delinquency. Just as breaches in informal social control, particularly in the family, expedite early sexual exploration, this frequently appears alongside other forms of delinquency, which further erode attachments to the social bond and exposes the youth to still more delinquent opportunities and hazards.

This conjunction of control theory with Udry's model of the conditions that initiate normal adolescent sexuality helps explain the otherwise anomalous early onset of coitus associated with girls who become involved with prostitution. It does so, on the one side, without basing the explanation completely on the theory of trauma, the evidence for which was so inconsistently reported in previous studies, and without, on the other, invoking a reductionistic account of female nature that sometimes equates sexuality with delinquency.

We had the opportunity to explore some of these hypotheses in a comparison of a sample of active street prostitutes (*n* = 42) and junior college students (*n* = 57) (Gibbs Van Brunschot & Brannigan, 1997). The results can be discussed here briefly. Controlling for age, race, and confining the analysis to females, we found that the prostitutes were far more likely to characterize their parental home life more negatively, to report higher levels of physical abuse, sexual abuse, non-traditional family structures, parental drug and alcohol abuse, more sexual experience prior to age 14, more personal drug use, higher levels of attempted suicide, higher levels of running-away behaviour and more frequent school expulsions and discipline, lower levels of completed education, more children, and sexual partners significantly older than themselves at first voluntary intercourse. These two groups were quite different on virtually every dimension we explored, including sexual abuse. But what does that tell us?

What was most revealing in our analysis were the results of a series of logistic models in which we predicted group membership (prostitute or student) based on background factors (non-traditional family structure, negative home life, sexual abuse, physical abuse, parental drug or alcohol abuse, and sexual precocity). The only factors that significantly predicted prostitution were negative home life and sexual precocity. In a similar model predicting running-away behaviour, the same two predictors were the only significant factors. What this means is that once sexual precocity and a negative home life have been measured, there is no further contribution to the model made by adding the much less prevalent associations represented by the more specific abuse variables.

Obviously, many of these factors are mutually confounding—an abusive parental relationship is likely to correlate highly with a hostile family atmosphere and negative home life. As a result, once the best fit has been identified in the model, the individual contribution of other factors, which similarly measure processes destructive of the social bond, diminish. These findings are more consistent with a general control perspective than an explanation based on the unique contribution of sex-

ual trauma. Notably, sexual abuse was in fact the *only* background factor in our models that predicted suicidal behaviour in respondents. This makes us conclude that such traumas may be important in de-coupling youth from family bonds, but their contribution cannot be assessed in isolation from other family tensions and processes of development.

SUMMARY

This paper has examined research that attempts to explain entry to prostitution in terms of the family experiences of young prostitutes. Though there is some evidence of rape, incest, and other kinds of sexual trauma in these backgrounds, this evidence is inconsistent and contradictory. A more plausible approach to the question is based on general control theories. Any traumas or conflicts that unattach children and youth from their families make youngsters highly vulnerable to delinquency. In the case of adolescent females, breach of family attachments appears to heighten the risk of early sexual involvements that, in the context of gender differences in sexual development, expose them to partners significantly older than themselves, and in significantly larger numbers than would otherwise be the case. These factors help explain the role of dysfunctional backgrounds in entry to prostitution without presupposing a role for unobservable traumas and psychiatric disturbances. They likewise recognize a role for the interaction between social control factors and the normal process of sexual development.

STUDY QUESTIONS

1. Why is it important to note differences in operational definitions when comparing studies on the same topic?

2. On page 35, the authors stated that "a problem with all these approaches is that they . . . tend to capture only prostitution as an outcome—

and miss cases in which the predictor . . . had no such effect." What is the importance of this observation? What implications does this have for researchers trying to find causal "determinants" rather than contributing factors?

3. What problems in the operational definitions used by the authors and other researchers might have contributed to the failure of their review to "establish that incest contributes uniquely to the onset of prostitution" (page 36)?

REFERENCES

Akers, R. L., Krohn, M.D., Lanza-Kaduce, L., & Radosevich, M. (1979). Social learning and deviant behavior: A specific test of a general theory. *American Sociological Review, 44,* 635–655.

Armstrong, E. G. (1978). "Massage Parlors and Their Customers." *Archives of Sexual Behavior, 7,* 117–125.

Bagley, C., & Young, L. (1987). Juvenile prostitution and child sexual abuse: A controlled study. *Canadian Journal of Community Mental Health, 6* (1), 5–26.

Bloor, M., Leyland, A., Barnard, M., & McKeganey, N. (1991). Estimating hidden populations: A new method of calculating the prevalence of drug-injecting and non-injecting female street prostitution. *British Journal of Addiction, 86,* 1477–1483.

Bour, D. S., Young, J. P., & Henningsen, R. (1984). A comparison of delinquent prostitutes and delinquent non-prostitutes on self-concept. *Journal of Offender Counselling, 9*(1–2), 89–101.

Boyer, D. K., & James, J. (1983). Prostitutes as victims. In D. E. MacNamara & A. Karmen (Eds.), *Deviants–Victims or Victimizers?* (pp. 109–146). London: Sage Publications.

Bryant C. D., & Palmer, D. E. (1975). "Massage Parlors and "Hand Whores:" Some Sociological Observations." *Journal of Sex Research, 11,* 227–241.

Buss, D. (1994). *The evolution of desire: Strategies of human mating,* New York: Basic Books.

Canada (1984). Report of the Committee on Sexual Offenses Against Children and Youths, Vols. 1 and 2 (Robin Badgley, Chair), Ottawa: Supply and Services.

Cates, J. A. (1989). Adolescent male prostitution by choice. *Child and Adolescent Social Work, 6*(2), 151–156.

Chesney-Lind, M. (1989). Girls' crime and woman's place: Toward a feminist model of female delinquency. *Crime and Delinquency, 35*(1), 5–29.

Coleman, E. (1989). The development of male prostitution activity among gay and bisexual adolescents. *Journal of Homosexuality, 17*(1–2), 131–149.

Csapo, M. (1986). Juvenile prostitution. *Canadian Journal of Special Education, 2,* 145–171.

Daly, M., & Wilson, M. (1988). *Homicide,* New York: Aldine de Gruyter.

De Schampheliere, D. (1990). MMPI characteristics of professional prostitutes: A cross-cultural replication. *Journal of Personality Assessment, 54*(1–2), 343–350.

Earls, C. M., & David, H. (1990). Early family and sexual experiences of male and female prostitutes. *Canada's Mental Health, 38*(4), 7–11.

Earls, C. M., & David, H. (1989). A psychosocial study of male prostitution. *Archives of Sexual Behavior, 18,* 401–419.

Fisher, J. (1989). *Missing Children Research Project: Findings of the study.* Executive summary. Ministry of the Solicitor General of Canada, no. 1989-07.

Gibbs Van Brunschot, E., & Brannigan, A. (1997). *Childhood maltreatment and subsequent conduct disorders: The case of female street prostitution.* Department of Sociology, University of Alberta, Canada.

Gibson-Ainyette, I., Templer, D. I., Brown, R., & Veaco, L. (1988). Adolescent female prostitutes. *Archives of Sexual Behavior, 17,* 431–438.

Glueck, S., & Glueck, E. (1934). *500 Delinquent women.* New York: Knopf.

Glueck, S., & Glueck, E. (1950). *Unraveling juvenile delinquency.* New York: The Commonwealth Fund.

Glueck, S., & Glueck, E. (1964). *Delinquents and non-delinquents in perspective.* Cambridge, MA: Harvard University Press.

Gottfredson, M., & Hirschi, T. (1990). *A general theory of crime.* Stanford, CA: Stanford University Press.

Gray, D. K. (1973). Turning-out: A study of teenage prostitution. *Urban Life and Culture, 1,* 401–425.

Hancock, L. (1985). *The involvement of young people in prostitution.* Melbourne: Crown Law Office.

Hindelang, M., Gottfredson, M., & Garafalo, J. (1978). *Victims of Personal Crime,* Cambridge, Mass: Ballinger.

Hirschi, T. (1969). *Causes of delinquency.* Berkeley: University of California Press.

Inciardi, J. A. (1984). Little girls and sex: A glimpse at the world of the 'Baby pro.' *Deviant Behavior, 5,* 7–78.

James, J., & Meyerding, J. (1977). Early sexual experience as a factor in prostitution. *Archives of Sexual Behavior, 7*(1), 31–42.

Klein, L., & Ingle, J. L. (1981) "Sex solicitation for Short Wave Radio." *Free Inquiry in Creative Sociology, 9,* 61–63, 68.

Kufeldt, K., & Nimmo, M. (1987). Youth on the street: Abuse and neglect in the eighties. *Child Abuse and Neglect, 11,* 531–543.

Laub, J, H., & Sampson, R. J. (1988). Unraveling families and delinquency: A reanalysis of the Glueck's data. *Criminology, 26,* 355–380.

Loeber, Rolf, & Stouthamer-Loeher, M. (1986). Family factors as correlates and predictors of juvenile conduct problems and delinquency. In M. Tonry & N. Morris (Eds.), *Crime and Justice: An annual review of research* (Vol. 7, pp. 29–149). Chicago: University of Chicago Press.

Lowman, J. (1987). Taking young prostitutes seriously. *The Canadian Review of Sociology and Anthropology, 24*(1), 99–116.

Luxenburg, J., & Klein, L. (1984). CB Radio Prostitution: Technology and the Displacement of Deviance. *Journal of Offender Counselling Services and Rehabilitation, 9,* 71–87.

Maiuro, R. D., Trupin, E., & James, J. (1983). Sex-role differentiation in a female juvenile delinquent population: Prostitute vs. control samples. *American Journal of Orthopsychiatry, 53,* 345–352.

McCarthy, W. (1990). *Life on the street: Serious theft, drug-selling and prostitution among homeless youth.* Doctoral thesis, University of Toronto.

McCord, J. (1979). Some child-rearing antecedents of criminal behavior in adult men. *Journal of Personality and Social Psychology, 37,* 1477–1486.

Mathews, F. (1993). Adolescent (juvenile) prostitution. Speech to the National Consultation on Prostitution in Canada (May 10). Calgary: Federation of Canadian Municipalities.

Newton-Ruddy, L., & Handelsman, M. M. (1986). Jungian feminine psychology and adolescent prostitutes. *Adolescence, 22,* 815–825.

Potterat, J., Phillips, L., Rothenberg, R. B., & Darrow, W. W. (1985). "On Becoming a Prostitute: An Exploratory Case-Comparison Study." *Journal of Sex Research, 21*(3), 329–335.

Price, V., Scanlon, B., and Janus, J-D. (1984) "Social Characteristics of Adolescent Male Prostitution." *Victimology, 9*(2), 211–221.

Raine, A. (1993). *The psychopathology of crime: Criminal behavior as a clinical disorder.* San Diego: Academic Press.

Riley, D., & Shaw, M. (1995). *Parental supervision and juvenile delinquency.* Home Office Research Study No. 83, London: HMSO.

Ross, C. A., Anderson, G., Heber, S., & Norton, R. G. (1990). Dissociation and abuse among multiple-personality patients, prostitutes and exotic dancers. *Hospital and Community Psychiatry, 41*(3), 328–330.

Sampson, R. J., & Laub, J. H. (1993). *Crime in the making: Pathways and turning points through life.* Cambridge, MA: Harvard University Press.

Savitz, L., & Rosen, L. (1988). The sexuality of prostitutes: Sexual enjoyment reported by 'Streetwalkers'. *The Journal of Sex Research, 24,* 200–208.

Schaffer, B., & DeBlaissie, R. R. (1984). Adolescent prostitution. *Adolescence, 19,* 689–696.

Seng, M. J. (1996). Sexual behavior between adults and children: Some issues of definition. *Journal of Offender Counselling, 11,* 47–61.

Seng. M. J. (1989). Child sexual abuse and adolescent prostitution: A comparative analysis. *Adolescence, 24,* 665–675.

Silbert, M. H. (1984). Treatment of prostitute victims of sexual assault. In I. R. Stuart & J. G. Greer (Eds.), *Victims of sexual aggression: Treatment of children, women, and men* (pp. 251–269). New York: Van Nostrand Reinhold.

Silbert, M. H., & Pines, A. M. (1981a). Sexual child abuse an antecedent to prostitution. *Child Abuse and Neglect, 5,* 407–411.

Silbert, M. H., & Pines, A. M. (1981b). Occupational hazards of street prostitutes. *Criminal Justice and Behavior, 8,* 395–399.

Silbert, M. H., & Pines, A. M. (1982a). Victimization of street prostitutes. *Victimology, 7*(1–4), 122–133.

Silbert, M. H., & Pines, A. M. (1982b). Entrance into prostitution. *Youth and Society, 13,* 471–500.

Silbert, M. H., & Pines, A. M. (1983). Early sexual exploitation as an influence in prostitution. *Social Work, 28,* 285–289.

Silbert, M. H., & Pines, A. M. (1984). Pornography and sexual abuse of women. *Sex Roles, 10*(11–12), 857–868.

Silbert, M. H., Pines, A. M., & Lynch, T. (1982). Substance abuse and prostitution. *Journal of Psychoactive Drugs, 14*, 193–197.

Simons, R. L., & Whitbeck, L. B. (1991). Sexual abuse as a precursor to prostitution and victimization among adolescent and adult homeless women. *Journal of Family Issues, 12*, 361–379.

Smith, C., & Thornberry, T. P. (1995). The relationship between childhood maltreatment and adolescent involvement in delinquency. *Criminology, 33*, 451–477.

Sullivan, T. (1985). Juvenile prostitution: An unspoken vocational option. *School Guidance Worker, 40*(5), 31–34.

Udry, R. (1988). Biological predispositions and social control in adolescent sexual behavior. *American Sociological Review, 53*, 709–722.

Van Voorhis, P., Cullen, F. T., Mathers, R. A., & Garner, C. C. ([988). The impact of family structure on quality of delinquency: A comparative assessment of structural and functional factors. *Criminology, 26*, 235–261.

Vitaliano, P. P., James, J., & Boyer, D. (1981). Sexuality of deviant females: Adolescent and adult correlates. *Social Work, 26* (6), 468–472.

Weisberg, K. (1985). *Children of the night: A study of adolescent prostitution.* Lexington, MA: D. C. Heath.

West, D., & Farrington, D. (1977). *The delinquent way of life.* London: Heinemann.

Williams, S. (1992). *Nobody's business: An analysis of the Calgary escort business,* Master's Thesis, University of Calgary Department of Sociology.

Zingraff, M. T., Leiter, J., Myers, K. A., & Johnsen, M. C. (1993). Child maltreatment and youthful problem behavior. *Criminology, 31*, 173–202.

Chapter 3

Book Review of *Philosophy of Social Science: The Philosophical Foundations of Social Thought* by Ted Benton and Ian Craib

Reviewed by Jonathan Joseph

Source: Book review by J. Joseph in *Capital and Class*: Spring 2003, Issue 79, p. 184. Reprinted with kind permission of the publisher.

This is an interesting and informative introduction to debates in the philosophy and methodology of social science. Intended for undergraduate students, it will also interest a wider audience because of the way it tackles familiar issues through new ideas.

Benton and Craib distinguish between two main philosophical approaches. One, emanating from the early days of modern science, sees philosophy as a foundational 'master-discipline'. By contrast, the more humble underlabourer view recognises that speculation about the nature of the world must be limited and that philosophy's main role is to provide help and support for scientists while letting them get on with their work.

The book opens with a discussion of positivism and empiricism, positions which regrettably are still dominant within social and natural science. In presenting alternatives to this view the book mentions how some Marxists see science as an expression of the alienated relationship between modern capitalism and nature. The Frankfurt School, for example, links this alienation to the growth of apparatuses designed to secure mastery over nature (p.51). This says a lot about the positivist approach.

However, it must be remembered that Marx and Engels themselves had a positive (if not a positivist) conception of science which contrasted it to the contaminated realm of ideology. Writers like Althusser develop this, but also fall into difficulties for science is a social practice, so how can a correspondence to the real objects of knowledge be maintained?

The solution proposed lies with critical realism which, it is claimed, can 'combine together the model of science as a social practice of production of knowledge with a realist understanding of knowledge as *about* something independent of itself' (p.57). It is claimed that in this way we can understand science 'as a historically changing and socially situated human practice with an acknowledgement of it as, distinctively, a social practice whose aim is the production of knowledge about objects, relations, processes and so on which exist and act independently of our knowledge of them' (p.58).

The discussion of critical realism is one example of allowing other, often marginalised approaches to have their say. The book also examines the relation between gender and science, raising the issue of whether the search for objective knowledge is tied to a (white, Western) masculine aggressive desire to dominate nature (p.63). Feminists are often more aware of the problems of knowledge creation and how this is a social process involving relations of power.

However, feminist debates are often not dissimilar to wider scientific debates. Thus feminist empiricists tend to criticise male-dominance in the interests of 'scientific objectivity' while postmodern feminists focus excessively on questions of language and identity.

Other alternatives to positivism follow the line of Kuhn and paradigms. This correctly stresses the social and historical basis of knowledge. The danger is that if paradigms carry their own standards of evaluating scientific explanation, then knowledge is relativised. This is the case with subsequent approaches, reaching its extreme in the anarchism of Feyerabend who argues that there is no objective basis for considering science to be superior to any other forms of life or practice.

The problem is, however, that such radical scepticism involves a performative contradiction. For example, Bruno Latour's attempt to dispense with such concepts as 'nature' and 'society' implicitly presupposes them, while his denunciation of reason employs reason itself (pp.73–4).

The book provides a useful description of Giddens as an 'ontological individualist' who sees the social world as made up of individuals interacting together (p.77). Weber's approach regards the object of sociology as meaningful, rational, social action while the phenomenological approach examines the way in which we give meaning to the world. The more instrumental approach of social interactionists like Mead and Goffman sees our relationship with others in terms of role-play. All these approaches draw a great dividing line between the natural and social sciences, regarding their objects as entirely different, and stressing meanings and understandings as an alternative to 'facts'. The irony is that such 'radical' approaches usually accept the positivist approach to *natural* science as entirely appropriate.

The influence of Wittgenstein and language-games is also noted. The question shifts from meaning to use. Again there is relativism here—in Winch, we understand cultures on the basis of the rules they follow. This makes it difficult to compare cultures where the rules are said to be different. How can we judge one set of rules from the perspective of a different culture? More generally, we might ask, where do these rules come from?

The critical realist approach argues that we can only understand cognitive practices if we recognise that they are about something that exists independently. It makes the transcendental argument that, given that science is possible, this presupposes something about the structure of the world itself. The identification of scientific laws, for example, is based on the tendencies of underlying mechanisms. This can be applied to the social as well as the natural world, and counters both the idealist view that social science is about subjective or intersubjective understanding, and the positivist view that there is something out there, but that it is reducible to the constant conjunctions of observable events. Reality is stratified or layered so that the occurrence of empirical events is dependent upon underlying structures and generative mechanisms.

In the social world, these structures need to be reproduced through human activity, thus allowing for the possibility of their transformation. The book also discusses critical realism's distinction between intransitive or independent structures, and the transitive or social and historical nature of the knowledge that we have of them.

The chapter on post-structuralism and postmodernism moves from the structuralist belief in underlying structures, to the post-structuralist abandonment of this position. Foucault and Derrida emphasise absence, difference, fragmentation and rhetoric. From here, postmodernists decide to abandon the basis of philosophy. Science comes to represent no more than a regime of power. Postmodernists make the argument that there is no point to argument—another self-refuting position (p.177).

Which again returns us to the status of philosophy. Is it, as the postmodernists argue, largely irrelevant? Or is it, as grand-metaphysicians would argue, the foundation of science? Given the vast gulf between these positions, as well as the wider array of different perspectives covered in this book, the answer would seem to lie with the underlabouring view. In fact, not only does critical realist philosophy need to provide help and support to the work of the scientists, but it would seem it needs to give a helping hand to the philosophers as well.

STUDY QUESTIONS

1. Define the following terms:

   a. critical realism

   b. relativism

   c. idealism

   d. positivism

2. Describe the approach taken by someone using each of the following perspectives when studying cognitive processes:

   a. a critical realist perspective

   b. an idealist perspective

   c. a positivist perspective

   d. a relativist perspective

3. What advantages does critical realism offer over other philosophical approaches to knowledge and scientific investigation?

Chapter 4

Limited Confidentiality, Academic Freedom, and Matters of Conscience: Where Does CPA Stand?

John Lowman and Ted Palys

Source: Reproduced by permission of the *Canadian Journal of Criminology* 43(4): 497–508 (October 2001). Copyright © by the Canadian Criminal Justice Association.

Normally, we would not request an opportunity to reply to another author's response (Zinger, Wichmann, and Gendreau 2001) to our commentary (Palys and Lowman 2001) on one of their articles (Zinger, Wichmann, and Andrews 2001). The purpose of this brief article is two-fold: (a) to clarify our position on limited confidentiality; (b) to address some fundamental (and more general) questions about the Canadian Psychological Association's (CPA's) approach to confidentiality. First, we clarify our position and then examine issues arising from the obligations that Zinger and his colleagues cite to justify the limitations on confidentiality they employed in their research on prisoners.

A CLARIFICATION

Research participants have a right to confidentiality. A question arises, however, as to what researchers should do when, in the course of research, they are faced with "heinous discovery," i.e., they receive information indicating that the research participant may pose a serious threat to him/herself or others. With respect to their research on segregation, Zinger *et al.* (2001: 272) assert our solution (Palys and Lowman 2000) offers a choice between "deceiving" research participants by guaranteeing confidentiality when actually we intend to violate it, or

ignoring threats, thereby exposing researchers and correctional authorities to liability. That is not the choice we presented.

Distinguishing our approach from that of Zinger and his colleagues on this issue requires that we address two issues. First is the breadth of behaviour that may be considered "heinous." Jurisprudence on this question (e.g., *Smith* v. *Jones*, 1999) always consider these issues in relation to threats of serious injury or death to identified third parties or, in the case of *Smith* v. *Jones* (1999), to clearly identifiable groups. When Zinger *et al.* limited confidentiality to include plans of suicide and escape, threats of injury that did not constitute "serious injury," and threats to the general security of a prison, they cast an overly broad net that deviated significantly from the standards set in common law. More importantly, the standard *expected of researchers* remains an open question, as the Canadian Psychological Association and American Sociological Association differ in this respect. The point we made about Zinger *et al.*'s approach is that, as researchers, they had a fiduciary duty to protect the rights and interests of research participants and not put themselves in a conflict of interest whereby they are obliged to fulfil other institutional "requirements," such as the institutional obligations of prison guards.

Second, the approach we articulated asserts we must distinguish between situations where heinous revelations can *not* be anticipated and situations where they *can* (Palys and Lowman 2000). An example of *un*anticipated heinous discovery might occur in an interview study of employees about their job responsibilities. One would not normally begin such a study expecting that some interviewee will spontaneously reveal plans to murder his/her boss. Indeed, if such a revelation occurred, it would lie outside the purview of the research, in which case it is arguable whether it is even covered by the guarantee of confidentiality. Most research is of this nature. Research where one can *anticipate* heinous discovery is unusual. One example is Zinger *et al.*'s research on the effects of solitary confinement on prisoners.

It would be unethical to deceive research participants in this context. In the case of *anticipated* heinous discovery, the choice we offered is between (1) making an unlimited guarantee of confidentiality and sticking to it; or (2) not doing the research, because limiting confidentiality would, in all likelihood, invalidate the data (*cf.* Palys and Lowman 2000).[1] In responding to this position, Zinger *et al.* claim to possess evidence that their limitation on confidentiality did not affect the validity of their data.

VALIDITY ISSUES

On the basis of research participants' scores on the Balanced Inventory of Desirable Responding (BIDR), Zinger *et al.* (2001: 273) conclude, "[W]e can report with confidence that segregated prisoners employed fewer tactics to deceive researchers (intentionally or not), and likely responded accurately throughout our data collection period."

The problem with this claim is that the BIDR barely speaks to the problem we have identified. We suggested that, because of limited confidentiality, prisoners simply would not disclose certain kinds of information to researchers. There is a vast difference between "self-deception" and "impression management," the constructs underlying the BIDR, and the wholesale omission of information about what prisoners *actually do* or *intend to do*. Information about prisoners' actions and intention is vital to assessing the "effects" of segregation. Why would they divulge this information to researchers knowing that it could have tangible negative consequences, such as further segregation or loss of privileges?

PROFESSIONAL STANDARDS

Zinger *et al.* argue that they had no choice but to limit confidentiality the way they did because various professional standards *required* them to "disclose any information [research participants] may provide if it's in regards to [their] safety or that of the institution. These areas include suicide plans, plans of escape, injury to others and the general security of the institution" (Zinger 1999: Appendix 4: 107). The standards they cite include (a) the *Corrections and Conditional Release Act (CCRA)*; and (b) the Canadian Psychological Association's (CPA) *Code of Ethics*. Also, they cite the Law Society of Upper Canada's (LSUC) *Rules of Professional Conduct* as support for their position. We consider each of these so-called obligations in turn.

The *Corrections and Conditional Release Act*

While the CCRA delineates the duties of the Correctional Service of Canada (CSC) and its employees in the custody of prisoners, it does not spell out the ethical obligations of researchers *as researchers*. A problem arises when a researcher's obligations to an *institution* conflict with the ethical obligations they have to *research participants*. If it imposes its own institutional obligations on researchers, CSC acts on its conflict-of-interest.

Zinger *et al.* (2001: 270–271) cite various statistics on violence and suicide in prisons as if these make it obvious why they see themselves as being obliged to report certain kinds of "threats." In many respects, the situation is similar to the allegory that Saul Alinsky (cited in Cohen 1985) recounts about a person, whom we will call the "Samaritan," standing on a riverbank who dives in to save a drowning man. As soon as the Samaritan is back on the bank another man floats by. The Samaritan rescues the second drowning man. But then another man appears, and another and another, at which point the Samaritan recognises that a better idea than trying to rescue each drowning man would be to walk up the river bank to find out why so many men are falling in. The problem is that by walking upstream the Samaritan increases the likelihood that the men floating by will drown. A similar dilemma characterises research on the effects of segregation on prisoners.

Clearly, there are bodies in the river at CSC, as Zinger *et al.*'s statistics attest. How many of these incidents were related to the effects of segregation? Could the yearly number of murders, suicides and serious assaults be reduced if we had valid and reliable information about the effects of segregation on prisoners?

When researchers tell prisoners that they will report "suicide plans, plans of escape, injury to others and the general security of the institution," they virtually guarantee that prisoners will not divulge this information, thus throwing doubt on the validity of the research. Because they do not learn about it, the researchers will not be able to prevent immediate acts of violence either. Doing valid research by giving an unlimited guarantee of confidentiality would not change the immediate situation, but it might help generate information that would stop so many drowning men from floating down the river and appearing in the statistics that Zinger *et al.* cite. In other words, far from providing an obvious reason to limit confidentiality, these statistics provide the justification for arguing that CSC should allow at least one researcher to walk upstream to try and determine the extent to which isolation contributes to there being so many drowning men in Canada's prisons.

As to Zinger *et al.*'s (2001: 272) concerns about liability, we assert that researchers should base their decisions about research confidentiality on ethics criteria rather than fear of liability (*cf.* Lowman and Palys 2000). Research requires the courage of our convictions. If researchers are concerned about liability, they need to educate courts about the reason for giving an unlimited guarantee of confidentiality in the first place, rather than sell the research enterprise short by prioritising liability over ethics.

LAWYERS' *RULES OF PROFESSIONAL CONDUCT*

Zinger *et al.* (2001: 272) also refer to the Law Society of Upper Canada's (LSUC's) *Rules of Professional Conduct* to show that solicitors (and, presumably, by extension, all other professionals who have or claim a privileged relationship) *must* report heinous revelations. The quote is worth repeating because it shows no such thing:

Where a lawyer believes upon reasonable grounds that there is an imminent risk to an identifiable person or group of death or serious bodily harm, including serious psychological harm that substantially interferes with health or well-being, the lawyer *may* disclose, pursuant to judicial order where practicable, confidential information where it is necessary to do so to prevent the death or harm, but shall not disclose more information than is required. [LSUC Rule 2.03(3), cited by Zinger *et al.*]

Clearly, Zinger *et al.* have taken a "may" and made it a "must" as part of their broader interpretation of the "obligations" that professional ethics codes bestow on their members. Far from imposing a formulaic rule, the LSUC's

Rules permit disclosure of confidential information in very limited circumstances, but they do *not* require it. This approach is consistent with the way that some laws relating to therapist-patient confidentiality operate in the United States (*cf. Thapar* v. *Zezulka*, 1998). Also, it is consistent with the way that U.S. confidentiality and privacy certificates for researchers deal with the problem of heinous discovery. And that is how it should be for researchers: a matter of case-by-case consideration and conscience.

THE CPA *CODE OF ETHICS*

Zinger *et al.* (2001:271–272) state that sections I.44, I.45 and II.39 of the CPA's *Code of Ethics* create an "obligation" for them to limit confidentiality. In the case of threats of serious injury or death (but only in those instances) the following passage from Ogloff (former Chair of CPA's Committee on Professional Ethics and, at the time of writing, President of CPA) and Olley (1998: 223) lends support to this interpretation:

. . . even though Canada has not had a case that mandates a "Tarasoff duty," the *Canadian Code of Ethics for Psychologists* (1991) does impose such a duty, one which closely parallels the duty first laid out by the Supreme Court of California in Tarasoff.

The "Tarasoff" case involved a University of California counsellor's client who during therapy indicated that he planned to kill Tatiana Tarasoff, his former girlfriend. The therapist became concerned when the client purchased a gun, and told campus police about the threat, thereby breaching client-therapist confidentiality. The campus police interviewed the former boyfriend, and decided no further action was warranted. Two months later, he murdered Tarasoff. The family sued the therapist, asserting that he had an obligation to warn the family of the threat. The "Tarasoff duty" has become shorthand for the idea that therapists are obliged to "do everything possible to stop or offset the consequences of actions by others when these actions are likely to cause serious physical harm or death" (CPA *Code of Ethics*, Section I.45).

If the CPA has created a "Tarasoff duty," it presumably would apply only where the threat involves "serious physical harm or death" to a *clearly identifiable target* (*Tarasoff* v. *Regents of Univ. of California* 1976; *Smith* v. *Jones* 1999). This duty surely cannot extend to the highly generalised "obligations" to which Zinger *et al.* lay claim, including plans of suicide and escape, threats of injury that do not constitute "serious physical harm," and threats to the general security of a prison.

More generally, however, it is not clear why the CPA would impose a Tarasoff-based duty on its members when some states in the U.S. have "rejected the whole concept and taken the position that confidentiality in therapy outweighs the value of this specific duty to third parties" (Owen 1998). Also, it is not clear why CPA would extend this duty from psychologists-as-clinicians to psychologists-as-researchers, who have overlapping but occasionally different obligations that can conflict. The absolute imposition of a Tarasoff-based duty on all researchers would seem to preclude the possibility of any researcher ever going "upstream" in order to try and understand the basis of the violent behaviour psychologists are ostensibly trying to prevent. In addition to unilaterally precluding some forms of research, our concern is that CPA may be walking down the path Bollas and Sundelson (1995) describe in relation to clinicians in their provocatively titled *The New Informants: The Betrayal of Confidentiality in Psychoanalysis and Psychotherapy*:

The gruesome paradox of the Tarasoff decision is that in some respects it will have the effect of preventing the truly violent person from seeking professional help and further prevent many a person who was not truly violent—but only full of destructive impulses—from discussing destructive parts of the personality. Tarasoff will ultimately increase levels of violence in certain individuals. The threat of punishment, however understandable a primitive feeling it is, is a less effective deterrent of the violent impulse than is professional treatment of these forms of mental conflict.

Extending a Tarasoff-based "duty to warn" to the research context does nothing to prevent the violence represented in Zinger *et al.*'s litany of prison statistics because it dissuades research participants from disclosing their violent intentions. In the process it may violate the academic freedom of university researchers to make choices of ethical conscience.

Having said this, we wonder if Ogloff and Olley (1998) are correct when they say that CPA has bestowed an absolute Tarasoff-based duty on its membership. While sections I.45 and II.39 of the CPA *Code of Ethics* appear to oblige members to violate confidentiality "as required or justified by law," standard IV.17 would appear to offer other possibilities. It says that psychologists should:

familiarize themselves with the laws and the regulations of the society in which they work, especially those that are related to their activities as psychologists, and abide by them. If those laws or regulations seriously conflict with the ethical principles contained herein, psychologists would do whatever they could to uphold the ethical principles. If upholding the ethical principles could result in serious personal consequences (e.g., jail or physical harm), decision for final action would be a matter of personal conscience.

Far from being a "requirement," standard IV.17 asserts that where law or regulations [or, we would add, liability considerations] conflict with ethical principles, psychologists' first obligations are to ethics. Further, it states that the CPA member's "decision for final action" is ultimately a matter of personal conscience. Why would CPA prohibit the same approach to heinous discovery?

WHERE DOES CPA STAND?

During the course of the research confidentiality controversy at Simon Fraser University (Lowman and Palys 2000), a research ethics committee dominated by psychologists began insisting that criminologists and other researchers who might learn of law violations during the course of their research issue the following warning to prospective research participants:

Any information that is obtained during this study will be kept confidential to the full extent permitted by law. . . . However, it is possible that, as a result of legal action, the researcher may be required to divulge information obtained in the course of this research to a court or other legal body.

The problem with this consent statement is that it could give the impression that, far from doing everything they can to uphold ethical principles in the event that law and ethics conflict, as the CPA *Code* requires, researchers will disclose information whenever a court requires them to. When we asserted that we would uphold ethical principles even if that meant violating a court order, and hence refused to use the limited confidentiality consent statement shown above, the committee refused to approve our research.

In light of this development, we wrote in 1998 to Dr. John Service, the Executive Director of the CPA, asking for the Association's interpretation of sections of the 1991 *Code* which correspond to sections I.43 and I.45 of the 2000 *Code*. The questions were phrased as follows:

We are writing to seek clarification as to how we should interpret the confidentiality provisions of the 1991 (Revised) CPA *Code of Ethics*, particularly in the situation where research ethics and law conflict. What would the CPA advise researchers to do in the event they are subpoenaed and ordered to divulge confidential information? What information about confidentiality should researchers give to potential research participants in the process of seeking informed consent? What should researchers do when their university ethics committee "requires" them to do something they believe is unethical? (Letter from Palys and Lowman to John Service, 30 April 1998)

In his reply, dated July 14th 1998, Dr. Service informed us that our inquiry had been referred to Dr. Carole Sinclair who had agreed to address the issues we brought forward. The letter stated that "It is not known how long this examination will take."

Three years later, we are still waiting for the reply. We hope the appearance of our interchange with Zinger *et al.* will hasten the reply. In light of the current interchange, we request that the CPA respond to some additional questions:

1. Does the CPA bestow a Tarasoff-based duty on its members engaged in research? If so, we are concerned that the CPA is violating the academic freedom of its members to choose an alternative ethical position, such as the one adopted by the American Sociological Association (Palys and Lowman 2001: 262) which offers researchers a choice.

2. If "yes," does the CPA require its members to act on information they receive from research participants about *any* threat that could result in serious physical harm or death?

3. If the answer to question (2) is "yes," does CPA bestow this obligation on its members when there is no clearly identifiable victim?

4. Does the CPA require its members engaged in research with prisoners to report to prison authorities all "suicide plans, plans of escape, threats of injury to others and threats to the general security of prisons"?

5. The *Garner* v. *Stone* case (Palys and Lowman 2001: 258–259) suggests that the liability issues arising from the "Tarasoff duty" are far

from clear, and that if the CPA *requires* its members to act in every case a threat is made, it may well be assuming liability itself. Given the complications that arise from *Garner* v. *Stone*, what guidelines can CPA provide to help researchers distinguish "real" threats from fantasies and braggadocio?

LEGAL ADVICE AND LEGAL ANALYSIS

One final point. Zinger *et al.* portray our work as offering "legal advice." We suggest a distinction should be made between a general analysis of law of the sort we made in our article on "Ethical and legal strategies for protecting confidential research information" (Palys and Lowman 2000) and "legal advice," which is something a "client" seeks from a member of the bar. The CPA *Code of Ethics* (Standard IV.17), like other disciplinary codes of research ethics, says that researchers should familiarise themselves with the laws and regulations relevant to their professional activity. Our article on ethical and legal strategies reported our findings when we did just that. The article refers to two legal opinions on academic privilege. It was submitted to a journal that sends out all articles for blind review before it accepts them for publication. Knowing nothing about the training of the authors, the reviewers focus their comments on the substance of the arguments presented in the article. And that is as it should be.

STUDY QUESTIONS

1. Researchers are required to protect the confidentiality of the participants, but what are some limitations on that obligation?

2. How are professional obligations around the issue of confidentiality defined in other professional organizations?

3. Why would limits on the degree of confidentiality a researcher can guarantee sometimes affect research results?

NOTE

1. We would add that in following the *Tri-Council Policy Statement* (MRC 1998), researchers should take a subject-centred perspective and ask research participants what they think the confidentiality rules should be, and adjust their research protocol accordingly. It is conceivable that this consultation might yield other options in addition to the ones we identify.

REFERENCES

Bollas, C. and D. Sundelson
  1995 The New Informants: The Betrayal of Confidentiality by Psychoanalysis and Psychotherapy. Northvale, New Jersey: Jason Aronson.

Cohen, S.
  1985 Visions of Social Control. Cambridge: Polity Press.

Garner v. *Stone*
  1999 Georgia State Court (DeKalb County). No. 97A-30250-1. Reported in Renaud (2000).

Lowman J. and T.S. Palys
  2000 Ethics and institutional conflict of interest: The research confidentiality controversy at Simon Fraser University. Sociological Practice.

MRC (the Medical Research Council), NSERC (Natural Sciences and Engineering Research Council), and SSHRC (Social Sciences and Humanities Research Council)
  1998 Tri-Council Policy Statement: Ethical Conduct for Research Involving Humans. Ottawa: Department of Supply and Services. [Available at http://www.sshrc.ca/english/programinfo/policies/Index.htm]

Ogloff, J.R.P. and M.C. Olley
  1998 The interaction between ethics and the law: The on-going refinement of ethical standards for psychologists in Canada. Canadian Psychology 39(3): 221–230.

Owens, H.
  1998 The Tarasoff case: Myths and misconceptions. Forensic Psychiatry, January. [Available at http://www.nyspsych.org/cybercol/jan98/owens.html]

Palys, T.S. and J. Lowman
  2000 Ethical and legal strategies for protecting confidential research information. Canadian Journal of Law and Society 15: 39–80.

Palys, T.S. and J. Lowman
  2001 Social research with eyes wide shut: The limited confidentiality dilemma. Canadian Journal of Criminology 43: 255–267.

Renaud, T.
  2000 Jury Awards $287,000 for Psychologist Telling of Client's Lethal Fantasies. Fulton County Daily Report, January 5. [Available at http://www.lawnewsnetwork.com/stories/A12736-2000Jan4.html]

Smith v. *Jones*, [1999] 1 S.C.R. 455.

Tarasoff v. *Regents of Univ. of California* [551 P.2d, 334 (Cal. 1976)].

Thapar v. *Zezulka* Supreme Court of Texas, No. 97-1208, 1998.

Zinger, I.
  1999 The Psychological Effects of 60 Days in Administrative Segregation. Doctoral Dissertation. Department of Psychology, Carleton University.

Zinger, I., C. Wichmann, and D.A. Andrews
  2001 The psychological effects of 60 days in administrative segregation. Canadian Journal of Criminology 43: 47–83.

Zinger, I., C. Wichmann, and P. Gendreau
  2001 Legal and ethical obligations in social research: The limited confidentiality requirement. Canadian Journal of Criminology 43: 269–274.

Chapter 5

The Development of an Applied Whole-Systems Research Methodology in Health and Social Service Research: A Canadian and United Kingdom Collaboration

Susan Procter, Bill Watson, Carolyn Byrne, Jeni Bremner, Tim Van Zwanenberg,
Gina Browne, Jackie Roberts, and Amiram Gafni

Source: From *Critical Public Health*, Vol. 10, No. 3, pp. 331–342 (2000). Reprinted with kind permission from Taylor & Francis Ltd. http://www.tandf.co.uk/journals.

INTRODUCTION

This paper combines concepts from social policy, health economics and health sciences to develop a model for researching health and social service utilization across the whole system of service provision. Social policy concepts of universality and selectivity are combined with health economic concepts of supply and demand, opportunity costs and substitution of goods (services). Indicators that reflect an integrated theory of health are incorporated into the model. The paper describes the model and the theoretical rationale for the model. It provides two examples of how the model can be used to research health and social service utilization across the whole system related to biopsychosocial indicators of health needs and outcomes. One example is taken from the UK, focusing on patients with chronic obstructive pulmonary disease (COPD), and one example is taken from Canada, focusing on single parents on welfare benefits.

BACKGROUND

Calls for community-based multi-agency/multi-professional approaches to service provision

have gathered momentum since the early 1960s.[1-6] These calls arose partly in response to acknowledged failures in tertiary services to adequately resolve the presenting problems and from a recognition that intervention at this stage is often ameliorative rather than preventive.[7-10] In the light of this evidence, increasing emphasis is being placed on health promotion and prevention which, it is recognized, requires coordinated multi-agency strategies encompassing integrated universal community-based provision, greater community involvement and control and more focus on health, social inclusion and quality of life.[5, 11-13] For those at risk of succumbing to the need for tertiary intervention due to deteriorating health and/or social circumstances targeted, early individual and community-centred proactive and preventive interventions are recommended.[14-17]

Calls for community-based multi-agency/multi-service approaches to service provision derive from evidence indicating that health is created by the level of resource to which individuals and their predecessors have access throughout their lifespan. Contemporary epidemiology reveals the importance of early life experiences in determining health in middle and old age. As individuals progress through life, there are critical periods when they are at risk of acquiring attributes or experiences that predispose towards illness. Critical life course events and predisposing factors include: inter-generational factors such as maternal nutrition during pregnancy;[18] unemployment; job insecurity; onset of chronic illness and exit from the labour market.[19-21] Without support from appropriate health and social policies these events can have adverse effects on future patterns of individual and community health. Accumulated evidence of the impact of socio-economic factors on health indicates that the number of healthy life years a person can expect is dependent on the level of socioeconomic support they receive throughout life across a broad range of factors.[22] Health in its broadest sense is not the product of health services but of access to a broad range of social supports which cumulatively give rise to the number of healthy life years a person can expect and simultaneously reduces the need for curative intervention services.

This evidence has been summarized to produce the salutogenic model of health. The salutogenic model challenges researchers to identify those factors that enable people to achieve and maintain health in their daily life regardless of whether or not they have already succumbed to a disease process.[23] It can be contrasted with the pathogenic model of health that distinguishes between healthy and ill people and adopts a research agenda confined to identifying risk factors that predispose to specific disease categories.

Within the pathogenic model the role of hospitals is to provide specialist tertiary interventions targeted at those for whom there is evidence that these interventions are effective.[24] The increasing effectiveness of medical technology[25] combined with the cost of supplying and maintaining this technology has led to healthcare policies aimed at limiting access to hospitals to those able to benefit from hospital care.[26-28]

Hospitals are increasingly characterized by high turnover, shortening length of stay, and advanced technology. As a consequence they risk becoming highly impersonal. In the absence of evidence of the impact of these changes on patient and population outcomes, cost savings rather than clinical concerns may drive hospital agendas, creating wards which are 'pressure chambers' rather than safe spaces for clinical care.[28]

In response to these concerns this paper describes a model of service utilization developed at McMaster University in Canada and adapted for use in the UK, which uses a biopsychosocial perspective on health to identify the factors that drive people to access services across the whole system of service provision. The model evaluates the cost-effectiveness of providing proactive, coordinated community services in resolving needs of individuals and families with two or more compounding problems, compared with the provision of fragmented, on-demand reactive services, found in hospital-dominated systems of care provision.

SERVICE UTILIZATION

There is evidence that access to and utilization of health and social services is affected by factors as diverse as where people live, ethnocultural diversity, variation, type and intensity of service provided and individual social networks.[29-34] Moreover, underutilization of services by individuals and families from the most socially deprived and disadvantaged communities has consistently been identified.[6, 16, 35, 36] Services have different routes and access points. Some services are more immediately available and less stigmatizing than others. Healthcare is an example of a service that is less stigmatizing than social care[37, 38] and, unlike social care, it is available on demand (through general practitioners and accident and emergency departments). In the UK and Canada, healthcare is free at the point of access.

Regardless almost of need, therefore, it is likely that healthcare will form the first and most acceptable point of service access for many people. Traditionally, individual agencies have been organized to meet specific and circumscribed needs.[39] The success of these agencies is measured in relation to indicators of effectiveness at meeting these needs. Healthcare is dominated by a biomedical model of health and measured on indicators of success at reducing the incidence and prevalence of organic disease processes.[40] People presenting to healthcare, however, may have multiple and complex problems mainly, but not always, stemming from organic disease processes, often compounded by social, economic and psychological problems. Access to agencies other than health frequently involves complex referral and selective processes and may be resource limited.[41] Conversely, however, access to hospitals is limited only by waiting lists and frequently is more immediately available through general practitioners and accident and emergency departments. Under these circumstances the line of least resistance and greatest likelihood of some form of positive, acceptable response for both service users and professionals is referral to hospital. Therefore, despite considerable efforts to reduce hospitalization the rate continues to rise.[26, 27] This rise is thought to be independent of the ageing of the population.[24, 29]

This paper presents a methodology which aims to test the model that hospital utilization will only decrease when the characteristics of hospitals are replicated in community settings, augmented by a proactive and integrated approach to service provision (see Figure 5.1). The methodology uses a biopsychosocial model of health and a measure of whole-

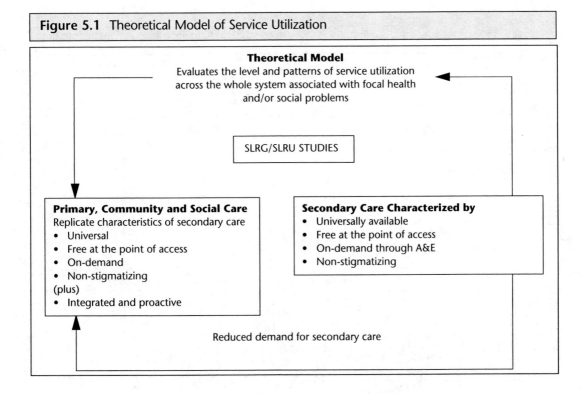

Figure 5.1 Theoretical Model of Service Utilization

Theoretical Model
Evaluates the level and patterns of service utilization across the whole system associated with focal health and/or social problems

SLRG/SLRU STUDIES

Primary, Community and Social Care
Replicate characteristics of secondary care
- Universal
- Free at the point of access
- On-demand
- Non-stigmatizing
(plus)
- Integrated and proactive

Secondary Care Characterized by
- Universally available
- Free at the point of access
- On-demand through A&E
- Non-stigmatizing

Reduced demand for secondary care

Table 5.1   Identification of Tools Used to Measure Variables across Two Studies

Measurement of	COPD	Single Parents on Welfare
Resource utilization	Health and Social Service Usage Questionnaire	Health and Social Service Usage Questionnaire
Quality of life measure	SEIQoL	Social adjustment scale Kessler UM/CIDI
Functional ability	St George's Respiratory Questionnaire	Time on social assistance
Psychosocial health	Psychological Adjustment to Illness Scale	The Minnesota Child Development Inventory

system service utilization.[42] Health needs are measured as variables along a continuum from individual physiology to family and social network support (see Table 5.1), reflecting an ecological approach recommended for community-based public health research.[6, 43] Each of these variables is correlated with service uti-lization, thereby allowing the relative costs of different mixes of service provision to be cal-culated and evaluated against the factors driv-ing service use. Taken together it is possible to identify which services maintain or improve outcomes across a range of variables and at what cost (Figure 5.2).

Figure 5.2   Cost-Effectiveness Grid

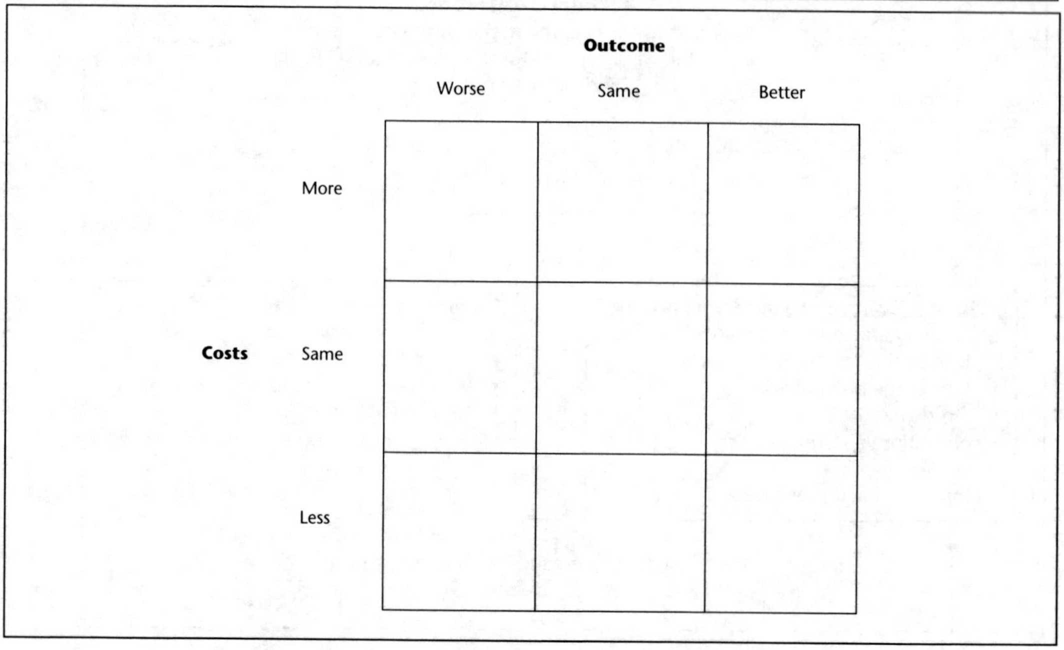

METHODOLOGY

The methodology described here was pioneered by the System-Linked Research Unit on Health and Social Service Utilisation (SLRU) and is currently being replicated by the Service Linked Research Group (SLRG) in Newcastle upon Tyne. The research uses survey methods which can take one of two forms. Large-scale, cross-sectional surveys of specified population groups are carried out to obtain data on each of the variables depicted in Table 5.1 and described below. Alternatively, service interventions are evaluated by repeating the survey data collection following changes in provision on the same study population or by establishing randomized or case-control trials of the service interventions. These interventions may be new interventions, existing or planned service developments or reductions in service provision.

Surveys are notorious for the collection and *post hoc* empirical analysis of data to identify possible correlations and causal factors. Developing a model prior to survey research requires explicit theory-making activity and has been described as 'the hallmark of scientific uses of surveys' ([44], p. 72) requiring rigorous thinking and logical clarity. In the methodology described here, the model underlying the survey is depicted in Figures 5.1 and 5.2 and Table 5.1.

SETTING

In order to achieve change and influence service development the survey method described in this paper is linked to an action-research process whereby the researchers work in collaboration with a cross-section of local agencies to identify and evaluate service interventions and to influence the future planning of services. The research is carried out within the geographic area provided for by the collaborating services. This process is described elsewhere.[45]

PARTICIPANTS

Participants in the studies conducted so far have been service users using services provided by the collaborating service providers. The study populations are identified from existing hospital and/or primary care records, or in the case of trials by referral. Ethical permission is obtained from relevant medical ethics committees before approaching potential participants.

DEVELOPMENT OF A COMMON METHODOLOGICAL FRAMEWORK

In developing a methodological framework that could be applied across different and diverse population groups it was necessary to focus on the dimensions of health underpinning the measurement tools used, rather than trying to identify a range of universally applicable tools. Consequently, the methodological framework encompasses a range of population-based indicators, depicted in Table 5.1 and described below.

In each study a range of demographic information is collected including occupation of respondent, housing tenure, marital status, number of dependants and number of rooms in the home. These data enable a differential analysis of the impact of current and planned configurations of service provision on vulnerable populations.

Previous research has found that the use of health services is independent of the type or the severity of the disease[46] but rather depends on functional ability and level of adjustment to illness.[47] Consequently, functional ability and disease severity are key indicators to measure. Functional ability has been defined as a person's ability to perform his/her normal activities of daily living.[48] Whilst this definition provides a useful starting point, it is limited to the measurement of loss of function arising from physical disability. However, physical disability may not always be the focal problem for lack of access to health. Different studies, therefore, measure disease severity and functional ability in different ways. For example, measures of functional status would differ for chronic obstructive pulmonary disease (COPD) versus single-parent mother on welfare. Functioning in the COPD study is measured as the patient's reported ability to perform activities of daily living and the impact of the disease on his/her social roles. Functional ability for welfare mothers is measured as time on or off social assistance as an alternative measure of the mother's self-sufficiency. Data on functional ability, and where appropriate, disease severity, are collected in order to provide a comparison that identifies when whole-system changes adversely impact on disease severity and/or functional ability.

The approach to the measurement of costs pioneered by the SLRU in Canada is based on measuring health and social care resource utilization through direct patient questioning and recall. The Health and Social Service Utilization questionnaire[42] is validated for differing periods of reliable recall specific to different categories of service utilization. Following data collection the level of each component of service utilization is annualized for each service user. Wherever possible, standard national prices are used, for example, in the UK, data compiled by the Personal Social Services Research Unit at the University of Kent at Canterbury were used. If national data are not available for a particular component, local average price is used as a substitute. These totals are then aggregated for each service agency and sector to provide a means of comparative analysis.

The service utilization data collection is designed to compare proportional costs within the system rather than calculate absolute costs. This approach to health service costing is a common feature of health service research.[49] What is distinctive about the Health and Social Service Utilization questionnaire is the breadth of costs covered that include direct, indirect, transfer and personal costs. Consequently the research is able to show the relative distribution of costs across the formal and informal system of care. The aim of using this measure is to show where the costs fall across the system rather than to reduce costs to any one agency's budget and to identify changes in service utilization following changes in any one part of the whole system of provision.

Psychosocial characteristics and resources are crucial factors determining the extent to which individuals are able to access and make effective use of statutory services, be those services education, health or social services. Therefore measures for psychosocial resource are identified for each population studied. For example, in the study of people with COPD, psychosocial adjustment to illness is used,[50] whilst in the Canadian study of mothers on welfare, the Minnesota Child Development Inventory was used.[51]

Quality of life has been used as an integral part of many cost-benefit analysis studies. It is used here as a way of broadening the scope of the research in order to take into account the impact of changes in service provision on the person's perceived emotional, physical and social lifestyle.[52] In both the survey and experimental phases of the research, quality of life provides a person-centred index of the effectiveness of a particular service format. Its use also ensures the research is able to identify where changes in service provision have deleterious effects upon individual circumstance.

STUDY OUTCOMES

This paper describes a research methodology that is able to identify the ways in which people use a range of statutory and voluntary sector services. The data collected on the variables given above can be analysed to produce a map of service use by different population groups including high, low and non- service users differentiated by age, gender, class, ethnicity, geography and correlated with patient outcomes as measured using physical, psychological and social indicators. Participants can be clustered according to specific characteristics and further data collected from individuals within each cluster, using qualitative interviews to obtain a more in-depth analysis of perceived need and service use.

MAIN FINDINGS

Two examples are presented, which demonstrate the diversity that the research methodology allows (see Table 5.1). In the UK, the SLRG has completed a study exploring the patterns of service use by people with chronic obstructive pulmonary disease (COPD). Disease severity was measured in terms of participants' ratings of symptomatic severity and forced expiratory volume and their ability to cope with their illness by measuring activities of daily living and their quality of life. Their current use of services was measured by the Health Utilization Questionnaire.[42] Results indicated that the high users of services, in particular hospital services, are not the individuals with the most severe disease but rather the individuals with poor psychosocial functioning. These results are now being used by partner agencies to design and test new service interventions for individuals with COPD.[53]

In Canada the SLRU has completed an intervention study where 765 single-parent householders with 1800 children aged 0–24 were randomly assigned to groups receiving home visits by public health nurses, job retraining and enhanced recreation and child care for children and compared with a group receiving usual services.[54] The study found that it was equally effective but less expensive to serve the whole family with proactive, comprehensive health and social services. In all, 25% of fami-

lies offered the full range of services exited social assistance compared with 10% outside the augmented services. The savings more than paid for the additional services and saved continued costs in social services.

These two studies provide examples of work in both Great Britain and Canada using a similar model, research methodology and ways of linking the research team with the local agencies.

DISCUSSION

Common to many recent policy documents at both an international and national level is a discussion of inter-agency collaboration and shared ways of working. Historically the function of a service has been defined in terms of its impact on a singular variable (i.e., in the case of hospitals, waiting lists, bed occupancy, compliance with medical instructions), and that variable reflects professional or organizational concerns rather than the needs or reality of the experience for the service user. The impetus underpinning inter-agency working requires agencies to collaborate in order to provide individual mixes of services designed to meet individual needs.[4] Multi-agency approaches to evaluation using measures of patient need and health and social care outcomes which do not privilege the contribution of any one agency are required to test the cost-effectiveness of inter-agency working. The model described earlier goes some way towards addressing these issues.

A strength of this model and approach to fostering inter-agency collaboration lies in providing outcomes which have a currency for all services involved in the research. By defining health as a multi-dimensional concept and developing a model that measures features of its biological, psychological and social components, the health outcomes for the service user can be seen as being affected by a number of agencies. This, in turn, gives rise to the potential for joint forms of service input customized to meeting the individual needs of the user more comprehensively.

To date, the SLRU team has carried out 12 studies (five historic cohorts and seven randomized control trials) in diverse sectors of public services. Findings from these studies consistently indicate that the main predictors of service utilization across the whole system are psychosocial characteristics rather than disease type or severity. Intervention studies built on these findings demonstrate that programmes of well-integrated, community-based interventions reduce whole-system costs whilst improving or maintaining health outcomes. The main conclusions emerging are that it is more or equally effective and less expensive to offer comprehensive, proactive packages of care rather than on-demand, fragmented services.[55]

While the results are promising, further work needs to be undertaken on testing the validity and reliability of the model presented here. The research carried out so far has addressed issues for members of particular social groups, e.g., single parents in receipt of state benefits, and diagnostic groups, e.g., people with a chronic disease. What is not yet established is whether this model of health and social service utilization has a role within other areas of health or social research, such as epidemiology where the focus is often whole populations rather than targeted population groups. The data collected provide evidence of the cost-effectiveness of integrating provision from different agencies; however, the issue of shifting resources from tertiary services to preventive primary services remains difficult, even with evidence of the cost-effectiveness of this approach. While the model provides some evidence for proactive targeted interventions, the issue of stigmatization needs to be understood if services that are acceptable to the targeted population are to be utilized effectively. The model has been able to demonstrate comparative outcomes arising from different forms of intervention for individuals presenting with

similar needs. To date it has not been developed to look at the long-term consequences on service utilization of early population-based preventive interventions. Meanwhile the ultimate strength of this model for public health research is the power to identify the impact on health outcomes using interventions from a multitude of disciplines and sectors.

STUDY QUESTIONS

1. What is the authors' operational definition of health?

2. How would you conduct this study if your operational definition of health was the absence of disease or injury?

3. How well does the theoretical model fit the general guidelines for a sound theory? Explain.

4. What are the advantages of doing comparative research? Use the study to explain fully.

5. How does the study apply outside of a traditional research setting? Explain. (Hint: applied research).

REFERENCES

1. Ministry of Health. *Report of the Committee of the Welfare of Children in Hospital* (Platt Report). London: HMSO; 1959.

2. Seebohm Report. *Report of the Committee on Local Authority and Allied Personnel Social Services.* London: HMSO; 1968.

3. Bulmer M. *The social basis of community care.* London: Allen & Unwin; 1987.

4. Audit Commission for England and Wales. *Community care: managing the cascade of change.* London: HMSO; 1992.

5. Department of Health. *Partnership in action: new opportunities for joint working between health and social services.* London: Department of Health; 1998.

6. Israel BA, Schulz AJ, Parker EA, Becker A. Review of community based research: assessing partnership

approaches to improve public health. *Ann Rev Public Health* 1998; 19: 173–202.

7. World Health Organisation. *Primary health care: a report on the Conference on Primary Care* (Alma Ata), Health for All Series No.1 WHO, Geneva; 1978.

8. World Health Organisation. *The Ottawa Charter for Health Promotion*. Ottawa, Canada: Canadian Public Health Association, Health and Welfare Ottawa; 1986.

9. World Health Organisation. *European health care reform: analysis of current strategies*. Copenhagen: WHO; 1997.

10. Council of Europe. *Organisation of prevention in primary care*. Strasbourg: Council of Europe; 1986.

11. Ashton J. *Healthy cities*. Milton Keynes: Open University Press; 1992.

12. van Londen J. *What has Europe done for us?* Public hearing on the future of public health policy, October. Brussels: European Parliament; 1998.

13. Donaldson RJ, Donaldson LJ. *Essential public health medicine*. London: Kluwer; 1993.

14. Kaplun A. *Health promotion and chronic illness*, WHO Regional Publications, European Series, No. 44. Copenhagen: World Health Organisation Regional Office for Europe; 1992.

15. The NHS Health Advisory Service. *Child and adolescent mental health services, together we stand*, The Commissioning Role and Management of Child and Adolescent Mental Health Services. London: HMSO; 1995.

16. Flaskerud JH, Winslow BJ. Conceptualizing vulnerable populations: health related research. *Nursing Res* 1998; 47(2): 69–77.

17. McWilliam CL, Stewart M, Brown JB, Desai K, Coderre P. Creating health with chronic illness. *Adv Nursing Sci* 1996; 18(3): 1–15.

18. Barker, D. *Fetal and infant origins of disease in adult life*. London: British Medical Association; 1992.

19. Blane D, Brunner E *et al.*, editors. *Health and social organisation*. London: Routledge; 1996.

20. Essen J, Wedge P. *Continuities in childhood disadvantage*. London: Heinemann; 1982.

21. Bartley M, Blane D *et al.* Health and the life course: why safety nets matter. *BMH* 1997; 314: 1194–6.

22. Grossman M. The demand for health: a theoretical and empirical investigation. New York: National Bureau of Economic Research; 1972.

23. Antonovsky A. The salutogenic model as a theory to guide health promotion. *Health Promotion Int* 1996; 11(1): 11–18.

24. Abel-Smith B. *Introduction to health policy, planning and financing*. London: Longman; 1994.

25. Walford D. The developed world: health policy and technological innovation. Newson-Davis J, and Weatherall, DJ, editors. *Health policy and technological innovation*. London: Chapman & Hall; 1994: 3–26.

26. World Health Organisation. *European health care reform: analysis of current strategies*. Copenhagen: WHO; 1997.

27. US Congress Office of Technology Assessment. *Hospital financing in seven countries*. Washington, DC: US Government Printing Office; 1995.

28. McKee M, Aiken L, Rafferty AM, Sochalski J. Organisational change and quality of health care: an evolving international agenda. *Qual Health Care* 1998; 7: 37–41.

29. Barer ML, Evans RG, Hertzman C, Lomas J. Aging and health care utilisation: new evidence on old fallacies. *Soc Sci Med* 1987; 24(10): 851–62.

30. Light E, Lebowitz BD, Bailey F. CMHCs and elderly services: An analysis of direct and indirect services and delivery sites. *Community Mental Health J* 1986; 22(4): 294–302.

31. McCance C, Paterson JG, Nimmo AW, Hunter D. Psychiatric geography: where people live and their use of services—a study of computerised mapping of case register data. *Health Bull* 1987; 45(4): 197–210.

32. Donaldson C, Wright KG, Maynard AK, Hamill JD, Sutcliffe E. Day hospitals for the elderly: utilisation and performance. *Community Med* 1987; 9(1): 55–61.

33. Starrett RA, Decker JT, Araujo A, Walters G. The social service utilisation behaviour of USA mainland Puerto Rican elderly: a causal model. *Ageing and Society* 1987; 7: 455–8.

34. Albert MA, Becker T, Mccrone P, Thornicroft G. Social networks and mental health service utilisation—a literature review. *Int J Soc Psychiatry* 1998; 44(4): 248–66.

35. Townsend P, Phillimore P, Beattie A. *Health and deprivation: inequality and the North*. London: Croom Helm; 1988.

36. Haynes R. Inequalities in health and health service use evidence from the General Household Survey. *Soc Sci Med* 1991; 33(4): 361–8.

37. Graham H. *Women, health and the family*. London: Harvester Wheatsheaf; 1984.

38. Twigg J. Models of carers: how do social care agencies conceptualise their relationships with informal carers? *J Social Policy* 1989; 18(1): 53–66.

39. James A. *Managing to care: public service and the market*. London: Longman; 1994.

40. Department of Health. *Health of the nation: a strategy for health in England* (CM 1986). London: HMSO; 1992.

41. Lipsky M. The paradox of managing discretionary workers in social welfare policy. In: Adler M, Bell C, Clasen J, Sinfield A, editors. *The sociology of social security*. Edinburgh: Edinburgh University Press; 1991: 212–28.

42. Browne G, Gafni A, Roberts J, Goldsmith A, Jamieson E. *Approach to the measurement of costs (expenditures) when evaluating health and social programs*, Systems Linked Research Unit Working Paper Series 95 11. Ontario, Canada: McMaster University; 1995.

43. Bronfenbrenner U. Ecological systems theory. In: Wozniak RH, Fischer KW. *Development in context: acting and thinking in specific environments*. Hillsdale, NJ: Lawrence Erlbaum; 1993: 3–44.

44. Marsh C. *The survey method: the contribution of surveys to sociological explanation*. London: George Allen & Unwin; 1982.

45. Watson B, Procter S, van Zwanenberg T, Byrne C, Browne G, Roberts J, Gafni A. Interdisciplinary, intersectoral and international collaboration in research. *National Academies of Practice Forum* 2000; 2(3): 217–222.

46. Browne G, Watt S, Roberts J, Gafni A, Byrne C. Within our reach: evidence-based practice resulting from alliances in health and social services. *Clinical Excellence for Nurse Practitioners* 1997; 1(2): 127–40.

47. Byrne C, Bell B, Roberts J. Problems of people who use primary care in Ontario, Canada: Implications for the complimentary role of the nurse practitioner. *Clinical Excellence for Nurse Practitioners* 1996; 1(1): 1–7.

48. Lareau SC, Breslin EH, Meek PM. Functional status instruments: outcome measure in the evaluation of patients with chronic obstructive airways disease. *Heart Lung* 1996; 25(3): 212–23.

49. Rees Jones I. Costing health services: health economics. In: Bowling A, editor. *Research methods in health: investigating health and health services*. Buckingham: Open University Press; 1997: 79–98.

50. Derogatis LR. The psychosocial adjustment to illness scale (PAIS). *J Psychosomatic Res* 1986; 30(1): 77–91.

51. Kopparthi R, McDermott C, Sheftel D, Lenke MC, Getz M, Frey M. The Minnesota Child Development Inventory: validity and reliability for assessing development in infancy. *J Dev Behav Pediatr* 1991; 12(4): 217–22.

52. Bowling A. *Research methods in health: investigating health and health services*. Buckingham: Open University Press; 1997.

53. Watson B, Stenton C, Bremner J, van Zwanenberg T, Procter S. Patterns of, and driving factors for service use in people with chronic obstructive pulmonary disease. British Thoracic Society Conference Paper, London, 1998.

54. Browne G, Byrne C, Roberts J, Gafni A, Watt S. Benefiting all the beneficiaries of social assistance: the 2-year effects and expense of subsidized versus nonsubsidized quality child care and recreation. *National Academies of Practice Forum* 1999; 1(2): 131–42.

55. Browne G, Roberts J, Gafni A, Byrne C, Weir R, Majumdar B, Watt S. Evaluating the outcomes of economic evaluations: lessons from 12 studies. Health and Risk Conference, St Catherines College, Oxford, 1998.

Chapter 6

Is Research-Ethics Review a Moral Panic?

Will C. van den Hoonaard

Source: From *The Canadian Review of Sociology and Anthropology*, Feb. 2001, Vol. 38, Issue 1, p. 19. Reprinted with kind permission from The Canadian Sociology and Anthropology Association.

Ethical review, as a broad-based approach to conducting scientific research, emerged from the aftermath of the horrors of World War II, when medical experiments furthered lugubrious social aims (Charbonneau, 1984: 20). The Nuremberg Code tried to forestall the use of such experiments by codifying viable, ethical guidelines for medical, scientific and social research, with particular emphasis on informed consent. While the Code remained an ethical hallmark, the history of scientific research would take at least another 50 years to catch up to the Nuremberg principles. As scientific experimentation with human subjects was thought to be directed toward more noble goals, the instances of such experiments ranged from exposing soldiers to atomic blasts (Welsome, 1999) to imposing medical procedures on prisoners or forensic in-patients,[1] to experimentation with drugs, whether LSD, DepoProvera,[2] or drugs near market entry.

When the latent effects of these experiments became manifest—often 20 or 30 years later—and with the subsequent rise of lawsuits, the public and government became acutely aware of the ethical implications of medical research and, indeed, of all research. First through professional societies and then more vigorously through the State, ethical guidelines became explicit.

During the latter years of this evolution of ethical norming, i.e., in the early 1990s, the Medical Council of Canada, the Natural Sciences and Engineering Research Council of Canada, and the Social Sciences and Humanities Research Council of Canada started the process of developing the *Tri-Council Policy on Ethics Involving Human Subjects* ("the *Policy*"). The first draft of the *Policy* was issued as a Memorandum on 16 November 1994. The draft was widely circulated but, under the force of opposition on the part of academics and other researchers, the draft seemed to have withered away. It resurfaced in 1998 in revised form, and the three Councils quickly adopted it in 1998. Universities now use the *Policy*, which was initially adopted to facilitate ethical approval of research funded by the three Councils, to cover non-funded research, including undergraduate research. The Councils required that the *Policy* be adopted no later than January 2000, within two years of its acceptance by the Councils.

EXPERIENCES OF QUALITATIVE RESEARCHERS

Long before research-ethics review became *de rigueur*, qualitative researchers were conscious of the ethical implications of their work. William Foote Whyte's *Street Corner Society*, first published in 1943, contains an extended discussion in the appendix about research ethics, although the word "ethics" was quite uncommon. More recently, Eliot Liebow's *Tell Them Who I Am*

(1993), already a celebrated classic in field research, exemplifies the highest ethical standards of research. Issues of "voice," representativity, and human dignity are now part and parcel of any discussion on qualitative research. Still, it is not a question of whether qualitative researchers are more ethical in their work than quantitative researchers.[3] It is a question of whether it is appropriate to judge the ethical merit of qualitative research using criteria derived from other paradigms of research: the question is a social-structural, not a personal, one.

Shula Reinharz (1993: 78) speaks eloquently about the problematic nature of the requirement to obtain written consent using "coercive" formal statements on official university letterhead. The coercive nature of ethical review on the "human subject" became the subject of an impromptu gathering at the 16th Qualitative Analysis Conference in Fredericton, New Brunswick, in 1999, at which emerged many sentiments of qualitative researchers when faced with the prospect, or the aftermath, of dealing with research-ethics committees. The experiences of these researchers fall into several broad categories: the political, epistemological, and the practical. Although not all of the experiences touch all of the researchers with the same degree of intensity, qualitative researchers do experience them.

Political

1. Gatekeeping and the Norming of Research
A number of researchers (e.g., Kellner, 2000) liken the control exercised by university ethics committees, and by the *Policy* in particular, to gatekeeping that favours deductive methods of research. There is no doubt that the standards envisaged in the *Policy* are normed in the natural, bio-medical sciences. The current *Policy* adopts a tenor that appears to be centred in these sciences. For example, the word "subject" is favoured over research "participant," a term

that finds more resonance among qualitative researchers, because the term "subject" has a pejorative connotation: for while it is true that one occupies the position of "researcher," there is a far greater sense of collaboration with interviewees than is customary in, for example, survey research. The *Policy* extends to judging the adequacy of the research design itself. The *Policy* speaks of the importance of maintaining a "common standard" of research, and scrutinizes applications on the basis of various levels of harm that might be inflicted on research subjects. The *Policy* speaks of research "protocols," a term that makes eminent sense to medical researchers, but is quite unfamiliar among qualitative researchers who see their work in a more collaborative sense. It is a comprehensive policy that streamlines the ethical strands of everyone's research under the aegis of the respective universities who have firmly adopted the biomedical model. As one qualitative researcher put it, "qualitative researchers have become the fall guys for ethical mistakes in medical research" (Anonymous D).

2. Advocacy Role as a Dilemma
As it is not atypical for qualitative researchers to immerse themselves in the setting they are studying, the boundaries between them and the community under study can become "blurred" (Pollack, 1999). Pollack notes in her study on women in prisons that the "notion of the self as a research influence is an important aspect of qualitative research that deserves further exploration." For her, the ethical issues of research centre on "the responsibility of the researcher to her/his subjects when one disturbs the equilibrium of a community." The complexity of this relationship is such that "protocols" cannot easily respond to it (Stokholm, 1999).

For some researchers, like Weinberg (1999), the practice of ethics in the field is not a one-dimensional issue. She conducted a focus group to understand the standpoint of the residents

of a maternity home, and three ethical dilemmas emerged. As a feminist, she became very
aware of her responsibility to challenge hege-
monic ideology, but "ran smack" into the realities of recognizing the need for some social
control in an institutional setting. Her "findings raised issues which reflected negatively"
on the institution. When conducting field work
in hierarchical settings, she found, conflicting
ethical demands arise, such as confidentiality,
causing no harm, and acknowledgement of
respondents in the study.

Epistemology

1. *Individualism* Research ethics, as they currently stand, are developed and used in the
context of a liberal democratic tradition that
emphasizes individual rights and freedoms.
The fetish of individualism (which lies at the
basis of medical research in particular) has
become a problem in sociological research for
several reasons. Such an individualistic tradition may be quite foreign to other cultures
where collectivism prevails and where individual rights are defined by the collectivity. In
such cases, the seeking of individual consent
may be an affront to the larger group.
Stokholm (1999), for example, using field work
in Kitchener-Waterloo with persons of Chinese
heritage, discovered that "such problems as
protection of participants and guarantees of
anonymity are treated not as simple ethical
rules." Rather, he finds, "failure to account for
this amounts to disciplinary self-delusion."
What the researcher needs, he believes, are the
"post-modernist and feminist preferences for
life histories and intense contextualization of
the individual."

2. *Issue of Voice* Increasingly, social researchers
have come to understand the unmitigated
nature of deductive approaches because, in
recording their findings, deductive researchers
amplify their own voice, rather than that of the
research participants. For qualitative researchers,
there is a growing recognition of the struggle
involved in finding the right place between the
autobiography of the researcher and the biography of the research participants (Mills, 2000;
Chahal, 2000). Using a life-history case study of
"Hazel," a dental assistant, Mills explores "the
contentious issues" surrounding voice, narrative,
and the "complex relationship" between the
biography of the research subject and the autobiography of the researcher.

Practical Considerations

1. *Limitations on Open Forms of Research* It
goes without saying that all research must be
guided by a relevant or appropriate research
question. While for many types of research it
is clear that such a question will emerge from a
review of the literature, or from some practical
issue, ethnographic research adopts, in some
instances, a different position. Researchers
using qualitative research methods find the
insistence on the part of ethics committees on
knowing the exact questions they are putting
to interviewees to be quite impossible to put
into practice. The nature and direction of questions in in-depth interviews are, in large part,
dictated by the interviewee him- or herself, not
by the researcher who defines the broader
research dimensions. Usually, the specific
research question emerges only *after* a series of
in-depth interviews. Typically, a review of the
literature comes at the end of the research
process. Anselm Strauss states that:

> . . . because the analysis of these [ethnographic]
> data begins (in our style of research) with the very
> first, second, or third interview or after the first day
> or two of fieldwork . . . It follows also that the next
> interviews and observations become informed by
> analytic questions and hypotheses about categories
> and their relationships. This guidance becomes
> increasingly explicit as the analysis of new data con-
> tinues (1987: 27).

Or, what may have seemed important during the initial stages of study becomes marginal in the course of the research, and so other areas open up for study. Scientists who are used to stating formal hypotheses and practising deductive reasoning may be appalled at such an approach. Nevertheless, ethnographic research has yielded significant insights because of its open, inductive approach.

2. Limitations on Participatory Research O'Neill (2000) and others see the hard architecture around current research-ethics review as limiting participatory models of research because, as it is impossible to specify in advance of the research either the questions or the risk of such research, it is difficult to receive consent to do such research. For many qualitative researchers this is perhaps one of the most significant obstacles in the current climate of research ethics. O'Neill avers that the idea "of a completely formulated proposal is a by-product of the medical model" and that "the demand that the researcher have a detailed proposal before starting . . . limits participatory models of inquiry." Typically, he claims, this sort of research, which involves a host community in planning a project "that serves local needs as well as scientific objectives," evolves over time.

3. Heterogeneity of Research Participants Defies a Common Ethical Template Karen Hancock (1999), amongst others, urges recognition of the heterogeneity of research participants. Even though she studied one social setting, namely the sex-trade industry in London, Ontario (focussing on the health and safety experiences of women living in the sex-trade subculture), her methodology included both observation and interviews of street prostitutes, exotic dancers, body-rub attendants, and escorts. As such, research ethics has differing implications for each group, requiring sensitivity on the part of the researcher.

4. Will the Policy Speak to Cyberspace Research? Research "on the Web" has increased to such an extent that even the current policies on research ethics seem out of place (GVU Center's WWW User Surveys, 2000). Barbara Waruszynski (2000) examines the interactions among groups conducting qualitative research via the Internet and the ethical implications that arise from the application of these innovative methods. She seeks to determine if certain research methodologies and activities in cyberspace would violate our professional ethics in conducting social-science research.

IS RESEARCH-ETHICS REVIEW A MORAL PANIC?

There has been an explosion of interest in "ethics." In Canada alone, in 1999, there were 5,000 ethics conferences, as opposed to 100 in 1994 (Curtis, 1999: D1). Similarly, there has been a staggering rise in the number of ethicists, ethics companies, and ethics policies in business, administration, sports, and science. According to Jenefer Curtis, the decline of religion and the rise of "intense individualism" have created a moral vacuum, which "ethics" is now trying to fill. In the process, however, the word has become "perverted" (Curtis, 1999: D1). Citing Tom Hurka of the Department of Philosophy at the University of Calgary, she points out that "because there is not much public trust, institutions put in place a code—cut and dried rules—instead of training people to have good judgment" (cited by Curtis, 1999: D4).

Under such circumstances, one wonders whether the parallel rise of research-ethics review might not be a case of a *moral panic*, which Cohen calls a "threat to societal values and interests" (Cohen, 1972: 9). A moral panic is indicated by hostility and sudden eruption of measured concern shared by a significant segment of the population, with disproportional claims about the potential harm moral deviants are able to wrought (Goode and Ben-Yahuda, 1994). Within the context of our paper, moral panic occurs throughout the research-ethics review, which so heavily relies on the deductive model of research as normative, proclaiming the rest as non-normative. As a member of a review board stated, "Today's academic research environment, with its public (and not public) scandals, provides a strong incentive toward regulation and monitoring. . . ." (Anonymous F, 1995). Moral panics involve exaggeration of harm and risk, orchestration of the panic by elites or powerful special-interest groups, the construction of imaginary deviants, and reliance on diagnostic instruments.

Exaggeration of Harm and Risk

Ethics-review bodies can overstate risks. In a study on teenage girls, for example, whereby the research topic invited disclosure of experiences "that require[d] professional follow-up or intervention," the researchers found that "the adolescent girls appreciated the opportunity to discuss their experiences and concerns with interested adults who inhabit a world outside their everyday realm of parents and school" (Anonymous C, 2000: 6). Social researchers like these, delving into emotive topics, have not found interviews cascading into the sort of troubled waters that require work by therapists. Still, it would be helpful to have phone numbers or persons available, but the premise should be that professional interviews are, for the most part, quite trouble-free. Many researchers are painfully aware that there might be many unintended results of one's research, but they also know that one cannot always know those results. While there is no perfect vision in that regard, risks might be exaggerated.

To show the level of difficulty in determining the risks and benefits of research, I refer the reader to a 1930s mapping expedition among the Aborigines of Australia, organized by Adelaide's Board for Anthropological Research, in the Warburton Range. The survey involved measuring and photographing individuals, eliciting their genealogies, drawing blood and hair samples, and even making plaster casts of parts or all of their bodies. As Woodward and Lewis (1998) point out, even though politicians and ethicists levelled criticism against the survey, the work was "done systematically and with care," later allowing Aborigines to find out "more about their family histories, their ancestry, and their land-based affiliations" (389).

Orchestration of a Moral Panic

Powerful elites or specific interest groups can orchestrate a moral panic (Victor, 1998: 547). The elites choose major institutions (in our case, universities and research-granting bodies) to generate a campaign that sustains scholarly methodological outrage about methodologies on the margins. It is common, when moral panics occur, for competition between the older and newer agencies of control to occur (Victor, 1998: 549). In many respects, quantitative researchers demand that qualitative research issues be rephrased in the language of the former, an unsettling form of colonization. Biomedical and legal authorities assert their dominance and define the shape of the moral panic. Newer authorities (like those represented by the community of ethnographers) must exert more effort to counter the social control exercised by the traditional authority.

Bolstered by legal enforcement, moral panic has assumed a legitimacy that has spread across Canada to other settings, such as Canada's North, and, indeed, to the Third World, where researchers are more likely to abandon traditional moral principles in favour of the ethical codes in which they were trained in Western society (Charbonneau, 1984: 21). Similarly, social research on Canada's North has been forced to undergo a process of ethical review that seems more appropriate for the hard sciences than the social sciences. For the stated purpose of protecting Inuit culture from researchers, granting bodies rely on a Western model of ethical review, reinforcing the very research approach that is being rejected. The setting up of such non-Western review bodies[4] still echoes the Western deductive template. At the heart of such orchestration are the issues of confidentiality and signed consent forms.

1. *Confidentiality*   Given the reliance on the biomedical model of research, aided by legal advice, it is understandable that the *Policy* gives much weight to the idea of anonymity and confidentiality. Legal enactments, in Canada and the United States, give the right of maintaining confidentiality (and anonymity) generally only to physicians, lawyers, priests, ministers, rabbis, and one's spouse. Social researchers in the United States, however, cannot invoke promises of confidentiality as a "scholar's privilege," as recently attested in a court case involving a doctoral student at Washington University whom the courts asked to surrender field data in connection with his research on a radical animal-rights group (Comarow, 1993: A44). Some, like Comarow, a lawyer and former federal official in the United States, suggest that sociologists ought to be prepared to spend time in prison if they wish to follow through on their promise of anonymity of sources and confidentiality of research data when faced with subpoenas or court orders (A44).

There has so far been only one case in Canada in which a court has asked a scholar— Russel Ogden, a graduate student in criminology at Simon Fraser University, who in 1994 was researching assisted suicides in cases of persons with HIV—to divulge confidential information in a matter involving a death (Lowman and Palys, 1998: 6).[5] The student defended the case successfully, arguing that he had passed the so-called Wigmore test, which sets out four criteria for disclosure of communication:

1. the communications must originate in the confidence that they will not be disclosed;

2. this element of confidentiality must be essential to the full and satisfactory maintenance of the relations between the parties;

3. the relation must be one that, in the opinion of the community, ought to be sedulously fostered; and

4. the injury that would ensue to the relation by the disclosure of the communications must be greater than the benefit thereby gained for the correct disposal of litigation (Lowman and Palys, 1998: 6).

The results, however, permeated successive research under the ethical aegis of the Simon Fraser Research Ethics Committee, which now insists that researchers can only offer "limited confidentiality" to research participants. In doing so, according to Lowman and Palys, the university ethics committee "traded away participants'" right to confidentiality by undermining their only legal protection, the Wigmore test (1998: 6). By undermining the criteria set out in the Wigmore test, university ethics committees are exposing research participants to harm (1998: 6).[6] By intertwining ethical and legal issues that prioritize institutional liability over ethics, the Committee leaves researchers

to twist and turn in the wind when they take seriously the responsibility to protect research participants from harm . . . [by which the university] abrogates its oblig8ation to create an environment in which researchers can collect and publicly disseminate information about all aspects of society (Lowman and Palys, 1998: 7).

In other ways, too, currently emerging ethical guidelines reaffirm the quantitative model of research. While Heather MacDonald, a Ph.D. candidate in nursing at the University of Manchester, was permitted to use a consent form that she, rather than the research participants, signed, she struggled with a move in the United Kingdom to store qualitative data for future review or for secondary analysis:

To gain access in one area I had to agree to have my data—and I mean transcripts—available for review for ten years. I had great difficulty with this since I am interviewing a vulnerable group and have taken great pains to provide anonymity (MacDonald, 1999).

2. Consent Forms The use of signed consent forms is one of the most highly contested areas from the perspective of qualitative researchers. It might be easy for ethics committees to stipulate the requirement of using the signed form of consent in all research involving interviewees, but the situation is far more complex and requires a lengthy and detailed understanding of the ethnographic field research method.

The idea of informed consent of the individual, which Charbonneau (1984: 20) describes as the *"cornerstone of all Western ethical codes,"* is extremely difficult to implement when studying groups living on the margins of society. Aside from problems of illiteracy (Charbonneau, 1984: 21), the difficulties multiply as one investigates not only those whose lives are touched by social problems, but also areas of secrecy, whether of marginal or even elite groups. It is ironic that just as society is devoting more resources to "applied" research, the legal emphasis on signed consent undermines the study of social problems.

The difficulty is heightened when both the advantages and risks are hard to assess and where potential participants must "have complete knowledge (to give informed consent)" (O'Neill, 2000). An insistence on using such forms may, in some cases, destroy natural anonymity. Whereas before, it would have been possible to retain the full anonymity of those being interviewed, it is now necessary to acquire a name and signature. One can imagine many instances where the insistence on a signed consent form may be unwise or tactless. In studies of street-corner men, poachers, prostitutes, fishers, drug users, professional thieves, the homeless and, in general, those with socially defined problems, this would simply

elicit an angry response. The difficulty even persists in obtaining signatures from those who occupy positions of power and prestige.

Ethnographic research, in the light of its purpose, is conducted from the point of view of "participant observation." A researcher of this methodological tradition endeavours to understand the whole subculture that surrounds the so-called subjects. To achieve such an understanding, the researcher endeavours to leave the culture intact. This involves a process whereby the researcher respects that culture with the least possible intrusion. The researcher must be careful not to aggressively assert his or her rights or views. The introduction of a signed consent form violates the very essence of ethnographic research, because human "subjects" would regard the requirement of such a form as *coercive*. The inappropriateness of using a signed consent form is further highlighted by the fact that ethnographic research does not entail experimentation. Such experimentation could, for example, involve the placement of "surface electrodes"[7] or, not infrequently, hidden tapes, whereby the "subjects" are told one thing, and the desired research plans are hidden from the persons under study. This approach to research is quite alien to ethnographic research. In the case of interviews, the datum rests within those interviews, consistent with the purpose of the research's being made clear to interviewees.[8]

In the experience of qualitative researchers, the requirement of using signed consent forms may paradoxically take away the right of an individual to participate in research. One colleague in one of Fredericton's universities, although eager to participate in a research project, would have been effectively barred because she refused to sign such a form even if the researcher had closely followed the approved procedure mandated by her ethics committee (Anonymous D, 2000). Here is an account from a nurse/sociologist who has taken on the task of interviewing people in home-care situations:

I gave each of them [caregiver and older person] a copy of the consent form and asked them to review it and then I would answer whatever questions they had. Both Mrs. McK [caregiver] and George [older person] read it carefully (took time).

George says that he has a question for me about the form. . . . He looks at me rather thoughtfully and asks, "What difference will it make whether I sign it or not?" Thinking he might be having second thoughts about my being there for the study, I reminded him that he could ask me to leave his home if he didn't want to participate. "No, you don't understand my question," he replies. "Will you do anything differently here this morning if I sign the form than if I don't sign it?" I can see that he is not concerned about my being there but seems to be questioning the need for his signature. I've just driven for 45–50 minutes to be at this home. If he's not objecting to my being there and knows why I am there, would I actually have to leave if he doesn't sign? These thoughts are racing through my head. While I'm thinking about this, George leans over and signs the consent. I still have another form for George to sign, the consent for the follow-up interview with the family caregiver (Anonymous E, 2000).

Some of the solutions proposed by ethics committees are just plain silly, but to be followed, nevertheless. For example, a member of a departmental ethics committee told a graduate student to turn her face the other way when she was doing participant observation in a group that had at least one human "subject" who did not explicitly give consent to the research. It is hard to know what to do under those circumstances. Such circumspect behaviour creates more problems than warranted and casts doubt among the subjects about their own behaviours and beliefs.

The researcher develops a natural bond with the interviewee: in all likelihood, the interviewee has been previously aware of the presence of the researcher, and a fair amount of common stock of knowledge is available about each other—this is not unlike any real-life situation. Reflecting on my own 30-year research experience, it is indeed difficult to imagine my relationship to the 200 or so interviewees without such a bond. Invariably, such ties either evolved out of, or became, natural friendships or relationships involving trust. The use of a signed consent form could break such a bond. Other interviewees will regard them as a disloyal act on the part of the researcher. This dilemma can occur even if one is known as a researcher, a fact that is stated in advance of any research project.

This vexing problem was brought to my attention recently by a graduate student doing fieldwork in Nunavut. She had obtained ethics approval from her department, and her proposal had been passed by the Nunavut Council on Research. Both groups insisted she use consent forms that "seemed to ferment the stereotype of a researcher from outside as self-centered" (Anonymous A, 1999). In addition to having a signed consent form and a mission statement, the student had to repeat the process for the interpreter, who also had to be provided with an "interpreter confidentiality" form. Each sheet was drawn up in two languages, and copies were to be made for all parties involved, including research agencies—a total of 22 sheets of paper had to be available and signed before the interview could begin. In the words of the researcher:

The woman looked at all of the papers, looked at the consent form, and refused to sign it, stating that her daughter had told her not to sign anything. I had to respect that . . . I wondered just how different the interview might have gone had I not felt the need to be so formal with her. When I left she refused to even keep the (unsigned) participant consent form.

Every other interview started with a confusing first five minutes and the interviewees would say, "whatever," whenever she would explain why she had all of these forms. The researcher concluded that the "consent forms were obtrusive and established an atmosphere of formality and mistrust" (Anonymous A, 1999).

The use of consent forms signed by interviewees becomes particularly problematic when one is engaged in research on sensitive topics. Grace Getty, who researches men who have sex with men, reports that she had devised a method of allowing interviewees to sign the form with a code that they had made up. She reports that "[f]ew of them would have been willing to have their name attached even to a consent form that was kept separate from the tapes, etc." (Getty, 1999). Obtaining signed consent forms is also problematic in other ways. As Felice J. Levine (1995) points out in the case of research on children:

parents often fail to sign and return written consent forms, not because they object to their children's participation in research, but simply because they do not have the time or take the time to read the forms and sign them (81).[9]

Each year, qualitative researchers bring similarly discouraging stories to the attention of their colleagues. In 1999, the issue became so compelling that qualitative researchers organized the impromptu session referred to above. One masters student, in correspondence, described the process of ethical review as "HORRIBLE, ridiculous [her emphasis]" (Anonymous B, 2000). She further stated that the person "in charge of approving or disapproving [research applications] knows nothing about social-science research."

If signed forms of consent create confusion on the part of the ethnographer, what could one say about the interviewees? Would not such forms be interpreted as a form of waiving control? Might not the interviewees guess that such forms are, after all, designed to protect a research grant–awarding body or some other institution, rather than them? Would not such an interpretation develop cynicism? How could one, moreover, be apprised of all the

risks involved in research? Remember that ethnographic research does not resort to experimental procedures where the effects may include physical or mental pain. It would be a gross overstatement of fact to claim to know, on the part of both the interviewee and the interviewer, what those risks are.[10] Both parties make an educated guess what those risks are, and both are free to enter into the interview situation; no more can be expected under such circumstances.

From the perspective of ethnographers or those who partially employ the ethnographic approach, mandated signed forms of consent interfere with academic freedom. While research-ethics committees insist on the use of such forms, the ethnographer will be precluded from practising his or her craft. Research funds will not be forthcoming and such research may have to move away from the protection of the university community. Ethnographers will have to practise their craft on a personal basis, leading to other sets of problems. It is beyond the scope of these pages to fully consider the development of the requirement of a signed consent form in its proper ideological, legal or political context.

The Construction of Imaginary Deviants

As Victor claims, "[f]alse accusations are a necessary part of a moral panic" (1998: 549). For a moral panic to be effective, it is essential to seize on highly publicized, ethically dubious cases. The social sciences do have available a number of such scapegoats. The highly publicized *Tearoom Trade* (Humphreys, 1975), for example, is a favourite target for those who criticize field methods. However, given the amount of research, there are remarkably few participant-observation studies that have been conducted unethically, and none in Canada has been subject to published discussions on research ethics.

Reliance on Diagnostic Instruments

The social construction of imaginary deviants, in a full-blown moral panic, "relies on diagnostic instruments and tests, which are oversimplified and ambiguous" (Victor, 1998: 549). Nearly everyone whose research has been subject to ethical review has experienced requests to answer a battery of questions on the research project. For example, in 1997, the University Ethics Committee prepared a six-page instrument (Office of Research, 1999). The section concerning the "Requirements for Informed Consent Forms" asks 13 questions, the "Checklist" specifies 15 items that require a statement (although not all 15 items may apply to a given research project), and the "Application" itself consists of 3 pages, including 17 additional questions (one question has 3 subsidiary questions). One faces a 45-item test.

"RAINBOW" POLICY AS A SOLUTION?

In light of the foregoing, it might be a daunting task to reset the course of formal research-ethics review: the template of biomedical research and the stirring of a moral panic are two powerful forces that seem to work against the benefits of doing qualitative research. Nevertheless, there are a few possibilities once ethical bodies decide to follow a more comprehensive model of research. In short, this paper suggests a "rainbow" policy for review of ethics in research, which entails the acceptance of a wider range of research methods and goals than is currently the case:

1. *Ethical review committees might wish to learn more about the collective, but still diverse perspectives of qualitative researchers.* It is fortuitous, for example, that the Research Ethics Board at the University of New Brunswick has responded so favourably to an invitation by the Organizers of the 17th Qualitative

Analysis Conference (Fredericton, 18–21 May 2000) to attend sessions devoted particularly to ethics in research.

2. As Arthur Kleinman (cited by Charbonneau, 1984: 21) proposes, *we should not rely on "supposedly universal moral codes" promulgated by clinical researchers.* Instead, he advocates bringing in anthropologists to denote the ethnographic moral context. Such an approach, he avers, is "more likely to resolve ethical problems than are philosophical debates on moral and legal codes for universal participation" (Charbonneau, 1984: 21). Rather than looking at a research setting from the perspective of "universal" moral codes, review committees should also consider looking at research proposals from the perspective of the populations being studied.

3. *Proposals from qualitative researchers should be evaluated for their ethical soundness by those who are qualified qualitative researchers.*

4. *Review committees might consider, on an annual or semi-annual basis, a colloquium on ethical questions in research.* Such a colloquium would be a means of bringing together the best ideas on research ethics, rather than a means of solely "educating" the researchers from the perspective of the prevailing paradigm.

5. Whether as researchers or as members of research-ethics review panels, *we should all become more cognizant of research ethics review as a "moral panic,"* to defuse the fear and anxiety that accompany the submission of research proposals for ethical review.

6. To assure anonymity, the researcher should not use real names on transcripts of interviews (pseudonyms can be either the researcher's or of the research participant's own choosing). *The ethnographic researcher would not need to offer a consent form, to be signed by the research participant. Instead, the researcher would provide an information sheet*

on which s/he would explain the research and the verbal consent needed to continue with the interview. The researcher would sign the information sheet, and the obtaining of verbal permission would be indicated on the transcription.

7. *Teachers in methodology courses might consider approaching their students on the issue of research ethics from an inductive perspective.* They could send their students out to collect field data in relatively safe places (such as in public or semi-public places, e.g., malls), return to class, and discuss what they noted about ethical dilemmas and possibilities. Rather than adopting a top-down approach, teachers would commence the instruction of research ethics at the experiential level, moving on to higher-order constructs of ethics. In more unfamiliar settings, students would regularly report back to their supervisors about the ethical implications of their data collection and analysis, and discuss them as a means of improving ethical sensibilities. In this manner, ethics would not be seen as routine, but as an ongoing social concern.

8. *Researchers might also consider submitting relevant portions of their drafts to the members of the community they have studied.* Factual errors would then be avoided and the opinions or observations of the researched community could be incorporated into either the main text or the endnotes. Such a dialectic provides a rich store of findings.

STUDY QUESTIONS

1. In this article, the author takes a very strong position. To what extent does he present evidence that supports all aspects of his arguments?

2. The author states that the "researcher develops a natural bond with the interviewee" (p. 70). Do you believe that this would happen in every study in which someone is interviewed? Why or why not?

3. To what extent is the author presenting an ideal qualitative research process?

4. What ethical concerns would be raised if we treated all researchers as if they would choose to act under and adopt procedures of the highest ethical standard?

5. Is there historical evidence to support the idea that researchers will always choose to act under and adopt procedures of the highest ethical standard?

6. What would be the risk of allowing only other qualitative researchers to review qualitative research proposals?

7. What would be the risk of allowing only quantitative researchers to review qualitative research proposals?

8. How might some of the author's concerns about ethics review of qualitative research proposals be dealt with, without reducing the level of ethical standards required?

9. Effective 2003, the *Tri-Council Policy on Ethics* mentioned in this article officially became the *Tri-Council Policy Statement: Ethical Conduct for Research Involving Humans, 1998 (with 2000, 2002 updates)*. The electronic version, available at www.pre.ethics.gc.ca/english/ policystatement/policystatement.cfm, is considered the official version of the policy document. Compare the *Tri-Council Policy Statement* to the problems described by the author. To what extent are the problems the author writes about a result of the practices of the individual Ethics Review Boards rather than the *Policy Statement* itself?

10. How should a researcher's desire to conduct a study be balanced with the need to safeguard the dignity and well-being of participants?

ENDNOTES

1. Regehr et al. (2000) cite the case of a forensic in-patient who was the subject of research without consent. The research resulted in a scale that was later used to deny his release.

2. DepoProvera is a three-month injection for birth control, used since 1967 on 2 million women in 80 countries, but the drug had not yet been approved by the FDA at the time Charbonneau (1984) wrote about it.

3. Indeed, Fine (1993) makes a number of references to ethically questionable field research.

4. The United Nations Conference on Science and Technology, held in Vienna in 1979, recommended such medical councils, and this was followed by a similar suggestion from the World Health Organization (Charbonneau, 1984: 21).

5. It is noteworthy that the case was brought against a graduate student; there are striking parallels with other cases brought against the less-powerful members of professional groups.

6. The reader can find the sequel to this development in Jones (1998: 24), who reports a decision by Judge Steinberg in June 1998 in which, although "the university was under no legal obligation to cover the legal fees in question," the university had stepped back from its opportunity to promote academic freedom and privilege.

7. "Consent Form—Digital Myoelectric Controls Study," provided to the author by the Ethics Review Committee of UNB, 30 October 1989.

8. One researcher (Anonymous D) who conducted research in a retirement community in Florida just could not visualize pulling out a consent form from her bathing suit as she chatted with community residents in a swimming pool.

9. In April 1995 the United States House of Representatives passed the Family Privacy Protection Act, which requires that in all cases parents give written consent before their children can participate in research (Levine, 1995: 81).

10. This point, of course, does not apply to illegal activities, which pose their own problems of having interviewees sign a written consent form.

REFERENCES

Anonymous A. 1999. E-mail from <[name omitted]> to <will@unb.ca>, Subject: consent forms. December.

Anonymous B. 2000. E-mail from <[name omitted]> to <will@unb.ca>, Subject: Qualitatives program and registration. February.

Anonymous C. 2000. "Detailed description of an application to the Social Sciences and Humanities Research Council of Canada." 6 p.

Anonymous D. 2000. Conversation with a colleague in the Gerontology program, St. Thomas University, Fredericton, January.

Anonymous E. 2000. E-mail from <[name omitted]> to <will@unb.ca>, Subject: notes re informed consent. April.

Anonymous F. 1995. Personal communication.

Chahal, K. 2000, "What will you do with this information?: Ethical issues and sensitive research." Unpubl.

Charbonneau, R. 1984. "Ethics in human research." *The IDRC Reports*, Vol. 13, No. 1, pp. 20–21.

Cohen, S. 1972. *Folk Devils and Moral Panics: The Creation of the Mods and Rockers*. New York: St. Martin's Press.

Comarow, M. 1993. "Are sociologists above the law?" *The Chronicle of Higher Education*, 15 December, p. A44.

Curtis, J. 1999. "The Business of Ethics." *The Globe and Mail*, Saturday 21 August, pp. D1–D4.

Fine, G.A. 1993. "Ten lies of ethnography: Moral dilemmas of field research." *Journal of Contemporary Ethnography*, Vol. 22, No. 3, pp. 267–94.

Getty, G. 1999. E-mail from <getty@unb.ca> to <will@unb.ca>, Subject: Personal Ltr to qualitative researchers at UNB and STU, Date Sent: Wed, 24 November, 13:60:44 - 0.

Goode, E. and N. Ben-Yahuda. 1994. *Moral Panics: The Social Construction of Deviance*. Cambridge: Blackwell.

GVU Center's WWW User Surveys. 2000. URL: http://www.cc.gatech.edu/gvu/user_surveys/.

Hancock, K. 1999. "London's sex-trade industry: The politics of the 'problem.'" Paper presented at the 16th Qualitative Analysis Conference, Fredericton, N.B., 13–16 May.

Humphreys, L. 1975. *Tearoom Trade: Impersonal Sex in Public Places.* Chicago: Aldine de Gruyter.

Jones, P. 1998. "Consultation underway at Simon Fraser following coroner's inquest." *CAUT Bulletin,* 24 October, p. 24.

Kellner, F. 2000. "Yet another current crisis: The ethics of conduct and representation in fieldwork-dependent social science." Paper presented at the 17th Qualitative Analysis Conference, Fredericton, N.B., 18–21 May.

Levine, F.J. 1995. "Consent for research on children." *The Chronicle of Higher Education,* 10 November, pp. 81–82.

Liebow, E. 1993. *Tell Them Who I Am: The Lives of Homeless Women.* Toronto: Macmillan Canada.

Lowman, J. and T. Palys. 1998. "When research ethics and the law conflict." *CAUT Bulletin,* June, pp. 6–7.

MacDonald, H. 1999. E-mail from keith@worrall17.freeserve.co.uk> to <will@unb.ca>, Subject: Re: Personal Ltr to qualitative researchers at UNB and STU, Date Sent: Wed, 24 November, 21:33:20 - 0000.

Mills, E. 2000. "Voices in harmony/voices in discord: Researching biography, writing autobiography." Unpubl.

Office of Research. 1999. "Requirements for informed consent form." 28 December, 6 p.

O'Neill, P. 2000. "Good intentions and awkward outcomes: Ethical gatekeeping in field research." Paper presented at the 17th Qualitative Analysis Conference, Fredericton, N.B., 18–21 May.

Pollack, S. 1999. "Conducting qualitative research with women in prison: Ethical issues and challenges." Paper presented at the 16th Qualitative Analysis Conference, Fredericton, N.B., 13–16 May.

Regehr, C. et al. 2000. "Research ethics with forensic patients." *Canadian Journal of Psychiatry,* Vol. 45, No. 10, pp. 23–29.

Reinharz, S. 1993. *On Becoming a Social Scientist.* 4th ed. New Brunswick, N.J.: Transaction.

Snyder, L. 2000. "Confidentiality and anonymity in qualitative research: Promises and practices." Paper presented at the 17th Qualitative Analysis Conference, Fredericton, N.B., 18–21 May.

Stokholm, S. 1999. "Beyond the consent form: The ethical nature of anthropological knowledge." Paper presented at the 16th Qualitative Analysis Conference, Fredericton, N.B., 13–16 May.

Strauss, A.L. 1987. *Qualitative Analysis for Social Scientists.* Cambridge: Cambridge UP.

Victor, J.S. 1998. "Moral panics and the social construction of deviant behavior: A theory and application to the case of ritual child abuse." *Sociological Perspectives,* Vol. 41, No. 3, pp. 541–565.

Waruszynski, B. 2000. "Pace of technological change: Battling ethical issues in qualitative research." Paper presented at the 17th Qualitative Analysis Conference, Fredericton, N.B., 18–21 May.

Weinberg, M. 1999. "Biting the hand that feeds you and other feminist research dilemmas." Paper presented at the 16th Qualitative Analysis Conference, Fredericton, N.B., 13–16 May.

Welsome, E. 1999. *The Plutonium Files: America's Secret Medical Experiments in the Cold War.* New York: The Dial Press.

Whyte, W.F. 1943. *Street Corner Society: The Social Structure of an Italian Slum.* Chicago: U of Chicago P.

Woodward, D. and G.M. Lewis. (eds.). 1998. *The History of Cartography: Cartography in the Traditional African, American, Arctic, Australian, and Pacific Societies.* Vol. 2, Book 3. Chicago: U of Chicago P.

PART 2

Qualitative

Chapter 7

Changing School-Community Relations through Participatory Research: Strategies from First Nations and Teachers

Seth A. Agbo

Source: From *The Canadian Journal of Native Studies*, XXIII, pp. 25–56 (2003).

The National Indian Brotherhood (NIB) (1972, 1980) engineered the accelerating process of First Nations control of education in Canada as an integrated school reform process that gives the right to First Nations to control the education of their children by exercising parental responsibility (NIB, 1972). The local control concept has proven powerful enough to be adopted nationally as a concurrent model of school governance and self-determination for First Nations. The testimony to the attractiveness of the local control concept as an integrated school improvement process should be provided by the intellectual and material support given to the communities to control their own education. One starting point would be to ask: What does local control mean to First Nations community-school relations?

Many educational researchers interested in First Nations education believe that local control will provide opportunities for local people to have a say in school governance, and restore to them the feeling that they are not powerless and are in control of their own schools (Matthew, 1990; Hampton, 1995). A basic purpose of local control is to move towards collaborative decision-making, involving principals, teachers, parents and students. Under Indian and Northern Affairs Canada (INAC) there could be a significant degree of unifor-mity in school practices, procedures, and salaries, notwithstanding local disparities in the educational needs of students. Schooling could also mean cumbersome bureaucracy and an impersonalization of the needs of students and teachers, and the federal government's monopoly of school functions could restrict parents from influencing the direction of their children's education. Therefore local control of First Nations schools should be more responsive to student needs and involve greater parent participation in the schooling of their children (Hampton, 1995; Matthew, 1990). The shift in the loci of power to First Nations communities means that the education of First Nations children will greatly depend on the feelings and aspirations of their parents.

The importance of local control is widely recognized, although the nature of the control process is currently the subject of considerable debate. The expected outcomes of local control depend on the conditions that define the particular schooling environment and on the particular interests of the First Nations communities. For First Nations, local control of education is a crucial movement towards Native self-determination (Senese, 1991). As the National Indian Brotherhood (1980) asserts: "The possession and control of one's education is vital to the development and survival of a people. If Indians in Canada are to survive as people we must develop and control our own education" (p. 5). The federal government or INAC and the local control systems can be different in terms of the degree of decision-making authority wielded by INAC and local authorities, respectively. The consequential blend of decision-making power with respect to education functions, decision-making modes, and levels of governance is what leads to the description of an entire educational system as federally controlled or locally controlled. According to Fantini & Gittell (1973), "The concept of community control represents an effort to adjust existing systems to new circumstances and needs. It seeks a balance between public, or citizen, participation and professional roles in the policy process" (p. 113).

In some contexts of local control such as site-based management (SBM), the transference of power is designed to enable schools and communities to manage changes in education within a framework that fits the overall objectives, strategic plans, policies and curriculum initiatives of the provincial government and education authorities. In this context, government and the central office determine key objectives and policies for education and empower communities and schools to work within a specific framework to provide education that is suited to each community (Spinks, 1990). Although teachers, parents, and principals may be involved in decision-making, the provincial governments assert more control and legitimacy over SBM schools. There are differences between SBM and First Nations control of education. In terms of First Nations control, decision-making authority is not merely distributed from the federal authorities to individual First Nations school sites. The devolution represents a nation-to-nation transference—that is, from the federal government to a First Nations government, each First Nations community representing a government. In First Nations

schools, band councils assume the political control of the school and delegate the administrative responsibilities to a local education authority. A potential increase in school autonomy at the local level should raise questions about school-community relations, of how community resources are serving the interests of the school. The Report of the Royal Commission on Learning (1994) found school-community relations as the number one priority for school improvement and describes it as the "first engine" (p. 11). As the report states:

We explored several ways to implement this concept [of school-community relations]. We think every school should have a school-community council, led by the principal and comprising parents, teachers, and students responsible for bringing appropriate community resources into the school to assume some of the obligations teachers now bear alone (p. 11).

This study utilizes a participatory research that draws on data collected through workshops, interviews, observations and discussions recorded as field notes to ascertain viewpoints of community people and school staff about school-community relations. I present perspectives of Euro-Canadian teachers as well as First Nations parents' viewpoints on community-school relations—parental involvement in schooling, communication between home and school, and teacher integration into the community. This paper concludes that both First Nations and school staff consider the extent of community involvement in education as a major factor for First Nations school improvement and suggests some strategies to deal with the problem.

PARTICIPATORY RESEARCH AS DIALOGUE FOR SCHOOL IMPROVEMENT

The approach and contexts to participatory research suggest that it is useful in helping dominated, exploited, and minority groups to identify problems and take action in solving them (Kemmis, 1991; Participatory Research Network (PRN), 1982; Maguire, 1987). Hall (1981) defines participatory research as a social action process that interconnects the activities of research, education and action. From this standpoint, participatory research provides a ground for collective empowerment that helps to deepen knowledge about social problems and helps to formulate possible actions for their solution. By its imagery and power, participatory research provides a type of anchor for thinking about participation in an active context. Participatory research is increasingly tied to and powerfully influenced by the concern with power and democracy and provides important social learning networks that are critical to issues of gender, race, ethnicity, sexual orientation, physical and mental abilities, and other social factors (Hall, 1993).

Kemmis (1991) studied Aboriginal and teacher education in the Northern Territory of Australia and found that participatory research with Aboriginal people resulted in some innovations that led them to maintain a central role in their own development. Maguire (1987) studied battered families in Gallup, New Mexico, U.S.A., and found women's participation in participatory research projects boosted self-esteem as well as the control and organizational power of women's groups. Jackson (1993) documents the significance of the specific role of participatory research in providing essential political infrastructures for land use claims for Canada's Aboriginal people in the 1970s. Horton (1993) has also written on how participatory research provided structures for changing the ownership and control of resources for the Appalachians in the United States.

Maguire (1987) asserts that participatory research goes beyond merely interpreting and describing social phenomena. Accordingly, the most peculiar aspect of participatory research is the direct link between research and action

(Maguire, 1987; Hall, 1981). Thus, in the project, we did not merely describe social reality, but radically tried to change it by combining the creation of knowledge about social reality with actual action in that reality. Therefore, our objective of this project was to collectively build a group ownership of information as we moved from being objects of research to subjects of our own research process (Maguire, 1987). By using an alternative social science framework, we employed data collection processes that combined the activities of research, education, and action (Hall, 1981; Maguire, 1987; Kemmis, 1991). As an educational process, the project educated us by engaging in the analysis of structural causes of selected problems through collaborative discussion and interaction. As an action process, the project enabled the participants to take collaborative action for radical social change in both the short and the long run. The common ethos of the project consists of an emphasis on cultural education and the desire for an assertion of cultural knowledge in matters of educational concern.

So, unlike a study using an externalist position, this project did not intend merely to produce information about Aboriginal education and remain on the shelves. Moreover, the project was also unlike more latent interpretive forms of critical theory. Our method was to apply thinking processes related mainly to the development of strategies for problem solving and decision-making. These strategies laid special emphasis on the learning of all the activities, institutions, social groups and networks that First Nations have progressively developed over the years (Kemmis, 1991).

The participatory research at Yellow Pond concerned forms of educational theory and research aimed at transforming the works of First Nations schools—"forms of research whose aim is not to interpret the world but to change it" (Kemmis, 1991, p. 102) or "to transform the social environment through the process of critical inquiry—to act on the world rather than being acted on" (Miles & Huberman, 1994, p. 9). The design for this project drew on an alternative research paradigm approach, the method of critical education research described by Kemmis (1991) and Miles & Huberman (1994), and the method of participatory research described by Hall (1975, 1981).

Community Profile

Yellow Pond is a relatively small isolated First Nations reserve in northwestern Ontario, Canada. The reserve attained a band status with its own chief in 1970. The community is reached only by daily scheduled flights when the weather permits or by a winter road during February and March. The main aircraft that ply the routes are Beech 99s and Cessna 180s. The community people also make considerable use of float and ski-equipped aircraft for trapping and hunting trips and traveling to other communities. About 2,000 kilometers from Toronto, the provincial capital, Yellow Pond, procures its essential supplies of merchandise from the metropolitan centers of Winnipeg and Thunder Bay, which are each about 700 kilometers away.

Before the coming of Europeans, Yellow Pond based its livelihood on hunting and gathering. There is a significant level of awareness of past traditions among the elders of the community although the young in general are not knowledgeable on matters concerning past traditional beliefs, cultural patterns and expectations for First Nations. Nevertheless, data from elders strongly confirm that even though children are raised to speak the local dialect, Ojibwe, there is a comprehensive pool of information on local traditions that is virtually unknown to the young and the Euro-Canadian teachers of the children.

As with all cultures, the culture of Yellow Pond is dynamic, changing and adapting to new times. The establishment of band councils by the government of Canada to administer First Nations communities and enforce law and order has much to do with the demise of First Nations culture on some reserves to which Yellow Pond is no exception. Euro-Canadian Law has replaced First Nations, and the values, customs and conflict resolution ideals of First Nations are giving way to Euro-Canadian ways.

The community's population has grown from 392 in 1986 to about 600 in 1995, an average annual growth of about 4 percent. The population lives in 85 households with about 55 percent under 20 years of age, and about 25 percent is at present in school in the community. While the population of the reserve continues to grow at a rapid rate, economic conditions have not kept pace with the population growth. Unemployment, alcohol and substance abuse, teenage suicide, broken families and starvation are serious problems in the community. The Band Council considers the improvement of the education system as one way of finding solutions to the social and economic problems.

The School within the Community

The present premises that harbours the Yellow Pond School was built by INAC as an Indian Day School. The school with its teachers' quarters lies on a sandy, gentle slope in the north-eastern corner of the community facing a sprawling lake on the south. A fence clearly defines the boundaries of the school and separates its elite residents from the community. Within the school and teachers' quarters are modern facilities of running water, showers, water closet toilets, and oil furnaces for heating. Until a few years ago, the school and its teachers' quarters were the only places in the community that had electricity from a small diesel generator. While the whole community slept in darkness, the lights from the school area illuminated the lake to the south and the coniferous forest that borders it to the north. Immediately beyond the fences are community houses with wood-stove heating systems, and little outhouses at the side of each of the homes. To the south of the community is the sprawling brown-water lake from which all community people acquire their water supply for all purposes all year round. During winter months, when the lake is frozen, families bore holes in the thick ice to collect water for their household chores.

Community people told me that during the period that INAC controlled the school, they did not have anything to do with what went on within the confines of the school fence. Community people looked upon the school as an ivory tower and whatever happened behind the fences was the business of professional teachers. As an elder, 63-year-old J.S., put it:

A bus would come round to pick our children to school in the morning and would bring them back after school. I knew they went to school but I didn't know exactly what they were doing there. They will be there, behind the fence until it is time for them again to come home (Interview with an elder in Yellow Pond).

Parents said they neither visited the school nor the teachers' homes either because they were never invited or felt that there was nothing they could do in those places. The comment by this 51-year-old parent, K.J., below, was instructive in regard to the perceptions most parents had about the school:

When there was no bus, we dropped the kids off at the gate. There will be one or two teachers waiting for them. We never went inside the fence except there was something wrong with your kid then the principal will invite you to the office. We had one principal here who will visit the kids' home every-day after school to talk to their parents. I think he was an Irishman. . . . No, we never went to their [teachers'] homes (Interview with community member in Yellow Pond).

So the present study explored whether the school still maintains the legacy as the fenced-in modern quarter of the First Nations reserve, that is, a community within a community, or

whether local control has changed the notion community people have about the school. Certainly the school has its own value systems, laws and regulations that are entirely different from those of the community-at-large. The present study uses participatory research to ascertain viewpoints of community people and school staff about school-community relationships—parental involvement in schooling, communication between home and school, and teacher integration into the community.

Research Procedures

This study proceeded in five phases: 1) negotiating the research relationship; 2) identifying the most significant problems; 3) collective educational activities; 4) classification, analysis; and 5) definition of action projects. Note taking and tape recording of interviews formed an integral part of all the phases of the research. Table 7.1 shows the research phases and activities initiated.

Phase 1: Negotiating the Research Relationship (September–October)

I arrived at the First Nations reserve of Yellow Pond during the last week of August to take up the building level administration of the school and at the same time embark on a participatory research study. The initial problem I encountered was how to establish myself, particularly, how to be accepted by the community people as a researcher and at the same time as someone closely connected with the school. I realized that being a person of minority origin and working in the school, I stood in a unique advantageous position as a researcher, compared with other researchers who community members might regard as outsiders and with whom they might not fully cooperate.

As soon as I entered the community I started gathering and analyzing information about the research area. This was a period during which I started establishing relationships

Table 7.1 Research Phases

Time	Phase	Activity
September–October	1. Negotiating Research Relationships	a) Gathering and analyzing information about research area b) Establishing relationships with groups c) Locating research problem within site d) Formed advisory group e) Journal keeping
November–January	2. Identifying Most Significant Problems	a) Setting up a problem-posing process b) Dialogue with groups and individuals c) Daily journal keeping and notes from interviews d) Workshops
February–April	3. Collective Educational Activities	a) Connecting participants' personal perceptions of issues b) Workshops c) Compiled themes for investigation d) Participants began to assume fuller responsibility e) Preparing for action
May–July	4. Classification, Analysis and Conclusion Building	a) Information gathering, analysis and conclusion building b) Meetings with participants c) Workshops d) Development of theories and search for solutions e) Data gathering, classification and analysis
August	5. Definition of Action Projects	a) Deciding on action projects b) Ongoing participation in school development

Table 7.1 shows the research phases of this study. It shows that in all, there are five phases. The sections that follow provide a more detailed description of the activities initiated during the phases.

with groups within the community and inviting these groups to participate in the research process. It was also a period during which I tried to locate the research problem within the community. I identified the small groups within the community that were active in school affairs and formed an advisory or reference group for the project. Data gathering was in the form of journal keeping and note taking during interviews and dialogue with people in the community.

Phase 2: Identifying the Most Significant Problems (November–January)

By November, I started setting up a problem-posing process that enabled us to start identifying the community's most significant issues about schooling of their children. It was a period of ongoing problem-posing in the form of dialogue with groups and individuals, leading us to a more complex and critical understanding of the problems and issues as perceived and experienced by us. It became quite clear to me during this period that the community people were aware that problems existed in the school and were prepared to work together for the improvement of the school. I started collecting data in the form of daily journal keeping and notes from interviews and dialogue with community people.

In December, an idea came from a member of the Local Education Authority (LEA) to conduct a problem identification exercise for the school. We agreed at a general meeting that we would all submit lists expressing problems about the school. I received lists from classroom teachers, support staff, LEA members and community people. In total I received 36 lists from respondents. Some respondents provided causes of the problems and suggestions for their solution, while others merely listed the problems. The high standard of responses, the efforts that respondents put into identifying the problems of the school and the number of suggestions reflected the importance members attached to the notion of school improvement and participatory research.

We decided to hold workshops to discuss the problems raised by participants. According to the Participatory Research Network (PRN) (1982), "Group discussions are probably the most widely used method in participatory research. They occur throughout the process, and are often used together with other methods" (p. 6). The PRN (1982) suggests small numbers of 8, 12 or 25 who meet to solve problems by sharing experiences, information and support. For this study, I targeted the small group of five people who form the Local Education Authority, who were active in school affairs, to act as an advisory or reference group for the project. Basically, this group advised on what to do in the course of the project.

The workshops were mainly group discussions that helped in problem posing, identifying causes, discussing possible solutions and evaluating actions (PRN, 1982). Group discussions also created circumstances under which people felt relaxed and free to speak. Researcher and participants used group discussions to build a sense of trust, support and cooperation among community people who shared the same ideas or problems; group discussions maintained communication between researcher and community members, and also acted as productive interviews (PRN, 1982).

We held the first two-day workshop in January. The themes of the workshops reflected the viewpoints of participants in relation to the problems they viewed as most pressing for the school. In order to identify most precisely the problems that were common in the submissions, we, as a group, analyzed the sub-

missions in two stages. First, we thoroughly scrutinized all the submissions identified by participants. Second, we subjected the submissions to a coding process. In coding the submissions, we categorized all the issues by using colored stickers to reflect common themes expressed by the participants. We then rearranged the themes and came up with categories such as school-community relations, school governance, curriculum and staff development, and traditional and cultural education.

Phase 3: Collective Educational Activities (February–April)

In the third phase, I attempted to connect participants' personal perceptions of issues to the wider context of the community. Having increased their understanding of the issues it became obvious at this stage that the school and the community were ready to mobilize themselves for school improvement. We all felt mandated and committed to develop an effective school program that would ensure students received high quality education.

In this way, by the end of this phase, we compiled the questions and themes for the investigation. Also in this phase, participants began to assume fuller responsibility for the project through further workshops that encouraged suggestions to deal with problems affecting the school. They also began to realize their potential and abilities to mobilize and act on school issues. It is important to note that as community people seemed to lack the literacy skills and information for critical analysis, we embarked on collective educational activities, such as showing videos and organizing open forums to which we invited presenters to educate us on various topics such as the role of the home and school in education, communication skills, and conflict resolution. For example, an educator from Sioux Lookout presented a workshop on the roles of teachers and parents in school discipline. Such forums helped participants to further examine their interpretations of issues.

Phase 4: Classification, Analysis and Conclusion Building (May–July)

During this phase, I involved participants, through various means, such as inviting them to regularly visit the school and talk to students and teachers, to gather information, classify, analyze, and build conclusions. That is to say, community people interacted in the school to observe what was going on and were free to ask questions and make suggestions. Above all, we attended two public meetings apart from participant and researcher meetings two times in every month, to investigate problems posed in Phase 3. Public meetings formed an integral part of this phase. I used public meetings to inform community members about the research as it progressed and to provide a chance for them to contribute to the plan and implementation of action projects. I used them to involve more community members in playing an active part in the research project by joining small group discussions, interviewing people and allowing themselves to be interviewed. Since the balance between First Nations and Euro-Canadian conceptions of schooling may be important for the development of education in the community, I met with Euro-Canadian contract teachers and community people together at certain times and met with them separately at other times. For example, questions that arose during meetings with the Euro-Canadian teachers concerned issues such as orientation of non-First Nations teachers into the community, e.g., What kind of orientation should new teachers be given by the community? How long should this orientation be? How can non-First Nations teachers integrate themselves into the community? Should they have host families? During these meetings, I encouraged teachers to write down observations in their own words while I jotted down notes on my observations about individual interactions, group activities, and statements by participants. I highlighted priorities in participants' comments and recorded overall reflections.

Phase 4 was a crucial period when participants began to develop their own theories and understanding of issues and began to find solutions for them. This phase was crucial to the study in that this was the phase where I put together information, classified, analyzed and started to build a thesis.

Phase 5: Definition of Action Projects (August)

The final phase, which at this time is still ongoing, has involved researcher and participants in deciding on what actions to take to address the issues they have collectively identified and analyzed. At this stage, community people have "moved from being objects to subjects and beneficiaries of the research" (Maguire, 1987, p. 51), I have become an involved activist in the school improvement program. Quite early in this phase, we designed some action projects that we implemented immediately. Because of the numerous issues that came up for us to address, it is inconclusive where we might be with our action projects a couple of years from the time of this study. In other words, although the process of the research has indicated direct immediate value for us, one cannot determine the final results of the research, since phase 5 is still ongoing. We should realize definitive results of our participatory research efforts by the end of this phase.

DATA ANALYSIS

In this study, the initial question that came up regarding data analysis was which is the best possible way to analyze data within the framework of an alternative research paradigm in order for the study to conform to traditional ideas of social science research. Like data collection, participatory research literature does not specify "one best way" of data analysis. As the data for this study came from the notes I took throughout the phases of the research process, submissions of participants, and the transcribed tape recorded interviews, I felt I had to analyze the data using qualitative approaches to research. However, Lather (1992) contends that data analysis of alternative research paradigms transcends the ordinary application of qualitative approaches because "their focus is the overriding importance of meaning making and context in human experiencing" (p. 91).

Miles and Huberman (1994) contend that because participatory research is an approach that aims at changing the social environment through a method of critical inquiry by acting on the world, data analysis should concentrate on descriptions in the initial stages, and go through to the search for underlying concepts or ideals. While there are several ways to analyze data collected from interviews, discussions, field work and workshops, the data analysis of this study essentially utilized qualitative procedures with a focus on generating meaning within a particular setting (Lather, 1992).

There were two major phases of data analysis, namely, the collection phase, and the analysis phase. Owens (1982) contends that in the early stages of the study, the researcher devotes about 80 percent of the time and effort gathering data and spends about 20 percent of the time on the analysis and vice versa in the latter stages. During the collection phase, while I continuously referred to, and reflected on the data being collected, I also compiled some systematic field notes that might be useful to the study. The analysis period entailed classifications, the formation and testing of ideas, making connections among ideas, and relating concepts to emerging categories.

For the interviews, I prepared summaries of the fifty-eight interviews for verification by respondents. First, I listened to each audiotape and made detailed notes or transcription of the interviewees' responses. I then subjected each of the responses to a coding system I developed to identify the respondent and the interview questions to which she/he responded. I separated each of the respondents/responses using as guidelines the research questions for the study. The objective was to categorize each of the responses according to common patterns, themes or ideas that fit into the research questions.

After reducing the interview data, I searched for patterns, repeated themes or views that conform to categories such as school-community relations, shortcomings and priorities of schooling, and educational governance. As the analysis continued, I recorded theoretical memos about what the patterns possibly meant, and drew from research questions and the analytic insights and interpretations that emerged during the data collection. I then assigned the emerging ideas and patterns to categories. For example, first, I assigned pieces of information relating to school governance, budgeting, accountability and efficiency in the schooling system to the category of control; second, I assigned issues relating to parental involvement in schooling, teacher orientation into the community, and communication between teachers and parents to the category of school-community relations; and, third, I assigned problems relating to curriculum, student attendance, school supplies, and facilities to the category of shortcomings of schooling.

In order to prevent incidents of single, possibly well-articulated or emphatic views of individual respondents from outshining the others, I counted the number of respondents who expressed a certain view or theme relating to a concept. Rather than considering the majority view of total respondents, the unit of analysis was each of the groups I invited to participate in the research. I considered groups such as the advisory committee, elders of the community, parents, teachers, and students as levels of analysis. To view a perception as a factor, a majority of participants belonging to each of the groups would have had to refer to it as an issue, and, therefore, deserving to be considered in the analysis and presentation of the results of this study. Apart from helping to shape meaning for the combined viewpoints of respondents, the counting also helped me to understand the viewpoints held by the majority of respondents. Thus, data analysis at this stage essentially involved coding and counting the data according to the categorized indicators and highlighting further indicators that became evident from the raw data (Miles & Huberman, 1994). Lastly, I verified the final conclusions by confirming and substantiating the interpretations that appeared in the data for their validity to establish some truth in the responses of participants. In order to establish and communicate meaning from the data, and to provide conceptual consistency by grouping details under more general ideas, I identified and labeled emerging themes and patterns (Miles & Huberman, 1994).

As an alternative paradigm research, it is not the intention to present the results of the study with the purpose of making them more reliable and valid than those of dominant research paradigms. It would, however, be helpful here to draw upon some of Lather's (1986) approaches used to validate alternative research paradigms to ensure credibility and trustworthiness of the study. Lather asserts that researchers should build into their research designs triangulation, face validity, and catalytic validity. First, Lather addresses triangulation as the inclusion in the research design of various data sources, procedures, and theoretical outlines that seek contrasting patterns as well as similarities. This research utilized various data sources, such as field notes, interviews, discussions, meetings and workshops. Second, face validity occurs by "recycling categories, emerging analysis, back through at least a subsample of respondents" (Lather, 1986,

p. 78). In this study, after typing the interview summaries for example, I took the summaries back to participants in order for us to review them and make necessary modifications. I also presented all participants with workshop summary reports in order for them to read them and make the necessary corrections. Furthermore, because I had to employ an interpreter to translate the answers of community people who could not answer the interview questions in English, there may be a possibility for misinterpretation. In order to minimize this possibility, I subjected the tape recordings in Ojibwe to a second interpretation. In all cases, the second interpreter confirmed the translation of the first one. Finally, catalytic validity follows when there is "some documentation that the research process has led to insight and, ideally, activism on the part of the respondents" (Lather, 1986, p. 78). Catalytic validity should be crucial to this study, as its main purpose was to promote participants' understanding of their own capabilities and right to control decisions affecting them. The suggested fundamental and detailed strategies suggested for action address this concern. Accordingly, this study meets Lather's (1986) criteria for judging the trustworthiness of a participatory research.

RESULTS

Results from this study indicated that most parents who participated in the study are informed of the fundamental principle of educational philosophy. That is to say, parents are aware that education should equip their children with the necessary tools for survival in both First Nations and Euro-Canadian society. Furthermore, parents believed that their children should be self-sufficient, competent, and able to confidently manage their lives and those for whom they are responsible.

Parental Involvement in Education

As in all cultural milieus, young First Nations children in Yellow Pond gain the basic concepts of the social order of traditional First Nations' cultural knowledge through interaction, first with parents and close family members and eventually with others in the community, that is, peers and other adults that the child notices outside the immediate family. The data in this study suggest that community people feel that in some cases teachers and school officials completely overlook First Nations' cultural values. The present study pointed out that some teachers do not see the difference between the purpose of education for First Nations and Euro-Canadian children. Whereas teachers support a view that the education of the children is supposed to continue to augment and reinforce the cultural and social experiences that the child brings from home to school, parents feel that the school is different from the home.

Results relating to school-community relations generally revealed that parents and teachers do not work together for the improvement of schooling. Parents think that they should not involve themselves in their children's schooling. Although the school is under local control, community people do not understand and are not aware of alternatives and how to involve themselves in choosing among them. Most teachers I interviewed indicated that the most frustrating aspect of their job was lack of parental involvement. As one of the female teachers, H.S., commented:

I find the apparent apathy in the community towards education and providing recreational opportunities for the children and the lack of parental involvement the most frustrating aspects of the job. It appears that if the non-Native people in the community did not do things for the kids, nothing would get done. There appears to be a general expectation of the community that the teachers can do everything where the kids are involved (Interview with Teacher, Yellow Pond).

Parents on the other hand feel that teachers continue to assume that as soon as children enter the schoolyard, they are expected not to behave as First Nations, but as "civilized" persons and could only be First Nations after school. The comments by this 49-year old parent, and a former LEA member, A.W., presented below were typical of how a majority of parents felt:

The children don't behave well at school. They carry their behavior at home to the school. Teachers shouldn't allow them to do that. They can do what they want to do at home but when they go to school, they should behave as school children. The other day X and I went to grade . . . classroom to see the teacher, and the kids were swearing at us. They were calling us names. If they do that at home they shouldn't be allowed to do it at school (Interview with parent in Yellow Pond).

The above quotation supports the perception that the school is a fenced-in enclave, which is different from the home. The present study revealed that the change from INAC to local control does not change many of the notions community people had about the school.

Although community people I interviewed showed considerable interest in the affairs of the school and the improvement of the school system, they accepted that there was little parental participation in school affairs. Some parents did not know that there was a local education authority in charge of the school. They still entertained the notion that the school was under INAC control and they did not have anything to do with the schooling of their children. Also, some parents did not know that they could visit the school at their own will and talk to teachers about the progress of their children.

Perhaps the comments of a community member about the seclusion of the school from the community prior to the takeover from First Nations and Northern Affairs Canada (INAC) can provide a reason for lack of parental involvement. As 67-year-old G.C. commented:

The only time we saw our children during school time was at recess when they played within the fence. Sometimes I would like to speak to my children during recess time but teachers would not allow them to cross the fence. They are all over the place guarding the fence and since I know that they don't want us to speak to the children, I don't want to offend them. Teachers know their job and we should leave them free to train our children (Interview with Yellow Pond community elder).

While parents felt that they were not welcome in the school, teachers thought that it was necessary for parents to participate in their children's education. Another female teacher, M.C., in her late twenties remarked:

To improve schooling for students, parents and teachers must get to know each other. Parents should feel that the teacher has the best interest of the child in mind, and teachers should feel that they have the support of parents in carrying out their programs. Parents should become involved in the daily programs of the school. When children see their parents taking an interest in school, they may begin to develop the attitude that school is important (Interview with a Euro-Canadian teacher).

In soliciting ideas from community members as to how much participation is fitting or preferred by community people, I found that many people felt that it was the duty of the Local Education Authority (LEA) to encourage parents to urge their children to go to school. They felt that as soon as the LEA got involved in schooling, parents would follow suit.

Another requirement that community people most frequently stated in our discussions regarding parental involvement in schooling was the need for more effective communication and more understanding between community people and the Euro-Canadian school staff. Respondents indicated that community people do not want to get involved in school affairs because there is lack of communication

between the school and the community. As W.T., a man in his thirties who worked in the school a couple of years ago, stated:

Community people don't want to get involved. People are afraid to communicate. They need lot of public education. Teachers need to sacrifice their time to get to know people and try to gain knowledge from Native people. They need to establish trust and respect. Teachers should invite parents and ask them questions. They should establish friendship with parents. I have never seen a teacher going to visit a parent except report card day. Teachers go from their houses to the school; they never bother to know what is happening in the children's homes. As I said earlier, the most important thing is getting to know people (Interview with community member, ex-worker in the school).

As I personally found out during this study, it is difficult to communicate with First Nations people without getting to know them. This study has the benefit of establishing a direct contact between personnel from the school and community people. I found that the personal contact I introduced between me and community people went a long way in enhancing the image of the school staff. Many respondents indicated that it would take trust, friendship and understanding on the part of teachers to get parents involved in schooling. This comment from a parent confirms how important it is to get to know people:

If my people don't trust you, they'll have nothing to do with you. Some of them feel that their children don't behave well at school and teachers will find fault with them so they won't get near the teachers. Teachers have to open up to parents and make them aware that they're here for the welfare of the children. As I said earlier, the only way by which to do this is . . . I guess, they should be friendly towards parents. Teachers should also learn to understand parents (Interview with community member).

W.T. suggested that a major problem facing parental involvement in school matters is lack of effective communication between the school and the community.

Communication

One of the drawbacks cited as facing schooling was lack of effective communication between parents and teachers. I asked a middle-aged man working at the Band Office, O.R., to tell me the way by which school could become more effective for the children:

The main problem of schooling in this community is lack of communication between parents and teachers. All of you teachers are new to our way of life. You don't know what we do with our kids at home. Ask your teachers, how many of them have ever attempted to visit a parent and spent a weekend with him, and, perhaps, go on the trap-line together and see what children and parents do over there. You are teaching children whose way of life you don't understand. You are just teaching them what you think they should know. It is only when teachers know about the home environment of the children that they can teach them well. I don't blame the teachers. It is poor parenting that brings about problems in the school. Some parents just don't care about what their children do. Teachers and parents have to work together (Interview with band worker).

The study revealed that teachers acknowledge the lack of communication between them and parents. Teachers believe that the school can build effective lines of communication with parents by hosting school events and inviting parents, visiting parents at home, and attending community events. They suggested that it is necessary for the school to create venues where parents can meet and discuss school issues together. Teachers felt the necessity of becoming well acquainted with parents. As a female teacher, S.D., commented:

Teachers and parents can work together to improve schooling by communicating with, and supporting each other. When the school plans an event, parents should come out and show their support. When possible, parents should be included in the planning process and volunteer to help. That way, they will see the effort that goes into the planning by the teacher, and not just the end result. Teachers and parents should communicate with each other, not

only when there is a problem with a student, but when there is good news also. I think a PTA would help because then parents would have an opportunity to get an inside look. It is good for the school to have an open door policy for parents. However, parents need to use it to come in. If an open door is not used, it only lets in the cold (Interview with Euro-Canadian teacher).

Respondents I interviewed felt that what makes the problem of communication between teachers and parents more serious is that the language and cultural backgrounds of teachers differ from those of community people. Participants recommend that the initial necessity is for teachers to become acquainted with parents and develop a new footing of trust, agreement, and cooperation. It is clear from the present study that community people want to feel that Euro-Canadian teachers are reinforcing family values, that is, respect for parents, elders and First Nations culture, rather than teaching children only western values. I asked 38-year-old M.G., a mother of two, what she would recommend for teachers to teach in school. As she stated:

Teachers should teach children our values. We were taught to respect our parents but these kids don't want to listen to us as parents. The other day, I saw some of your school children in front of the school teasing that old man . . . I asked them to stop, they won't listen. Some of them were even throwing snowballs at him. These kids don't respect elders. They just do what they like. I think teachers should teach them all these things like respect for elders, and our culture too (Interview with a parent).

Respondents also indicated that in order to communicate effectively with parents, teachers need to understand the cultural differences, First Nations' way of life, their problems and aspirations. As B.M. of the Band Office remarked:

Teachers are different from us and they've got the way they do things and we also have our own way of doing things. I know parents won't come to teachers if they don't go to them. Teachers have to show understanding of our way of life and our problems. If teachers invite parents and they come late you should understand that they're on First Nations time [laugh] (Interview with band worker).

Teachers believe that the problem of communication partly lies in parents' refusal to involve themselves in school affairs. Teachers expressed that all attempts they make to invite parents to school events prove futile. Thus, teachers feel that while they try all they can to keep an open door policy, parents would not make efforts to visit the school. As 30-year-old male teacher H.D. stated, when I asked the question: "How can the school build effective communication lines with the community?":

I think this question is a reflection of the problem that now exists. The onus is put on the school to build effective communication. If you look at a relationship between two people, one person cannot make it work by him/herself. If one person is a great communicator, and does everything possible to make the relationship work, yet receives little or no response from the other person, the relationship will eventually die. No matter how great a communicator you are, you cannot carry on forever alone. Quite often, teachers put a great deal of work into planning events to involve parents but they receive little or no support, and little or no turnout for their efforts. After awhile, they get tired of it, and they don't want to try any more because there seems to be no purpose. Nobody communicates anything good that is done, only complains when they don't like something. This is very discouraging for teachers. For a relationship to work, between two people, both partners must put effort, support, and communication into making it a good relationship. Each person has an equal responsibility. I believe for effective lines of communication to exist between the school and the community, each has to accept the responsibility for making this happen. Each has to work at making it become a reality (Interview with Euro-Canadian teacher).

Even though a number of parents said that teachers are unable to communicate effectively to parents, some indicated firmly that the problem of communication does not lie with the teachers because students convey messages of invitation by notes to homes. However, it is clear from the study that because many parents are illiterate and do not read as well as speak English, they have a problem comprehending messages sent by teachers. Some parents feel that it is the responsibility of the LEA and the Band Council to be actively involved in school events, and draw the community into accepting to be part of the school. As 66-year-old J.S. commented:

The Band Council should provide effective relationship to community people. The Band should communicate effectively with the people, for example, who are the teachers? What are they doing? What have they planned for the school? How should community people support the plans for the school? The Band Council is unable to report about the school to the people. They don't deal with the school properly. The Band doesn't inform us about what happens in the school. There should be a regulation that the LEA and the Band Council should report periodically to the people what the school is doing. They can communicate with the people through radio shows, community meetings or newsletters (Interview with community elder).

While a majority of respondents indicated that lack of communication was a major drawback for schooling, at the same time a few respondents blame parents for apathy. Those respondents felt that most parents do not care about the school and nothing could involve them in schooling matters. As LEA member S.V. remarked:

The parents just don't care. They have other things bugging them and won't worry about school (Interview with community member).

What this respondent suggested was that problems associated with deplorable living conditions, lack of job opportunities, lack of recreational facilities and adjoining problems of gas sniffing and alcohol abuse could contribute to parental apathy towards school matters.

Teacher Orientation and Integration into Community

Teachers felt that the two-day orientation they receive in Sioux Lookout before coming into the community is inadequate to prepare them to understand their students and parents. They recommended that they need two types of orientation: 1) prior to their arrival in the community; and, 2) after their arrival in the community. The first orientation should be at least one week long. It should thoroughly explain differences in culture; it should offer some training for teaching English as a second language; it should provide an information package of the community including pictures and videotapes; and above all, it should spell out teacher expectations. As teacher H.S. simply put it:

The orientation prior to arriving in the community should include suggestions as to how to 'break the ice' with the local people, what the community views as the role of the teachers both in and outside of the school environment; the duties and responsibilities of the Education coordinator and the LEA; administrative procedures/paper-work and brief synopsis of the Windigo Education Policy (Interview with Euro-Canadian teacher).

Teachers indicated that the orientation after they arrive in the community should be ongoing. They said they could use the first few days to familiarize themselves with community people and the environment. As teacher M.C. stated:

Once in the community the teachers could be taken on a walking tour of the place, to familiarize themselves with the layout; they could be introduced to the families. This could be done in one morning or afternoon. The potluck dinner this year was a good idea. It would be nice to have someone tutor the teachers for about half an hour once a week in Ojibwe, so we could learn some common greetings, expressions and phrases (Interview with Euro-Canadian teacher).

Some teachers also indicated that as part of the orientation process in the community, it is

necessary for non-First Nations teachers and community people to discuss issues directly pertaining to the education of the children. As teacher S.D. remarked:

The orientation in the community should include: a discussion of the local goals of education; an introduction to local resource people for cultural activities, traditional values, and those willing to assist in the classroom and extra-curricular activities when needed; a list of community activities in which teachers could participate; and a list of band officials and their responsibilities, and an introduction to these people (Interview with Euro-Canadian teacher).

Teachers expressed the need to have families volunteer to prepare them for some aspects of community lifestyles, such as hunting, fishing, cooking and craftwork. These families could 'adopt' teachers and bring them up to know the First Nations way. Teacher H.D., in an answer to the kind of orientation to receive in the community, stated:

If possible, various families in the community could adopt a teacher and invite them to go hunting, fishing, trapping and participate in their everyday life—hauling water, getting wood, and eating with the family. The teachers would gain valuable information and understanding of local life that would benefit them in teaching their children. This adoption would create a better rapport between the parents and the teachers and would promote cooperation. Teachers would be made to feel welcome in the community and would feel as if they were part of the community. A great benefit to the teachers would be first hand experience/assimilation into the local way of life (Interview with Euro-Canadian teacher).

When I asked teachers about how much they thought they should know about First Nations people before teaching their children, almost all of them agreed that it is important for them to understand the social and cultural realities in the community. They also indicated that they need to have some understanding of the general learning styles of First Nations children and how they could adapt curriculum

and resources to local needs. As one of the female teachers, M.C., maintained:

I think it is important to be aware of the realities that exist both socially and culturally in the community. We need to know what kind of behaviour is acceptable. Also, we should have an understanding of the general learning styles of Natives (Interview with Euro-Canadian teacher).

While community people felt that teachers are unwilling to learn about their way of life, teachers, on the other hand, indicated that they are willing to learn all that they can, provided community people are prepared to teach them. A majority of teachers expressed that it is the duty of the community people to find ways and means of imparting their culture to non-First Nations teachers. Teachers further indicated that as part of its involvement, the community should help teachers to learn the culture, language and history of the local community.

Discussions with the Euro-Canadian teachers revealed that most of them did not know anything about First Nations and their culture before arriving in the community. Teachers would have preferred to learn about First Nations people and their culture at the university. They felt that the university should play a vital role in improving the quality of teachers for First Nations children. As female teacher S.D. remarked:

I believe all education programs should include courses on Native students. Some of these should be taught by Native people, and some taught by non-Natives who have worked with Native students. This would provide teachers with culturally relevant information, as well as information that will help prepare them for what they will face in working in Native communities (Interview with Euro-Canadian teacher).

Teachers stated that universities should devote research towards collecting material from First Nations communities for use in courses such as sociology of education and educational psychology. Also, teachers felt that universities should organize seminars and give presentations in classes about First Nations education. H.D, whom I asked how much teachers need to know before teaching First Nations students, put it this way:

The focus of knowledge, I think should deal with psychology. How Native children think is crucial to designing approaches to helping them learn and especially for classroom management and discipline. Teachers need to know a lot about children, their relationship with the community and how the community responds to the needs of children not as it was traditionally, but as it is today, or maybe both (Interview with a Euro-Canadian teacher).

When I asked another teacher, D.T., what he thinks should be the role of universities in improving the quality of teachers for First Nations children, he said:

With the help of Native organizations and committees, content can be collected and submitted to universities to use in conjunction with sociology and psychology course content; otherwise, faculties of education should hold seminars, have presentations in classes, and hold a Native awareness day or week annually at the universities in order to kindle the interest of student teachers in Native education (Interview with a Euro-Canadian teacher).

FUNDAMENTAL STRATEGY SUGGESTED TO ADDRESS SCHOOL-COMMUNITY RELATIONS

Participants indicated that parents and teachers needed to work together to bridge the gap between home and school. They revealed the need for more understanding and better communication between parents, school staff and community-at-large. Participants also felt that parental involvement should be a strong impetus for student success.

One of the fundamental strategies suggested to address school-community relations was the need to inform parents about the importance of active participation in school affairs. Participants suggested that parents should provide management goals for the education system. They should participate in school activities such as open houses, professional development days, helping in the classrooms, sports activities, and so on. Participants also recommended that the Band Council should be actively involved in advertising school events to community people and should encourage them to take part in the events. Teachers should use various means such as the community radio and billboards to inform parents about school events and encourage them to attend. Parents and school staff should socialize at the beginning of each year and get acquainted with each other.

Specific Implementation Strategies for Dealing with Community-School Relations

As part of this study, participants sought the best possible ways to maximize parental involvement and the general relationships between the school and the community. Having established that community people are willing to communicate with teachers and involve themselves in the education of their children, and that teachers are also willing to learn the culture of the community, the participants deliberated issues concerning how to bring parents and teachers together to work for a common goal. In order to establish a continuity of parent-teacher cooperation, participants suggested that the following specific implementation strategies should be ongoing:

a. Teachers should organize parent-teacher events in teachers' homes.

b. Teachers should periodically invite parents to their classrooms to teach a skill or tell a story to the students.

c. The school should maintain a school-community newspaper that reports both school and community news with teachers and parents on the editorial board.

d. School should regularly send a newsletter or school newspaper to parents' homes.

e. School should organize parent-teacher games nights; parents should submit a list of skills they can offer the school.

f. The LEA should clearly understand issues arising in the school and should properly communicate these issues to the parents.

g. Teachers should reach out into the community by visiting parents of their students at least once a month.

h. Band Council should provide more social gatherings and make it possible for teachers and parents to meet outside the school.

i. Teachers should make learning relevant to home conditions of student.

j. School should involve children's extended family members such as grandmothers, uncles, aunts, and elder brothers and sisters in school affairs.

DISCUSSIONS

This study went beyond simply locating problems about schooling. Identifying perspectives and suggesting solutions for the improvement of relations between the school and the community, First Nations and Euro-Canadian teachers sent a message that, together, they can do a good job in school decision-making roles if they are offered the opportunity to know more about each other. In other words, because community people and Euro-Canadian teachers generally poorly understand each other's worldview, it is necessary for the teachers to have appropriate preparation for teaching in First Nations schools. DeFaveri (1984) and Hampton (1995) sum up the differences between First Nations and the Euro-worldviews. DeFaveri asserts that while the First Nations worldview symbolizes unity with creation, the Euro worldview symbolizes individualism and isolationism. Thus, while the First Nations worldview espouses that all things are integrated and united in some way, the White worldview maintains that reality does not necessarily constitute related or connected components. For Hampton (1995), there is the need for a radical change because differences are not only in terms of ethnicity, race, values, personal differences in viewpoints, and socialization but also in terms of historical antecedents rooted in colonization.

One important theme that constantly emerged and guided participants' recommendations about school-community relations was the part the school could play to rejuvenate traditional values in the school and the community. Suggestions implied that the school should be a repository and clearing-house for traditional values. This recommendation supports those of NIB (1972) and the Report of the Royal Commission on Learning (as will later appear in this paper). As the NIB (1972) paper states:

Indian children must have the opportunity to learn their language, history and culture in the classroom. Curricula will have to be revised in federal and provincial schools to recognize the contributions which Indian people have made to Canadian History and life (p. 29).

Recommendations offered by community people in the present study suggested that the teachers need more training into First Nations culture. The present data also showed that Euro-Canadian teachers in Yellow Pond would like to have had exposure to material on First Nations culture and traditions while at the university. Drawing from observations among First Nations parents and Euro-Canadian teachers, this study reduces all the concerns to the central issue of training and orientation of teachers to First Nations culture. The results of the present study support the sentiment echoed by the Royal Commission on Learning (1994) and NIB (1972) about the need to pre-

pare teachers of First Nations children. Recommendation 127 of the Report of the Royal Commission on Learning (1994) strongly advocates the inclusion of First Nations content in teacher preparation programs. The report recommends "that the province include in its requirements for pre-service and in-service education a component related to teaching aboriginal students and teaching about aboriginal issues to both Native and non-Native students" (p. 77). The National Indian Brotherhood (1972) also addresses the concern by stating:

Federal and provincial authorities are urged to use the strongest measures necessary to improve the qualifications of teachers and counsellors of Indian children. During initial training programs there should be compulsory courses in inter-cultural education, Native languages (oral facility and comparative analysis), and teaching English as a second language. Orientation courses and in-service training are needed in all regions. Assistance should be available for all teachers in adapting curriculum and teaching techniques to the needs of local children. Teachers and counselors should be given the opportunity to improve themselves through specialized summer courses in acculturation problems, anthropology, Indian history, language and culture (p. 19).

While many universities in Canada offer a variety of courses in First Nations studies, these courses are mostly offered to students of First Nations origin. However, the irony is that First Nations schools are mostly made up of Euro-Canadian teachers (see Agbo, 1990; Canadian Education Association (CEA), 1984). The CEA Report (1984) indicates an almost classic failure of the Euro-Canadian teacher to attend to the needs of First Nations children. As the report states:

Too often, non-Native teachers have little or no professional understanding of the lifestyles, values and cultures of Native people. There is no doubt that Native education must recognize and respect these differences and obviously Native teachers and counselors are ideally suited to meet the needs of the

Native student. However, the need for Native teachers is only partially being met and it is the non-Native teachers, often ill-prepared to deal with the cultural and linguistic differences, who are responsible for providing the greatest share of Native children's education (p. 75).

The issue of appropriate orientation into the community through proper training involves not merely one of theoretical knowledge or methods of teaching, but of acquiring the necessary tools for shaping and implementing a culturally- and socially-oriented concept of teaching that teachers can sustain from within, recognizing the community resources in context and reinforcing and maximizing their teaching and their own self actualization. Put simply, the training of non-First Nation teachers of First Nations children should develop the teachers' interethnic and intercultural skills in analyzing and finding alternatives in teaching and contribute to a complete education of the teachers by giving them the opportunity not only to better adapt themselves to the First Nations community but also to act on it.

The strength of the effect of this study was particularly noticeable in the high level of recommendations community people offered for the solutions to problems facing the school. Notwithstanding the present difficulties in understanding the different worldviews, these recommendations are a manifestation of the growing consciousness of community people's roles towards the organization of their school.

CONCLUSIONS

Local control of First Nations education has owed much of its origins and spread to the need for parental involvement in schooling, no less than its political equivalent, First Nations self-determination. In fact, the National Indian Brotherhood (1972) bases the handing of schools over to First Nations bands on the claim that local control may yield considerable

parental input in school decision-making. This claim involves two basic expectations: 1) that local control will mobilize the community to create resources that the federal and provincial governments may not be able to generate; and, 2) that local control will support cultural education that symbolizes interests and values of First Nations (NIB, 1972). The concentration of ownership and management of the school in the hands of the community is therefore predicated upon the notion that parents are further moved towards the decision-making processes that affect their children. In fact, the NIB (1972) document set forth five purposes for *Indian Control of Indian Education* at the local level: 1) to incorporate First Nations cultures into the school system; 2) to foster greater involvement of parents; 3) to harmonize education with local development; 4) to make community people accountable for the education of their own children; and 5) to assert the right of First Nations parents to circumscribe the type of education necessary for their children. From the view of the NIB, the common ethos of local control consists of an assertion of the community will in matters of schooling and an emphasis on cultural education that fosters the identity and ethnicity of the First Nations child.

This aspect of "self-reliance" as part of the philosophy behind *Indian Control of Indian Education* (NIB, 1972) should enable First Nations schools to become less dependent on the Euro-Canadian system of education in their efforts to provide relevant education for First Nations children. However, the school in Yellow Pond continues to bear all the hallmarks of the mainstream Canadian educational systems. Obstacles to effective school-community relations seem so much a problem handed down from the INAC era. From the standpoint of the Indian Education Paper—Phase 1 (1982), difficulties facing First Nations education authorities were inherited from federal agencies and became more aggravated as "Aboriginal education organizations were not supported or developed to assume functions associated with provision of quality of education" (p. 3). Discussions with community people revealed that in contrast to the present local control model that emphasizes community involvement in schooling and encourages genuine community input into the conduct of school affairs, the INAC era tended to underscore the primacy of puppet school committees such as the Parent Teacher Associations (PTA) that had nominal influence in confined areas of the school programs and had no decision-making authority. The concentration of ownership and management of school in the hands of INAC and Euro-Canadian in-school administrators and teachers during the INAC period predicated upon the notion that all power belongs to INAC and its cronies, the school administrative and teaching staff, while the PTA becomes merely a rubber-stamp. There is thus a linkage between the present school-community relations and those of the INAC era. That linkage can perhaps best be understood in terms of a tradition of school-community relationships built over time and for the fact that the fence surrounding the school and the teachers' quarters at Yellow Pond remains intact, even during local control, it is not surprising that interviews and observations revealed that parents never liked to interfere with the school.

To conclude, developments in the long quest for a culturally relevant education, following First Nations disappointment with the Euro-Canadian educational system, have strengthened the need for effective school-community relations. The Yellow Pond community and Euro-Canadian teachers have exposed a whole range of opportunities for collaborating with each other for school improvement. Given the enormous disparities in the economic, political and cultural conditions of reserve schools, the local rather than the provincial or federal context provides an arena for school improvement. The present study reveals that the fate of the school is increasingly tied to and powerfully influenced by its relationships with the community. As First Nations communities are more familiar with local conditions and needs, effective community-school relations should help local people to pool together those local resources that are critical and relevant to school improvement. Apart from the numerous strategies suggested by parents and teachers for cooperation, it would, in addition, seem reasonable for parents and for the community-at-large to have a substantial interest in knowing how the school system procures and uses its resources. It would also seem reasonable for them to know how well students are gaining the knowledge and skills that will equip them to function in their own society and the outside world (NIB, 1972). Likewise, it would seem reasonable to expect the education authorities and community people to have a substantial interest in how well particular students perform and the roles that teachers and parents are playing in student learning and whether parents are satisfied with the results. Perhaps the most important thing for now is for the school to cease becoming a fenced-in enclave by tearing down the fence.

STUDY QUESTIONS

1. How does the literature review help explain the purpose of the study?

2. What are the rationales for using a participatory approach? What advantages/disadvantages does the approach offer within the context of the study? Explain fully.

3. How does Agbo endeavour to maintain his objectivity while conducting the study? How effective do you feel he was? Explain fully.

4. What kind of sampling approach does the author use? Are there alternative sampling strategies that might have been more effective? Explain fully.

5. How does the study contribute to the discipline?

REFERENCES

Agbo, S.A.
1990 Teacher satisfaction in isolated communities of North-western Ontario. Unpublished Master's Thesis. Thunder Bay (ON): Lakehead University.

Canadian Education Association Report (CEA)
1984 *Recent Developments in Native Education.* Toronto: University of Toronto Press.

DeFaveri, I.
1984 Contemporary ecology and traditional Native thought. *Canadian Journal of Native Education*, 12(3), 15–21.

Fantini M. & Gittell M.
1973 *Decentralization: Achieving Reform.* New York: Praeger Publishers.

Hall, B.L.
1993 Introduction, In Park, P. et al. (Eds.), *Voices of Change: Participatory Research in the United States and Canada* (pp. xiii–xxii). Westport (CT): Pergin & Garvey.

1981 Participatory research, popular knowledge and power. A personal reflection. *Convergence, 3,* 6–19.

1975 Participatory research: an approach for change. *Convergence,* 24–32.

Hampton, E.
1995 Towards a redefinition of Indian education. In M. Battiste & J. Barman (Eds.) *First Nations Education in Canada: The Circle Unfolds* (pp. 5–46). Vancouver: UBC Press.

Horton, B.D.
1993 The Appalachian land ownership study: research and citizen action in Appalachia. In Park, P. et al. (Eds.), *Voices of Change: Participatory Research in the United States and Canada* (pp. 85–103). Westport (CT): Bergin & Garvey.

Indian Education Paper Phase 1
1982 Ottawa: Department of Indian Affairs.

Jackson, T.
1993 A way of working: Participatory research and the Aboriginal movement in Canada. In Park, P. et al. (Eds.), *Voices of Change: Participatory Research in the United States and Canada* (pp. 47–64). Westport (CT): Bergin & Garvey.

Kemmis, S.
1991 Critical Education Research. *Canadian Journal for the Study of Adult Education* (Winter) Vol. V, Special.

Lather, P.
1992 Critical frames in educational research: Feminist and post-structural perspectives. *Theory into Practice*, Vol. XXXI (2), 87–99.

1986 Issues of validity in openly ideological research: Between a rock and a soft place. *Interchange,* 17(4), 63–84.

Maguire, P.1
1987 *Doing Participatory Research: A Feminist Approach.* Amherst: The Center for International Education, University of Massachusetts.

Matthew, N.
1990 Jurisdiction and control in First Nations schools evaluation. *Canadian Journal of Native Education,* 17(2), 96–115.

Miles, M.B. & Huberman, A.M.
1994 *Qualitative Data Analysis: An Expanded Sourcebook* (2nd Edition). Thousand Oaks (CA): Sage Publications Inc.

National Indian Brotherhood (NIB)
1980 *Indian Control of Indian Education.* Winnipeg: National Indian Brotherhood.

1972 *Indian Control of Indian Education—Policy Paper Presented to the Minister of Indian Affairs and Northern Development.* National Indian Brotherhood: Ottawa.

Owens, R.G.
1982 Methodological Perspective; Methodological Rigor in Naturalistic Inquiry—Some Issues and Answer. *Educational Administration Quarterly,* 18 (2), 1–21.

Participatory Research Network (PRN)
1982 *An Introduction to Participatory Research.* ICAE: Toronto.

Royal Commission on Learning
1994 For the Love of Learning: Report of the Royal Commission on Learning. Toronto: Queens Printer for Ontario.

Senese, G.B.
1991 *Self Determination and the Social Education of Native Americans.* New York: Praeger.

Sprinks, J.M.
1990 Collaborative decision-making at the school level. In J. Chapman (Ed.), *School-Based Decision-making and Management* (p. 121–145). Bristol, PA: The Falmer Press.

Chapter 8

Discussing Sexual Health with a Partner: A Qualitative Study with Young Women

Jennifer Cleary, Richard Barhman, Terry MacCormack, and Ed Herold

Source: Reprinted from *The Canadian Journal of Human Sexuality*, 2002, Vol. 11(3–4), p. 117–132.

ABSTRACT

Twenty-two females, heterosexual, undergraduate students were interviewed about the health protective sexual communication (HPSC) that did or did not occur with their most recent sexual partner prior to first intercourse. The narratives derived from this qualitative study provided insight into the content and extent of HPSC occurring prior to intercourse, the perceived barriers and facilitators to HPSC, and to the strategies used to initiate such discussions. The analysis of the narratives resulted in the development of ten themes that appeared to encompass the various influences on this communication process. The findings reveal that typically, very little (if any) HPSC occurred prior to first intercourse, that there were numerous perceived barriers to this communication process, and that most of the participants did not have the communication skills necessary to initiate such discussion.

INTRODUCTION

Health protective sexual communication (HPSC) refers to communication content that includes discussion about sexually transmitted infections (STIs), human immunodeficiency virus (HIV) and birth control (Catania, Binson, Dolcini, Moskowitz & van der Straten, 2001). In an instructive discussion of the behavioural epidemiology of HIV/STIs, Catania et al. (2001) identified several reasons for the importance of HPSC:

1. HPSC may facilitate the translation of shared intention into action (e.g., mutual intention to use condoms);

2. HPSC may act as a reminder of HIV and influence the saliency of safer sex concerns over other sexual desires;

3. HPSC may have a persuasive function, for example, by changing the mind of an unmotivated person;

4. HPSC may, in fact, reduce uncertainties regarding safer sex behaviour, and increase social support by allowing an expression of support, perhaps even encouragement, for safer sex; and

5. HPSC may reinforce subjective norms about condom use which, in turn, facilitates the enactment of the behaviour (p. 25).

Some may argue that as long as individuals are using condoms there is very little utility in HPSC. This belief is challenged when we recognize that although there are enormous health benefits associated with condom usage, there are also two well-established limitations. These are: user failure (non-usage, incorrect usage, breakage, slippage) (Lindberg, Sonenstein, Ku & Levine, 1997), and method (condom) failure (Davis & Weller, 1999). Taking the widely documented inconsistency in the use of condoms (Civic, 2000) together with the current rates of HIV, STIs and unwanted pregnancies among heterosexual young adults (Dryburgh, 2000; Health Canada 1999a, 1999b, 2001), these data indicate that there are important reasons to talk about sexual health issues with a new partner.

It is important to note that these discussions do not ensure that people will be honest about their STI history, especially if they are (or have been) infected. Pliskin (1997) found that among her sample of adults infected with genital herpes, 49% reported never discussing STDs with a potential partner. For this particular sample, this lack of communication could have put them at risk for contracting another STD or transmitting herpes to their partner. In addition, Payn, Tanfer, Billy and Grady (1997) found that 25% of the 466 participants in their study (all of whom had had an STI) reported having sex while infected. The importance of HPSC, however, is illustrated by the fact that 85% of the men in Payn et al.'s study (who were aware that they had an STI) did report informing their partner prior to intercourse. Although having health-related discussions with a potential partner is not a *guarantee* that you will receive accurate information, the likelihood of being able to make more informed decisions does increase.

Sexual communication has been identified as one of the key components in understanding the interpersonal interactions that facilitate or impede sexual health protective behaviours, including condom use (Edgar, 1992). To date, much of the research in this area has focused on discussions specifically about condom use and the positive health protective implications of such discussions. Numerous studies have shown a direct correlation between communication about condom use and higher rates of actual condom use (Hillier, Harrison & Warr, 1998; Sheeran, Abraham & Orbell, 1999).

Barriers and Facilitators to Health Protective Sexual Communication

Despite the importance of communicating with one's sexual partner, researchers have found that the initiation of sexual health related discussions is difficult for most people and that the seeming reluctance to talk about these issues appears to be fuelled by numerous perceived personal and relationship barriers. The personal barriers include (but are not limited to): (1) lack of comfort, feelings of awkwardness and ineptness with sexual health related discussions, including condom use (Welch Cline, Johnson & Freeman, 1992); (2) lack of effective communication skills (Buyess & Ickes, 1999; Polit-O'Hara & Kahn, 1985); (3) lack of a belief in their ability to communicate (Dilorio, Dudley, Lehr & Soet, 2000; Freimuth, Hammond, Edgar, McDonald & Fink, 1992); (4) use of drugs and alcohol (Freimuth et al., 1992); (5) expected negative outcomes of having such discussions (Dilorio et al., 2000) and (6) fear of embarrassment and shame (Metts & Cupach, 1989).

The possible negative relationship implications of discussing sexual health issues with a partner are among the most commonly cited reasons for people to avoid such communication. The reasons for this avoidance include concern about: (1) threatening their relationship (Welch Cline, Freeman & Johnson, 1990); (2) ruining the romance, intimacy and spontaneity in their relationship (Galligan & Terry, 1993; Hocking, Turk & Ellinger, 1999); (3) potential partner's anticipated reaction (Dilorio et al., 2000); and (4) implying a lack of trust in a potential partner (Hocking et al., 1999).

Health Protective Sexual Communication in New Relationships

Most of the research on HPSC has found that discussions about sexual health issues, including contraception and STI protection, rarely *precede* first intercourse (Mitchell & Wellings, 1998; Polit-O'Hara & Kahn, 1985). To date, however, little is known about the factors influencing HPSC in the context of new relationships (Catania et al., 2001; Galligan & Terry, 1993).

A study by Edgar, Freimuth, Hammond, McDonald and Fink (1992) is among the few studies that have focused on developing a better understanding of this communication process in the context of new sexual relationships. Edgar et al. (1992) were particularly interested in how college students sought sexual health information from their partner and the particular strategies that they used to persuade their partner to use a condom during their first sexual encounter. In accordance with previous research findings, only 57% of their participants had used a condom the last time that they had sex with a new sexual partner and only a third of the non-users said that they had wanted to use a condom. Among non-users, women who wanted to use condoms were less likely than men to communicate their wishes to their partner. The most commonly cited reasons for not communicating included embarrassment or discomfort with asking a partner to use a condom, fear of 'ruining the moment' and the belief that condom use was not necessary because other birth control methods were being used. Among those who did use condoms, women most often used a direct request to ask their partner to use a condom, whereas men used primarily nonverbal strategies. Many of the men reported that they often used condoms without their partner knowing. Nonverbal strategies, such as simply putting on a condom, were used to avoid the need to verbally communicate with their partner.

More recently, Catania et al. (2001) explored the demographic and psychosocial correlates of HPSC with a sample of heterosexuals who had had a new sexual partner within the past year. They found that high levels of HPSC were significantly related to perceived STD risk, greater sexual self-regulation skills and condom regulation skills, a history of being tested for HIV, age (younger individuals = more HPSC), drug and alcohol use (intake = less HPSC), gender (females = more HPSC) and eth-

nicity (nonwhite = more HPSC). Sexual guilt, personal commitment to use condoms, and HIV risk were found to be unrelated to HPSC.

Although both of these studies (Edgar et al., 1992; Catania et al., 2001) explored some aspects of HPSC, their use of quantitative designs yielded only limited insight into the substance and character of this communication. They did not give the investigators access to such process issues as the content and timing of such discussion or detailed insight into the barriers and facilitators of HPSC.

Use of a Qualitative Methodology

Increasingly, researchers have noted the need for qualitative research on the communication that occurs between partners before their first occasion of intercourse. To date, however, there are very few qualitative studies that have explored this aspect of communication. Among the few that have, a qualitative study by Wong et al. (1994) explored the perceived barriers and facilitators reported by sex workers in Singapore in negotiating condom use with their clients. The findings from these in-depth interviews provided detailed, practical information about what differentiated successful and non-successful negotiators. The richness of their findings highlights the potential value of qualitative methods in exploring this communication process.

Research Objectives

The objective of the present study was to describe what a sample of young university women discussed about sexual health with their most recent sexual partner, prior to first intercourse. A secondary objective was to explore what the participants believe had facilitated or hindered their engaging in such discussion. Specifically, the investigation addressed the following research questions:

1. What sexual health issues do female university students report having discussed with

their most recent sexual partner, prior to their engaging in intercourse for the first time? What is the extent and substance of this discussion?

2. What factors do they identify as having inhibited or facilitated that communication?

3. What strategies do female university students report using to initiate sexual health related discussions with their partners?

METHOD

Participant Characteristics

All of the twenty-two participants met the inclusion criteria (female, undergraduate students, born in Canada, self-identified as having sex only with men, and having had a new sexual partner within the past twelve months). They ranged in age from 19 to 23 years (mean = 20.2 years).

Recruitment of Participants

The first author made brief presentations to several undergraduate classes each with between 50–300 students. It can be estimated that almost one thousand students were invited to participate in this study (although an unknown number of these participants would not have fulfilled the inclusion criteria). It is important to note that because of the methods of distribution and some use of participants being recruited by their peers, there is no way of knowing precisely how many students were approached. Of the approximately 45 participants who took an information package about the study from in-class announcements about the study, 22 actually volunteered for the study. In an attempt to increase variability in the sample, students were recruited from various disciplines. Very few, however, volunteered from outside of the social sciences.

As an incentive for participation, all participants were entered into a draw for one of three monetary prizes (1st prize = $80.00, 2nd prize = $50.00 and 3rd prize = $30.00).

Interviews

Each of the twenty-two interviews took between 40 to 60 minutes to complete, depending on the extent of the elaboration and detail provided. A series of semi-structured questions was used to guide the discussion. In accordance with grounded theory methodology (Glaser & Strauss, 1967; Strauss & Corbin, 1990, 1998), as themes emerged from the discussions, the researcher added questions to provide further insight and development of those themes. The interviews were tape-recorded for subsequent analysis. The interviews were conducted by the first author who was attentive to the emergence of new themes at each interview. With the goal of attaining theoretical saturation (Strauss & Corbin, 1998), recruitment continued until the researcher concluded that no new themes were emerging. This was then followed by the formal data analysis.

Data Analysis

Grounded theory methodology, originally developed by Glaser and Strauss (1967) and further developed by Strauss and Corbin (1990, 1998), was used to analyse the narratives. This qualitative method was chosen for several reasons, including its ability to take a qualitative study beyond a purely descriptive level.

The first author transcribed each interview. Consistent with the practice of grounded theory, the researcher was aware of the desirability of collecting and analysing data simultaneously (Cutcliffe, 2000; Glaser & Strauss, 1967). However, student volunteers' increased willingness to participate in such a study at the beginning of the semester prevented the analysis of each interview from preceding the next scheduled interview. The researcher did, however, take notes during and following each interview. These memos summarized the researcher's reflections on how each interview seemed to fit with the themes emerging from the interviews. In addition, this in-field analysis allowed the researcher to make decisions about additional areas that needed to be explored during subsequent interviews and to recognize the diversity existing within categories. Although the traditional recursive nature of a grounded theory study was not feasible, the constant comparison between and within the data was pursued throughout the data collection process. In conducting the analysis, the researcher worked through the three steps used in grounded theory: open coding, axial coding and selective coding (Strauss & Corbin, 1998).

Open coding is a preliminary process of generating descriptive categories (often referred to as codes) out of narrative data so that these can then be grouped into even larger conceptual categories. In the present study, open codes included descriptions such as "assumes partner does not have an STD", "attitudes about HPSC—doesn't fit into the atmosphere," and "facilitator—knowing partner won't get upset." The subsequent process of axial coding is a more interpretive process in which the various descriptive categories are subsumed by broader conceptual ones, out of which themes or core ideas begin to emerge from the narratives. Some axial codes were "education," "responsibility for sexual health" and "use of assumptions." Selective coding is yet a higher-level search for larger and more meaningful connections among the axial codes. As is described in the results section below, here the researcher "tied together" the open and axial codes into more encompassing themes that reflected, more broadly, what participants were saying about their sexual health communication experience.

At a later point in the analysis, in separate meetings with the first author, two of the participants provided feedback about whether or not they were able to hear their own story within the narrative account of sexual communication which emerged from the overall analysis of the interview scripts. Participants reported that the researcher had understood their experience and that their experience was well represented within the overall summary of the research findings.

It is integral to the use of such methodologies that researchers acknowledge and speculate on how their knowledge, values and beliefs might have influenced the process of theory development. As a young woman, with many demographic attributes similar to those of the participants, the researcher often felt that she understood their experiences. Sometimes these assumptions resulted in her not asking questions that might have required the participants to state their feelings more explicitly. Such statements might potentially have been different in some degree from the researcher's understanding of the same phenomena. Throughout the interviews, the researcher constantly reflected on how she might have been influencing the process and possible ways to minimize this influence.

RESULTS

The participants reported very little HPSC occurring prior to first intercourse. In fact, many reported *no* discussion about sexual health issues prior to first intercourse with a new partner. The participants who *did* report such communication indicated that it was not extensive and was typically focused only on ensuring condom use to protect themselves from pregnancy. Rarely did they discuss sexual histories, STI history, perceived HIV risk, STI testing and/or participation in high-risk sexual behaviours. The analysis of the narratives resulted in the development of 10 themes (see Table 8.1). It should be noted that the complexity of the relationships between the specific issues explored in this study inevitably resulted in themes that are not mutually exclusive; there is some degree of

Table 8.1	Ten Key Themes Identified from the Transcripts of In-depth Interviews with 22 Heterosexual Female Undergraduate Students about Their Experiences with HPSC Prior to Intercourse with a New Partner
Education	Peer influences
Responsibility for sexual health	Experience
Importance of feeling comfortable	Relationship expectations and commitment
Feelings of fear	Personal characteristics
The use of assumptions	Partner influences

overlap between the identified themes. The 10 themes identified do, nevertheless, provide detailed insight into the reported barriers and facilitators to HPSC and the strategies used to initiate such discussions. Each theme is described below.

Education

Although there were a few participants who reported extensive sexual health education from formal (school based) and/or informal (family, peers and the media) sources, the majority claimed to have little knowledge of sexual health issues. This reported lack of knowledge was seen, through the analysis, to be directly associated with a lack of HPSC with their partners:

I think that probably having some education prior to it, knowing what you are talking about . . . it is kind of hard to ask someone about being tested when you don't know yourself what it entails. (participant 19)

Participants who felt knowledgeable about sexual health issues often observed that this knowledge increased their confidence in having these discussions with their partners because they felt confident that they knew what they were talking about.

Some of the young women reported having developed these skills through informal educa-

tion from their parents. Those who grew up in environments in which their families were open to and welcomed discussions about sexuality were much more likely to feel comfortable with, and confident in, their abilities to have such discussions with their partner:

My family has been comfortable not just with sex conversations but with anything that you want to talk about . . . it's what's comfortable for you . . . there was nothing that you couldn't talk about which is why there is nothing that I can't talk about with someone that I am with . . . (participant 4)

Conversely, those who grew up in families where discussions about sexuality were taboo often reported carrying those same attitudes regarding sexual communication with them into their sexual relationships:

Some of the barriers just, um. When I was brought up, it was always like you don't really talk about that. It is kind of a non-issue. (participant 2)

Most participants, in this sample of university female students, reported growing up in families in which sexuality was *not* discussed. This lack of exposure to such discussion was closely associated with a self-reported lack of comfort and confidence in discussing sexual health issues with their partners.

In addition, *none* of the participants reported having any sort of formal training in how to communicate with a partner (what to say, how to say it, and when to say it). They stated that the focus of the curriculum was on teaching the biological basis of sex and did not address the interactive context in which sexual relationships occur, or the skills needed to talk about sexual health and safety with a potential partner:

Our education is too strict and too technical for any of us to get that out of it. All you got out of it was like, "The condom goes on the banana and pinch the end," you know, like there was no, "What are you going to say before you put that on?" you know, because that is that space before that happens that you are like, uhhhhh . . . they say that we have to do this now and they don't talk about it. (participant 4)

Many of the participants in this study were unaware of why HPSC is important prior to having sexual intercourse with a new partner. When asked why they did not believe that such discussion was necessary, they gave various explanations that revolved around their perception of low perceived risk, not knowing what they would talk about, and their belief that they were protecting themselves adequately. They rarely perceived a need to talk about sexual issues if they knew that they were protecting themselves in other ways (such as being on the pill and/or having condoms available). They frequently reported that condom use took place with no formal discussion about its use. For many, the use of condoms *replaced* the need for conversation:

Although I might not talk about it doesn't mean that I don't protect from it . . . I don't have sit-down conversation about what I think of STDs . . . how to . . . but I mean condoms . . . they almost . . . kind of, eliminate the conversation . . . I use the condom thing as a way of not talking about it. It overtakes the conversation, sort of, in my point of view. (participant 3)

Responsibility for Sexual Health

It became evident early in the research process that women not only reported having to be the initiators of HPSC (if it took place) prior to intercourse, they also reported being the ones who often provided the condoms and insisted on condom use and STI tests:

Because if I didn't bring it up (wearing a condom) I don't know when it would have been brought up . . . yeah, I am in charge of birth control completely. I go and get the pill and I buy the condoms. He will give me money for it but it is left up to me . . . yep, we split the cost evenly but other than that it is up to me to actually go out and do it. (participant 21)

Throughout the study, the researcher explored why women take on this responsibility. There were several reasons, including: (1)

the focus placed on women to protect themselves from pregnancy; (2) the fear of becoming pregnant; (3) being more aware of their reproductive health; (4) the perceived need for the women to set the boundaries; (5) how it bothers them when they do not have these discussions prior to sex; and the fact that (6) men were not taking responsibility, so the women felt that they had to. It is unclear if this is actually what is occurring within these relationships or if this is how the young women perceive it (potentially contrary to what young men might report).

It is important to note, however, that although these young women seemed to be taking much more responsibility than men, this responsibility did not generally involve having sexual health related discussions with their partners and was often associated only with condom use and/or being on the pill. As previously stated, this is evidenced by the fact that the majority of the participants reported minimal (to no) HPSC occurring prior to intercourse with a new partner.

Importance of Feeling Comfortable

The few young women who were able to initiate HPSC explained that they felt comfortable in doing so. These feelings of comfort often developed over time, in more committed relationships, and with experience having such discussions. For most in this sample, this comfort level developed some time *after* a sexual relationship had begun.

In addition, their partner's perceived comfort level also contributed to their feelings of comfort in having such discussions. It was commonly noted that their partner's *lack* of comfort in HPSC was a major barrier to the communication process. Clearly, the women sought to avoid making their partner feel uncomfortable:

It is hard for me because I don't like prying or making him feel uncomfortable. (participant 15)

Sexual self-disclosure was difficult for many of the young women and they often reported feeling very uncomfortable discussing their personal sexual histories with a potential partner:

R—How did you feel about disclosing that information about yourself?

P—A little uncomfortable [laugh] um, I am always going to feel a little uncomfortable whether he is going to view me as being slutty and you know . . . stop at that, like . . . okay, then I am not going to have sex with you kind of thing. (participant 18)

Although few participants were aware of using strategies to facilitate HPSC prior to intercourse, it became apparent that among those that did, the communication strategies revolved around making it more comfortable for themselves and their partner.

Feelings of Fear

Many of the participants were fearful about initiating and having sexual health related discussions with their partners. This fearfulness appeared to be a result of several factors including: (1) their concern about losing the relationship/sexual encounter; (2) a concern about being judged; (3) their wish to avoid offending their partner; and (4) being scared about talking about sex. A common fear was of losing their relationship by "scaring him off":

Like you want to keep that person, you don't want to cross that line, you know and if you bring it up you might embarrass them or make them run away and you might embarrass yourself. (participant 4)

Especially for the young women with more extensive sexual experience, the fear of being judged if they sexually self-disclosed was a barrier to the communication process.

One of the most commonly cited reasons for feelings of fear and embarrassment about the communication process was fear of offending their partner. Many of the participants were concerned about what initiation of these

discussions would imply about their partner and his sexual history:

I didn't want to offend him and I didn't want to like scare him and I didn't want to bother him kind of thing . . . (participant 17)

The Use of Assumptions

Very early in the interview process the researcher noticed the frequent use of the word "assume" to describe the process of evaluating risk and the need to have health related discussions with a partner. Generally, the young women believed everything that they were told by a potential partner, and they based decisions about sexual health protective behaviours, such as condom use, on this information:

P—We kind of talked about it a bit more and he told me that he had been tested and he had been safe in his past and everything so . . .

R—Did you believe him?

P—Yeah. (participant 5)

Participants also made assumptions about their partner's previous sexual experiences based on their current behaviours. For example, one young man was very concerned about STIs, so his partner assumed that he was "safe":

I assumed that, I guess I made an assumption, but I assumed that the fact that he was so paranoid about it meant that he didn't exactly have one himself so . . . (participant 3)

Assumptions were also used to avoid discussions about condom use, and the potential awkwardness often associated with HPSC. Instead of initiating conversations related to condom use, young women assumed that their partners would know that they needed to use a condom. In other cases, the men seemed to assume that the women would be taking care of the contraception:

It is just sort of an assumed thing. He assumed thatI was on the pill so he didn't get a condom. (participant 7)

It was evident that many of the participants did not think that there were any substantive risks involved in having a sexual relationship with their partner. Most used untested assumptions in making their own decisions on condom use and contraception. Under these circumstances, they felt quite safe.

Peer Influences

Many of the women were unaware of whether or not their peers had sexual health related discussions with their partners because this was not a common topic of conversation within their peer group. This lack of discussion was interesting because their peers seemed willing, and able, to discuss most sexuality issues *except* HPSC. As one participant said, "We talk about the good stuff, not the scary stuff." (participant 16)

It is important to note, however, that there were some participants who reported that their peers shared their insight with each other about how to initiate such discussions: what to say, when to say it, and what to expect. These discussions were most common among young women whose peers had become pregnant or they themselves had previously contracted an STI. These participants seemed more likely to realize the importance of having health related discussions before having sex with a new partner.

In addition, participants noted that they sometimes used peers' reported experiences to help facilitate HPSC with their own partners. They felt as though this was a more effective way to initiate such discussions because it provided a genuine reason why they were concerned enough to want to have such discussion:

It helped it go a little smoother because he knew that I knew what I was talking about; I wasn't just kind of like throwing out random shots in the dark. (participant 12)

Experience

While many young women reported having difficulty engaging in a discussion on sexual health issues with a new partner prior to intercourse, some reported that previous experience in initiating such discussion made it an easier thing to do with subsequent partners. They explained that this experience made them feel more comfortable, confident, taught them how to communicate more effectively, gave them the opportunity to "practice," let them know what to expect, how to handle it, and they learned what they would do differently in future relationships:

I think just mostly the experience (helped facilitate the communication with her partner). I have been through it once, I know what to expect and how to handle it. (participant 21)

Their belief about the number of sexual partners that their partner had had was also used to evaluate that person's potential risk, and the perceived need to have health related discussions. It was repeatedly noted that partners who (they believed) had had no previous partners, or only one or two, were not perceived to pose a risk to the young women's health and in these cases HPSC was judged to be unnecessary.

Relationship Expectations and Commitment

Since this study explored the HPSC that occurred *prior* to first intercourse, this early phase of the couple relationship was certainly an influential factor in whether or not they talked about sexual health issues prior to intercourse. Many of the participants were concerned that initiating such discussions *prior* to having sex would make their partner think that they were ready (and wanting) to have sex:

If I had just discussed it and discussed protection then he would assume that it was going to happen

. . . I think that if we had discussed it then he would have assumed that I was ready . . . (participant 1)

Due to the level of self-disclosure necessary in such discussions, many young women did not want to discuss such personal aspects of their life with someone that they did not know very well. They were not willing to raise these discussions when they were still uncertain about the relationship potential.

Casual relationships, such as one-night stands, were *not* associated with HPSC because of the lack of time to have such discussions, the mutual understanding that it is only about sex, and the belief that condom use was sufficient protection:

If it is a one-night stand it is kind of hard to get too involved . . . well, because there just isn't enough time. If it is a one-night stand you meet them at 8:00 at night, you hang out and you are gone by 8:00 in the morning or something like that. There just isn't enough time to do that . . . You don't want to be asking them their whole life story when you know good and well that you are only having a one-night stand . . . (participant 12)

In most cases, the necessary comfort level to have such discussion came after a sexual relationship had begun and when they knew that they had established a committed relationship:

There is no point telling such personal details to someone that you are going to break up with in the next week . . . (participant 9)

Interestingly, being in a committed couple relationship both facilitated *and* hindered the communication process. The perceived facilitators included the availability of time (which was often several months) to have such discussion, the agreement and acknowledgment by the partners that a sexual relationship was likely going to take place at some point, and the fact that participants felt more comfortable in initiating such discussion. For some participants, however, these more committed couple relationships proved to be a barrier. Several noted that the longer the relationship progressed before intercourse, the less concerned they were about the sexual health risks associated with having sex with that partner, and thus the less likely they were to initiate such discussion. This was due to the positive feelings and trust that they developed towards their partner rather than any objective knowledge they had gained about their partner's sexual health.

Personal Characteristics

Confidence in initiating HPSC was often cited (or indirectly referred to) as being a facilitator to the communication process, and lack of it as being a barrier. Participants frequently discussed their lack of confidence in their own communication skills and their inability to initiate such discussions:

But how do you ease into a conversation about . . . you know we talk about computers, he's in computer engineering . . . go from that to something more personal . . . I have thought about ways but I haven't come up with anything. (participant 6)

Not surprisingly, those who perceived themselves to be at risk were more likely to initiate such discussion. The majority, however, reported a low perceived risk about contracting an STI or becoming pregnant. This low perceived risk was often attributed to the fact that they did not participate in the behaviours that they believed were necessary to put people at risk:

I know for me personally I am not concerned for myself because I . . . I am tested regularly. I am not like this, I don't sleep around or anything. (participant 16)

This lack of perceived risk was almost always associated with a lack of HPSC occurring prior to intercourse, and a general lack of concern about sexual health issues:

Like I never really thought "I wonder if he has an STD," it just wasn't an issue . . . there hasn't been an excessive amount of discussion because it really just doesn't seem like . . . not an issue . . . I don't really feel that we need to. (participant 17)

Partner Influences

Even the most articulate, educated, skilled young women were not able to have discussions with partners who were unwilling to so engage. Participants reported that partners who inhibited the communication process did not want to talk, at all, about sexual health issues, sexual pasts and/or to sexually self-disclose:

And sometimes he would say things like, "Well, is that really necessary for us to talk about" because he hated talking about the past. Obviously, you don't want to talk about the past with someone new . . . but he would be like, "Do we have to talk about this? I don't want you to get upset blah blah blah" . . . (participant 4)

A perception that their partner would be open, and willing, to engage in a sexual health related discussion was the most frequently cited reason why some felt able to initiate them:

I think that it was mainly because of him (that she was able to initiate a discussion). He was really open . . . (participant 11)

I think that the biggest reason that I was confident was because he made me comfortable . . . I wasn't embarrassed to talk about it because he wasn't embarrassed to talk about it. (participant 4)

DISCUSSION

Content and Extent of HPSC Reported Prior to Intercourse

In accordance with much of the previous research (Polit-O'Hara & Kahn, 1985; Mitchell & Wellings, 1998), few participants in this study reported any HPSC occurring prior to first intercourse with a new partner. For most of the par-

ticipants, sexual health topics were considered to be off limits for discussion within the context of a new relationship.

These findings are of potential concern because of the established relationship between HPSC and health protective behaviours such as condom use (Catania et al., 1994; de Visser & Smith, 2001; Quina, Harlow, Morokoff, Burkholder & Dieter, 2000). Contrary to such research findings, however, the majority of the participants (all except three) in the current study did report using condoms during their first sexual encounter. It appears that for the majority of this sample of young women, HPSC with their new partner was not essential to facilitate condom use. It is important to note, however, that these high levels of condom use during first sexual encounters were reported by participants to have decreased over time, often with little (if any) discussion about sexual health issues before the practice of using a condom with that partner was ultimately abandoned.

Although it is a positive indicator that so many of the participants used condoms, regardless of the lack of HPSC that occurred during these first sexual encounters, there is still a need for having sexual health related discussions with one's partners. There are risks associated with sex, regardless of whether or not a condom is used. For these women, this lack of HPSC prior to intercourse seemed directly related to their lack of understanding of the purpose in having such discussions, and their over-confident sense of security associated with condom use. Many of the participants seemed completely unaware that condom use does not protect from breakage and failure, or from *all* STIs. Nor is its use a guarantee that you will not get pregnant. We cannot expect young women to have health related discussions if we never teach them *why* these discussions are important and *how* they can help protect their sexual health. There are compelling grounds to develop programs that emphasize the importance of condom use, contraception *and* HPSC. Individuals must realize that these are best understood as complementary behaviours rather than behaviours that replace each other.

Perceived Barriers and Facilitators to HPSC

Participants reported numerous barriers and facilitators that they believed had influenced the HPSC that did, or did not, occur with their most recent partner prior to intercourse. This present discussion will focus on some of the key findings that emerged from this study and will attempt to provide some explanations for and possible implications of these findings.

The Reported Deficiencies in Formal Sexuality Education

It became evident early in this study that participants generally believed that their formal sex education was inadequate, and certainly gave no attention to the development of the knowledge, skills and attitudes necessary to facilitate HPSC with a new partner. A recent review of HIV/STI intervention programs concluded that the inclusion of specific behavioural skills training was a commonality among effective intervention programs (McKay, 2000). Health Canada's (1994) *The Canadian Guidelines for Sexual Health Education* states, among other things, that sexual health education should enable learners to "acquire the skills they may need to maintain and enhance sexual health and avoid sexual problems" (participant 18). *None* of the participants in this study, however, reported any formal sexual communication skills training. So although Health Canada's advice is that curricula should include skill development within their sexual health education programs, these findings are consistent with previous reports that adolescents are still rarely given any formal training to develop these communication and negotiation skills (Troth & Peterson, 2000).

As noted in the literature, many people, including the participants in this study, *assume* that their partners are "low" or "no" risk. Such assessments are based on assumptions rather than objective knowledge (Civic, 2000; Williams et al., 1992). Researchers have noted that there is a need for prevention programs to focus on emphasizing the need to assess a partner's STI/HIV risk objectively (Civic, 2000). It is possible that part of the reason that people do not generally use objective knowledge in assessing a partner's health status (which inevitably involves HPSC with their partners) is because of their lack of comfort, self-confidence and desire to initiate such discussions. The development of these skills should be a priority for inclusion in a credible sexual health and education program.

The Reported Deficiencies in Informal Sexuality Education

In this sample, very few women had had open and substantive communication about sexuality, and more specifically sexual health, modelled for them by their peers, family and the media. This seemed to further reinforce the deficiencies in school-based education programs. Consequently, the women reported fears, anxiety and a lack of skills which all contributed to their reported reluctance to talk about sexual health issues with a new partner, even in cases where they wanted to have such discussion.

Consistent with the findings of previous research (Dilorio et al., 2000; Moore & Davidson, 2000), participants in the current study who did report open communication about sexuality in their own family were also more likely to feel comfortable initiating HPSC with a new sexual partner. This observation highlights the important role that parents can potentially play in developing the knowledge, skills, attitudes and comfort needed to facilitate HPSC.

Gender Differences in Taking Responsibility for Sexual Health

There was evidence of reported gender differences with respect to who typically took responsibility for sexual health within the participants' relationships. Although previous research has indicated that *men* tend to provide condoms (Carter, McNair, Corbin & Williams, 1999; Mitchell and Wellings, 1998), the majority of the female participants in this study reported purchasing and providing condoms in addition to initiating their use. A recent study by Carter et al. (1999) also reported that women tended to initiate condom use. These researchers concluded that the male college students in their study played "a more reactive role in the negotiation of condom use, waiting for their partner to initiate condom use" (participant 223). It is unclear, then, if the participants in this current study reflect evidence of a changing trend in who provides the condom, or if this finding is simply indicative of a small sample bias. Why is it that the women were comfortable providing condoms and initiating their use but were not comfortable in initiating HPSC? The answer may be that they are *not*, in fact, particularly comfortable carrying condoms but that they are more motivated to use them (due to their commitment to not becoming pregnant) than to initiate sexual health related discussions with their partner. The findings from this study support the view that these young women may not be motivated to have sexual health related discussions in large part because they are not aware of its purpose and potential benefits. Many of them are much more fearful of damaging their relationship than of contracting HIV or another STI.

Very few participants reported that their male partners asked them any questions about sexual health issues prior to intercourse. This is consistent with previous findings by Catania et al. (2001) that higher rates of HPSC were related to being female, and also with both of Jadack, Hyde & Keller (1995) and Lear (1995), who found that men are significantly less comfortable than women in initiating safer sexual activities such as asking their partner about her sexual history. This might be a result of traditional and practical attitudes that emphasize the need for women to protect themselves from an unwanted pregnancy, HIV and other STIs, and also the regular inclusion of internal examinations during their annual physicals. All of these factors seem to make young women much more aware (and seemingly concerned) about their sexual health.

It is important to note that women are faced with an additional challenge when negotiating condom use, namely the need for them to get their *partner* to use a condom. As Catania et al. (2001) state, "In the context of AIDS, women are told that they should protect themselves when having penetrative sex, even though men control the means of protection" (participant 30). In this study, the women's narratives showed very little evidence of men taking any responsibility for their sexual health. It appears that young men need to be educated about their role in ensuring that their sexual encounters are not placing them, and their partner, at risk.

The Influence of Immediate Rather than the Less Immediate Implications

Consistent with numerous previous research findings (Buyess & Ickes, 1999; Fay & Yanoff, 2000; Galligan & Terry, 1993), many of the women reported being anxious about the immediate, possibly negative, implications of HPSC (such as: fear of ruining the relationship, embarrassment and his perception of her changing), rather than the less immediate benefits of having such discussions. The participants in this study reported that their fear was magnified within the context of a new sexual relationship. Potential negative implications (relational and personal) of HPSC prior to intercourse were of greater concern than their fear of contracting an STI. For this sample, HIV was of minimal (if any) concern.

The Influence of a Partner on HPSC

This study made it very clear that we cannot understand HPSC, or more specifically, the negotiation of health protective behaviours such as condom use, without considering how one's partner influences this process. One-way discussions do little to increase knowledge about a partner's sexual health. An active discussion (with both partners involved) is necessary but was often reported by these women to be difficult with their male partners. As reported in previous research findings (Dilorio et al., 2000; Herold & Way, 1988), participants emphasized that partners who are willing and comfortable in discussing sexual health issues were perceived to facilitate such communication by increasing their own comfort and confidence in having such discussions. Very few participants, however, reported having a partner who made them feel this way.

The Role That the Interviews Had on Challenging Some of the Identified Barriers

Many of the women noted how they had never talked or thought about many of the issues that had been raised in the research interview. Several commented on how that discussion had made them more aware of the importance of HPSC and the risks that they have taken by *not* having such discussions with their partners. This self-reflection process raises an interesting question: Are these types of discussions about HPSC part of what is missing from sexual health programs? It would be interesting to determine if such a discussion or informal group forum would, in fact, increase confidence in and awareness of the importance and timing of HPSC within the context of new relationships.

These six key findings identified above may help identify areas where program develop-

ment, curriculum change and widespread changes in skill development relating to talking about sex appear to be needed.

Strategies Used to Initiate HPSC with a Potential Partner

The findings have provided only minimal insight into the strategies that this sample of women used to initiate sexual health related discussions. This is primarily because of the lack of HPSC that typically occurred in the participants' sexual relationships prior to intercourse. Among those who did know that it was important to have these discussions, most reported that they did not know how to bring such topics up with their partner. This finding in itself provides some insight into the lack of accessible strategies available even to participants who knew that there were important sexual health issues which they should discuss.

There were a few participants, however, who did use particular strategies to help initiate HPSC. In general, these participants perceived themselves to be at risk, and also recognized the purpose and benefits of HPSC prior to intercourse. They reported using games, bringing up an issue within the context of their peers' experiences, and joking around about sex in general in order to lead the discussion to more serious, personal issues. More frequently cited were strategies that involved planning and even practising discussions, although it was often the case that this planning was not very helpful and they ended up questioning their partner directly. Edgar et al.'s study (1992) found a similar use of direct strategies to initiate such discussion. Some other investigators have reported that questions about sexual health are typically characterized by ambiguity and indirectness (Metts & Fitzpatrick, 1992; Pliskin, 1997).

It is evident from the participants who did (and did not) report using strategies to initiate HPSC that there is a need for educators to implement, for example, some role-playing exercises that would give students a forum in which to practice both articulating, and also developing effective, realistic strategies that they can use to initiate talk about safer sex.

Common Threads

During the final stage of analysis, the researcher revisited consideration of the common threads between the ten identified categories. Although there were a few participants who reported discussing sexual health issues with their partners prior to having sex, the majority described very little (to no) HPSC occurring prior to intercourse. Each participant told a very different story about the extent, content, timing of these discussions, or lack of them, and the factors that they believed had influenced the communication process. However, underlying all of their stories was their internalization of the norms and attitudes about sexual communication that they had learned through their families, schools, peers and the media. None of the participants explicitly addressed the broad *societal* influences on the communication process. Rather, not surprisingly, these influences were underlying most of the experiences that they shared with the interviewer. Having had so little experience, themselves, with sexual communication, they were highly dependent on what they had and had not learned and observed from others specifically in relation to communication about sex.

Future Directions

It would be particularly interesting to replicate this study with young men. Very little is known about men's experience with HPSC (Lear, 1995). The research could be designed to provide insight into the perceived barriers and facilitators to HPSC that men report experiencing. Are they different from or similar to those identified by young women? Do young men not initiate such discussions because they are anxious about being perceived as being a 'typical guy who just wants

sex'? Do men support young women's belief that they do not take responsibility for sexual health in their relationships? If there is a discrepancy in their accounts, why do young women feel as though the responsibility is left up to them? The findings from such enquiries would subsequently enable researchers to study couples more effectively because they would have at the foundation of their work an understanding of women's *and* men's experiences with HPSC.

To date, research has not specifically addressed individuals' attitudes towards the importance and need to have such discussions with a partner. The findings from this study raise an important question. Is it the case that these discussions do not occur because people do not realize their potential importance and purpose? Future research might carefully investigate attitudes towards HPSC.

Larger scale quantitative studies should be undertaken to explore research questions that are grounded in the overall findings from the current study. For example, is the frequency of HPSC generally as low as was reported in this small sample? Can its use before the first instance of intercourse be shown to be reliably associated with prior skills training in sexual communication and negotiation? Is it the case that engagement in discussion of sexual health in broader contexts is strongly associated with the conduct of HPSC with a sexual partner prior to an occasion of first intercourse? In addition, future research might explore the potential benefits of talking about sexual health and safety, and also how one can open up such a discussion without sacrificing either the relationship or one's sexual health.

Most of the research on HPSC has employed quite small and narrow population samples. Researchers need to venture beyond this primarily university student, heterosexual, Caucasian sample, to other populations that are no less challenged by such discussions, and which are faced with their own sexual health risks.

Limitations of This Study

As is the case with qualitative studies having a small sample size, generalizations to the wider population cannot be made from the findings of this study. Furthermore, the participants cannot be considered representative of the diversity in HPSC experiences due to their willingness to participate in this type of study. Although representing a limitation of the sample, it is worth noting that despite their comfort discussing such personal aspects of their lives with the researcher they still reported a lack of HPSC within *their* own relationships.

Contrary to findings in many other studies, (Catania et al., 2001; Freimuth et al., 1992; Williams et al., 1992), drugs and alcohol use reportedly had minimal influence on the communication process. This appeared to be related to the lack of excessive consumption by the participants prior to intercourse, rather than the lack of any outcome from alcohol consumption. This lack of reported drug/alcohol use might be a reflection of the types of people who volunteered to participate in this study. Most of the participants were obviously not embarrassed about their most recent sexual experience and, more frequently than might be expected, reported being in some sort of established relationship prior to the first instance of intercourse with that partner.

The use of retrospective self-reports can be influenced by many forms of bias including recall bias and social desirability bias. It is worth noting that when follow-up discussions with some of the participants were conducted, many months after the initial interview, there was evidence of a very high level of consistency in their stories over time.

CONCLUSION

The findings from this study have provided a new level of confirmation of the findings that have emerged from previous quantitative studies. In particular, they have provided a relatively detailed insight into the sexual health related discussions that this sample of women had with their partners before their first occasion of intercourse. They have also provided insight into the diversity of barriers and facilitators to that communication which this sample reported.

Especially in view of the substantial educational advantage of the sample used in this study, our society appears to be failing in enabling its young people to know why HPSC is important, and how timely communication may help protect their sexual health.

STUDY QUESTIONS

1. The Tri-Council guidelines encourage researchers to be as inclusive as possible of diverse social groups. Is the reason that the authors interviewed only heterosexual women sufficiently justified?

2. How effective is the Abstract in conveying the purpose and findings of the study? Consider contrasting it with the American Psychological Association (APA) guidelines.

3. Could the authors' use of a lottery to pay research participants be seen as constituting undue influence on potential participants to volunteer for the study?

4. If the authors attempted to gather information on the same subject with a survey, do you think participation rates would increase or decrease?

5. What kind of sampling strategy did the authors use? What, if any, are its strengths and weaknesses? How might the sampling method be enriched?

6. What is the advantage of using an established method, such as Grounded Theory (p. 102), to conduct the analysis? Explain.

7. If the authors had used a quantitative design, what findings might have been lost?

REFERENCES

Buysse, A., & Ickes, W. (1999). Communication patterns in laboratory discussions of safer sex between dating versus nondating partners. *The Journal of Sex Research, 36,* 121–134.

Carter, J., McNair, L., Corbin, W., & Williams, M. (1999). Gender differences related to heterosexual condom use: The influence of negotiation styles. *Journal of Sex & Marital Therapy, 25,* 217–225.

Catania, J., Coates, T., Golden, E., Dolcini, M., Peterson, J., Kegeles, S., Siegel, D., & Fullilove, M. (1994). Correlates of condom use among Blacks, Hispanics, and White heterosexuals in San Francisco: The AMEN longitudinal study. *AIDS Education and Prevention, 6,* 12–26.

Catania, J., Binson, D., Dolcini, M., Moskowitz, J., & van der Straten, A. (2001). Frontiers in the behavioral epidemiology of HIV/STDs. In A. Baum, T. Revenson, J.E. Singer (Eds.), *The Handbook of Health Psychology* (pp. 777–799). Hillsdale, NJ: Lawrence Erlbaum Associates.

Civic, D. (2000). College students' reasons for nonuse of condoms within dating relationships. *Journal of Sex and Marital Therapy, 26,* 95–105.

Cutcliffe, J.R. (2000). Methodological issues in grounded theory. *Journal of Advanced Nursing, 31,* 1476–1484.

Davis, K., & Weller, S. (1999). The effectiveness of condoms in reducing heterosexual transmission of HIV. *Family Planning Perspectives, 31,* 272–279.

deVisser, R., & Smith, A. (2001). Inconsistent users of condoms: A challenge for traditional models of health behaviour. *Psychology, Health & Medicine, 6,* 41–46.

Dilorio, C., Dudley, W., Lehr, S., & Soet, J. (2000). Correlates of safer sex communication among college students. *Journal of Advanced Nursing, 32,* 658–665.

Dryburgh, H. (2000). Teenage Pregnancy. *Health Reports* (Statistics Canada, Catalogue 82-003-XPB); *12,* 9–19.

Edgar, T. (1992). A compliance-based approach to the study of condom use. In T. Edgar, M.A. Fitzpatrick, & V.S. Freimuth (Eds.), *AIDS: A Communication Perspective* (pp. 47–67). Hillsdale, N J: Lawrence Erlbaum.

Edgar, T., Freimuth, V., Hammond, S., McDonald, D., & Fink, E. (1992). Strategic sexual communication: Condom use resistance and response. *Health Communication, 4,* 83–104.

Fay, J., & Yanoff, J.M. (2000). What are teens telling us about sexual health? Results of the Second Annual Youth Conference of the Pennsylvania Coalition to Prevent Teen Pregnancy. *Journal of Sex Education and Therapy, 25,* 169–177.

Freimuth, V., Hammond, S., Edgar, T., McDonald, D., & Fink, E. (1992). Factors explaining intent, discussion and use of condoms in first-time sexual encounters. *Health Education Research, 7,* 203–215.

Galligan, R., & Terry, D. (1993). Romantic ideals, fear of negative implications, and the practice of safe sex. *Journal of Applied Social Psychology, 23,* 1685–1711.

Glaser, B.G., & Strauss, A.L. (1967). *The Discovery of Grounded Theory: Strategies for Qualitative Research.* Chicago, IL: Aldine.

Health Canada. (1994). *Canadian Guidelines for Sexual Health Education.* Ottawa, ON: Health Canada.

Health Canada. (1999a). *Epi Update: Genital Chlamydia in Canada.* Ottawa: Bureau of HIV/AIDS and STD and TB Update Series Division, Laboratory Centre for Disease Control, Health Canada.

Health Canada. (1999b). *Epi Update: Gonorrhea in Canada.* Ottawa: Bureau of HIV/AIDS and STD and TB Update Series Division, Laboratory Centre for Disease Control, Health Canada.

Health Canada. (2001). *Epi Update: HIV and AIDS Among Youth in Canada.* Ottawa: Bureau of HIV/AIDS and STD and TB Update Series Division, Laboratory Centre for Disease Control, Health Canada.

Herold, E., & Way, L. (1988). Sexual self-disclosure among university women. *The Journal of Sex Research, 24,* 1–14.

Hillier, L., Harrison, L., & Warr, D. (1998). "When you carry condoms all the boys think that you want it": Negotiating competing discourses about safer sex. *Journal of Adolescence, 21,* 15–29.

Hocking, J., Turk, D., & Ellinger, A. (1999). The effects of partner insistence of condom usage on perceptions of the partner, the relationship, and the experience. *Journal of Adolescence, 22,* 355–367.

Jadack, R., Hyde, J., & Keller, M. (1995). Gender and knowledge about HIV, risky sexual behavior, and safer sex practices. *Research in Nursing and Health, 18,* 313–324.

Lear, D. (1995). Sexual communication in the age of AIDS: The construction of risk and trust among young adults. *Social Science Medical Journal, 41,* 1311–1323.

Lindberg, L., Sonenstein, F., Ku, L., & Levine, G. (1997). Young men's experience with condom breakage. *Family Planning Perspectives, 29,* 128–131.

McKay, A. (2000). Prevention of sexually transmitted infection in different populations: A review of behaviourally effective and cost-effective interventions. *The Canadian Journal of Human Sexuality, 9,* 95–120.

Metts, S., & Cupach, W. (1989). The role of communication in human sexuality. In K. McKinney & S. Spreacher (Eds.), *Human Sexuality: The Societal and Interpersonal Context* (pp. 139–161). Norwood, NJ: Ablex.

Metts, S., & Fitzpatrick, M. (1992). Thinking about safe sex: The risky business of "know your partner" advice. In T. Edgar, M.A. Fitzpatrick, & V.S. Freimuth (Eds.), *AIDS: A Communication Perspective* (pp. 1–20). Hillsdale, N J: Lawrence Erlbaum.

Mitchell, K., & Wellings, K. (1998). First sexual intercourse: anticipation and communication. Interviews with young people in England. *Journal of Adolescence, 21,* 717–726.

Moore, N.B., & Davidson, J. (2000). Communicating with new sex partners: College women and questions that make a difference. *Journal of Sex and Marital Therapy, 26,* 215–230.

Payn, B., Tanfer, K., Billy, J., & Grady, W. (1997). Men's behavior change following infection with a sexually transmitted disease. *Family Planning Perspectives, 29,* 152–157.

Pliskin, K. (1997). Verbal intercourse and sexual communication: Impediments to STD prevention. *Medical Anthropology Quarterly, 11,* 89–109.

Polit-O'Hara, D., & Kahn, J. (1985). Communication and contraceptive practices in adolescent couples. *Adolescence, 10,* 33–43.

Quina, K., Harlow, L., Morokoff, P., Burkholder, G., & Dieter, P. (2000). Sexual communication in relationships: When words speak louder than actions. *Sex Roles, 42,* 523–549.

Sheeran, P., Abraham, C., & Orbell, S. (1999). Psychosocial correlates of heterosexual condom use: A meta-analysis. *Psychological Bulletin, 125,* 90–132.

Strauss, A., & Corbin, J. (1990). *Basics of Qualitative Research: Grounded Theory Procedures and Techniques.* London, UK: Sage.

Strauss, A., & Corbin, J. (1998). *Basics of Qualitative Research: Grounded Theory Procedures and Techniques* (second edition). London, UK: Sage.

Troth, A., & Peterson, C.C. (2000). Factors predicting safe-sex talk and condom use in early sexual relationships. *Health Communication, 12,* 195–218.

Welch Cline, R., Johnson, S., & Freeman, K. (1992). Talk among sexual partners about AIDS: Interpersonal communication for risk education or risk enhancement? *Health Communication, 17,* 39–56.

Welch Cline, R., Freeman, K., & Johnson, S. (1990). Talk among sexual partners about AIDS: Factors differentiating those who talk from those who do not. *Communication Research, 17,* 792–808.

Williams, S., Kimble, D., Covell, N., Weiss, L., Newton, K., Fisher, J., & Fisher, W. (1992). College students use implicit personality theory instead of safer sex. *Journal of Applied Social Psychology, 22,* 921–933.

Wong, M., Archibald, C., Roy, K., Goh, A., Tan, T., & Goh, C. (1994). Condom use negotiation among sex workers in Singapore: Findings from qualitative research. *Health Education Research, 9,* 57–67.

Chapter 9

An International Survey of Death Education Trends in Faculties of Nursing and Medicine

Barbara Downe-Wamboldt and Deborah Tamlyn

Source: Copyright ©1997 From "An International Survey of Death Education Trends in Faculties of Nursing and Medicine" by Barbara Downe-Wamboldt and Deborah Tamlyn. *Death Studies,* March 1997, 21(2), 177–190. Reproduced by permission of Taylor & Francis, Inc., http://www.taylorandfrancis.com.

ABSTRACT

The purpose of this study was to identify and describe the availability of death education, including teaching and evaluation methods, specific content areas, issues being addressed, and the background and expertise of the faculty members involved in teaching death and dying content. A questionnaire was developed based on the current literature and sent to 80 faculties of nursing and 36 faculties of medicine in Canada and the United Kingdom. The majority of nursing and medical schools that responded to the survey included death education, an integrated approach, through all years of their programs. Despite recent criticisms of Kubler-Ross's model of grieving, the majority of programs reported using her theory most frequently. The findings identify the current status of death education for health professionals in Canada and the United Kingdom, and implications for curriculum changes are discussed.

Death education emerged as a topic for discussion, research, and education in the late 1960s and has continued to be an educational challenge in the 1990s. Health professionals require appropriate educational experiences to acquire the necessary knowledge, attitudes, and skills to meet the physical, psychological, and spiritual needs of the dying and their family members. Although death education for health professions in the United States has been described, there is a paucity of such information for similar programs in Canada and the United Kingdom.

Death education surveys of health-related faculties conducted in the United States over the last decade (Dickinson, Sumner, & Durand, 1987; Dickinson, Sumner, & Frederick, 1992) and in Canada (Caty & Downe-Wamboldt, 1983) have found that the majority of professional schools provide students with some exposure to content related to death and dying within required courses. Full courses on death and dying are generally electives taken by less than 25% of the health professions students in the United States (Dickinson et al., 1992). A multidisciplinary approach is frequently used; however, most schools tend to use primarily professionals from their own academic disciplines to teach death and dying content. Dickinson et al. (1987) found that American nursing schools did not generally use physicians or pharmacists as instructors; but 19% of medical schools and 11% of pharmacy colleges used nurses to teach death education classes. Lectures and discussion formats were the most popular teaching approaches, and seminars were the least popular.

Tandy and Sexton (1985), in a survey of health education departments in the United States, compared institutional and expert opinions regarding topics that were considered to be essential to death education courses. Both groups identified 12 essential topics, including cultural aspects, the dying process, euthanasia, funerals/burials, the grief process, hospice, legislation, gender differences, preparation for death, suicide, terminal illness, and wills. There was no consensus concerning the topics of death history, religion and death, out of body experiences, or ethnic group perceptions.

In the United Kingdom, despite the existence of death education content in many programs, medical and nursing students have reported that their preparation to provide terminal care was inadequate (Doyle, 1987). Hospice staff members have also noted that there was inadequate professional training in palliative care for all health professionals working with the dying (Doyle, 1987).

The present investigation was designed to address the gap in the literature on the nature of formal death education within nursing and medical schools in Canada and the United Kingdom. The purpose of this descriptive, exploratory study was to identify and describe the current availability of death education, including teaching and evaluation methods, specific content areas, and the professional background of faculty members involved in teaching death and dying content in university programs of nursing, medicine, and social work in Canada and the United Kingdom, and to identify priorities for future education planning.

METHOD

A listing of university-based programs for nursing, social work, and medicine was obtained from the respective professional or national academic associations. Questionnaires were mailed to all of the programs listed in the association rosters, including 80 university nursing programs, 65 university social work programs, and 36 university medical programs in Canada and the United Kingdom. The seven-page questionnaire was developed by the authors based on

the relevant literature and was assessed for content validity and clarity by a panel of four local hospice nurses and faculty members with expertise in the content area.

SAMPLE

A total of 50 (63%) questionnaires were received from nursing programs, 17 (26%) from social work programs, and 15 (42%) from medical programs. Because of the low response rate from the social work programs, these data were deleted from further analysis. The response rate from Canadian programs was 93% and 38% for nursing and medical programs, respectively; for the United Kingdom the response rate was 45% for both nursing and medical programs. Responses from nursing programs were received from all regions of Canada; for medicine, responses were received from all regions except Atlantic Canada. United Kingdom responses were received from nursing programs in England, Northern Ireland, Scotland, and Wales, and from medical programs in England and Scotland.

FINDINGS

Curriculum Approach

Death education content was included in all of the responding Canadian nursing programs and 96% of the U.K. nursing programs. All of the Canadian medical programs and 89% of the medical programs in the United Kingdom that responded reported including death and dying content in their curricula. The frequency with which death education was addressed by integrating it throughout the curriculum and/or using elective or required courses or workshops is described in Table 9.1. Nursing programs reported allocating a greater number of hours for both classroom teaching and clinical practice than did medical programs (Table 9.2).

Table 9.1 Curriculum Approaches to Death Education (*n* = 65)

Approach	Nursing (*n* = 50)		Medicine (*n* = 15)	
	n	%	*n*	%
Canada				
Integrated throughout curriculum	25	93	16	100
Elective courses	7	26	2	33
Required courses	2	7	2	33
Required workshop	0	0	2	33
United Kingdom				
Integrated throughout curriculum	22	96	6	67
Elective courses	4	17	1	11
Required courses	7	33	1	11
Required workshop	5	22	1	11

Table 9.2 Average Number of Hours for Death Education

Country	Nursing		Medicine	
	C	CP	C	CP
Canada	24.50	36.25	6.60	5.50
United Kingdom	44.25	100.00	6.75	5.50

C = Classroom instruction; CP = Clinical practice.

Teaching Strategies

The death education teaching strategies reported by the nursing and medical programs in Canada and the United Kingdom are described in Table 9.3. Self-directed activities were used more than twice as often in U.K. nursing programs as in Canadian programs. Lectures, case studies, and small-group discussion were used most frequently in Canadian medical programs, whereas medical programs in the United Kingdom preferred lectures and small-group discussion. The majority of Canadian (66%) and U.K. (57%) nursing programs reported that most or several students had the opportunity to work with dying patients. Opportunities to work with dying patients were also made available for many Canadian (50%) and United Kingdom (55%) medical students.

Program Content

Table 9.4 provides a summary of the content areas most frequently addressed in nursing and medical programs. Nursing programs in Canada and the United Kingdom covered very similar content areas, including grief and bereavement, communication, pain and symptom control, legal/ethical issues, and family needs. However, there was a greater emphasis on the hospice movement and the topic of body image in U.K. programs. Medical programs in both countries addressed similar content, with Canadian programs placing greater emphasis on the topics of loss and grief, ethical issues, and the role of the health professional. Gender issues were reported as a content area only in the United Kingdom.

The specific theorists most frequently cited as being used by Canadian nursing programs

---

Table 9.3   Teaching Strategies for Death Education (*n* = 65)

| | Nursing | | | | Medicine | | | |
| | Canada (*n* = 27) | | United Kingdom (*n* = 23) | | Canada (*n* = 6) | | United Kingdom (*n* = 9) | |
Strategy	*n*	%	*n*	%	*n*	%	*n*	%
Lectures	19	70	17	74	5	83	5	56
Case studies	16	59	16	70	4	66	1	11
Small-group discussions	16	59	16	70	4	66	5	56
Audiovisual aids	16	59	16	70	3	50	1	11
Self-directed activities	12	44	23	100	1	17	0	0
Role playing	8	30	11	48	1	17	0	0
Clinical experience	5	19	7	30	2	33	2	22
Journal writing	1	4	1	4	0	0	0	0

Table 9.4   Content Included in Death Education (*n* = 65)

| | Nursing | | | | Medicine | | | |
| | Canada (*n* = 27) | | United Kingdom (*n* = 23) | | Canada (*n* = 6) | | United Kingdom (*n* = 9) | |
Content	*n*	%	*n*	%	*n*	%	*n*	%
Family needs	23	85	18	78	3	50	4	44
Bereavement	22	82	18	78	4	66	5	56
Loss/grief	22	82	18	78	5	83	4	44
Communication	22	82	18	78	4	66	6	67
Pain/symptom control	21	78	18	78	6	100	6	67
Role of health professional	21	78	17	74	4	66	2	22
Spiritual issues	21	78	17	74	1	17	2	22
Dying with cancer	20	74	15	65	5	83	6	67
Ethical issues	19	70	19	83	6	100	5	56
Hospice movement	17	63	19	83	4	66	6	67
Cultural diversity	17	63	18	78	3	50	4	44
Death anxiety	17	63	17	74	4	66	5	56
Dying with AIDS	16	59	15	65	3	50	2	22
Legal issues	15	56	17	74	5	83	5	56
Body image	14	52	16	70	2	33	1	11
Gender issues	11	41	12	52	0	0	2	22

---

were Kubler-Ross (52%), Aries (19%), Saunders (15%), and Engel (11%). Stress adaptation and coping theories were also identified as being used by several programs (15%). Canadian medical programs most frequently reported using the work of Kubler-Ross (33%). In the United Kingdom, nursing programs most often reported using the theoretical approaches of Kubler-Ross (57%), Parkes (44%), Worden (22%), and Saunders (13%). Only one medical program in the United Kingdom reported using any specific theorists or theory; that response identified the work of Parker, Kubler-Ross, Glaser and Strauss, Foucault, and Elias.

Ethical and Legal Issues

The ethical and legal issues addressed in both nursing and medical programs were strikingly similar in Canada and the United Kingdom. Euthanasia, living wills, assisted suicide, abortion, and reproductive technology were issues that the majority of programs consistently included in their programs. Most respondents stated that these issues were addressed in a required or elective ethics course. Seminars, tutorials, small-group discussions, case studies, role playing, and, less often, lectures were formats that many of the programs used to discuss these ethical and legal issues.

Evaluation Methods

Table 9.5 provides a summary of the methods used for evaluating students' knowledge and attitudes. For Canadian nursing and medical programs, written tests and papers, clinical practice, and case studies were frequently used to evaluate the cognitive domain of learning. In

the United Kingdom, only nursing programs used written tests or papers and case studies, with medical programs reporting relying exclusively on clinical practice to evaluate cognitive learning. Methods to evaluate the affective domain of learning in nursing programs frequently included discussion and observation during clinical practice, and less often attitude and death anxiety measurement. For medical programs, only discussion and clinical practice were reported to be used to evaluate student learning in the affective area.

Professional Background of Faculty

Consistent with earlier findings from Dickinson et al. (1992), many programs used professionals from their own discipline to teach classes. Eighty-nine percent of nursing programs in Canada and 83% of nursing programs in the United Kingdom most frequently used nursing faculty members to teach death and dying content. Similarly, 100% of the respondents from medical programs in Canada and the United Kingdom used medical staff most frequently.

Sixty-five percent of nursing schools in the United Kingdom and 83% of medical schools

---

Table 9.5 Methods for Evaluating Students' Knowledge and Attitudes (*n* = 65)

| | Nursing | | | | Medicine | | | |
| | Canada (*n* = 27) | | United Kingdom (*n* = 23) | | Canada (*n* = 6) | | United Kingdom (*n* = 9) | |
Method	*n*	%	*n*	%	*n*	%	*n*	%
Cognitive domain								
Tests	20	74	6	26	3	50	0	0
Papers	18	67	13	57	2	33	0	0
Clinical practice	17	63	12	52	1	17	3	33
Case studies	14	52	11	48	4	66	0	0
Affective domain								
Discussions	22	82	17	74	3	50	1	11
Clinical practice	17	63	12	52	2	33	3	33
Attitude measurement	7	26	4	17	0	0	0	0
Death anxiety measurement	6	22	2	9	0	0	0	0

in Canada stated that they used an interdisciplinary approach to death education; conversely, only 33% of Canadian nursing programs and U.K. medical programs indicated that an interdisciplinary approach was used. Respondents identified the benefits of an interdisciplinary approach to death education as including enhanced opportunities for interprofessional communication and problem solving, the development of broader perspectives around theoretical and philosophical issues, the promotion of teamwork and collaborative practice, and demonstration of a holistic model of care. Limitations of an interdisciplinary approach included a loss of depth and continuity of content, role confusion, and organizational and financial problems associated with using team members from diverse backgrounds.

Future Curriculum Planning

Priority areas for future curriculum planning for nursing programs were similar, as follows: affective/emotional issues (Canada, 41%; United Kingdom, 43%); provision of focused clinical experiences (Canada, 26%; United Kingdom, 17%); addition or refocusing of theoretical approaches (Canada, 22%; United Kingdom, 26%); inclusion of palliative and hospice care (Canada, 15%; United Kingdom, 17%); issues of cultural diversity (Canada, 11%; United Kingdom, 9%); use of an interdisciplinary approach (Canada, 4%; United Kingdom, 4%); and more formalized approach to death education (Canada, 4%; United Kingdom, 4%). Medical programs identified very few priority areas, as follows: affective/emotional issues (Canada, 0%; United Kingdom, 33%); focused clinical experience (Canada, 17%; United Kingdom, 0%); interdisciplinary and more formalized approach to death education (Canada, 17%; United Kingdom, 0%); and communication skills (Canada, 0%; United Kingdom, 11%).

DISCUSSION AND CONCLUSIONS

Most nursing and medical schools in Canada and the United Kingdom that responded to this survey included death education content in an integrated fashion throughout all years of their programs, and most frequently programs used professionals from their own disciplines to teach death and dying content. These findings are consistent with those reported in a survey of health profession schools in the United States (Dickinson et al., 1992).

Elective death education courses were more common in Canadian medical and nursing programs than in U.K. programs. As was found for American programs (Dickinson et al., 1992), required death education courses were rarely reported.

Consistent with Dickinson et al.'s (1992) findings for American programs, lectures were the most common teaching strategy reported by both medical and nursing programs in both Canada and the United Kingdom. Despite research (Hutchison & Scherman, 1992; Tamlyn & Caty, 1984) that points to the superiority of experientially based learning to didactic approaches, there was less emphasis on role playing, journal writing, and clinical experience. Self-directed activities were more commonly reported by nursing programs, especially in the United Kingdom, where they were used by all of the programs that responded.

Sixteen or more topics were reported as being addressed, many of which were similar to those identified as being important for health education students in an American study by Tandy and Sexton (1985). Despite recent criticisms of the Kubler-Ross stage model of grieving, her theoretical model was identified as being used by the majority of programs. Theory-based instruction was not strongly evident in U.K. medical programs. Some authors have indicated that health profession programs do not incorporate theory as a foundation for the design of death education programs, and this has been identified as a significant problem (Durlak & Riesenberg, 1991).

Evaluation of cognitive learning was generally achieved through tests, papers, discussion of clinical practice, and case studies. Affective changes were assessed through class discussions and observations in the clinical area. Only selected nursing programs attempted to measure changes in attitude toward death and dying or death anxiety.

The findings identified eight priority areas for future curriculum planning that provide direction for curriculum development. Affective issues such as attitudes toward death and dying and death anxiety were seen as the greatest priority for nursing programs. Canadian nursing programs ranked as their second priority the provision of focused clinical experiences. This finding is consistent with the finding that a structured clinical experience with dying individuals and their family members was provided in few programs. The addition or refocusing of theoretical approaches was the third priority identified by Canadian nursing programs and the second priority for U.K. nursing programs. Medical programs gave limited responses to this question, making it difficult to provide any meaningful interpretation of these data.

There are several conclusions that can be drawn from this survey of Canadian and U.K. nursing and medical programs. Many of the approaches to death education in Canada and the United Kingdom are similar to those reported in American surveys. Most programs integrate relevant content within required courses rather than offering separate death and dying courses, and lectures are the most frequently used format.

There needs to be a greater focus on theory-based educational approaches, and further research is needed to determine which approaches are most effective in meeting specific educational objectives. The uncritical adoption of Kubler-Ross's stage model of grieving should be addressed. The majority of programs in both Canada and the United Kingdom cited Kubler-Ross most frequently as the specific theorist used, despite recent criticisms of her model.

An interdisciplinary approach to death education was not identified as current practice or a future priority by most of the programs. As acknowledged by Crase (1989), death and dying transcend disciplines. The present authors recommend further research to determine the effectiveness of an interdisciplinary approach to death education, both in promoting collaborative practice and in enriching the discussion of theoretical and philosophical issues.

In summary, if educators are to make significant improvements in the area of death education, systematic research is needed to determine which curriculum contents and approaches are most effective in preparing health professionals to meet the needs of the dying and their families.

STUDY QUESTIONS

1. Why was this study needed?

2. What was the sampling procedure for this study?

3. Why did the authors delete the responses from social work programs? Explain fully.

REFERENCES

Caty, S., & Downe-Wamboldt, B. (1983). A look at death education in Canada. *Dimensions in Health Services, 60,* 37–39.

Crase, D. (1989). Death education: Its diversity and multidisciplinary focus. *Death Studies, 13,* 25–29.

Dickinson, G., Sumner, E., & Durand, R. (1987). Death education in U.S. professional colleges: Medical, nursing, and pharmacy. *Death Studies, 11,* 57–61.

Dickinson, G., Sumner, E., & Frederick, L. (1992). Death education in selected health professions. *Death Studies, 16*, 281–289.

Doyle, D. (1987). Education and training in palliative care. *Journal of Palliative Care, 2*, 5–7.

Durlak, J., & Riesenberg, L. (1991). The impact of death education. *Death Studies, 15*, 39–58.

Hutchison, T., & Scherman, A. (1992). Didactic and experiential death and dying training: Impact upon death anxiety. *Death Studies, 16*, 317–330.

Tamlyn, D., & Caty, S. (1984). Positive results from a death education seminar. *The Australian Nurses Journal, 13*, 47–49.

Tandy, R., & Sexton, J. (1985). A death education course survey. *Health Education, 16*, 35–36.

Chapter 10

Suicide and Prostitution among Street Youth: A Qualitative Analysis

Sean A. Kidd and Michael J. Kral

Source: From S.A. Kidd and M.J. Kral (2002). *Adolescence,* 37(146): pp. 411–431. Reprinted with kind permission from Libra Publishers, Inc.

In recent years, increasing attention has been paid to the problem of street youth suicide in the research literature. Most studies report a suicide attempt rate for that population between 20% and 40% (Adlaf & Zdanowicz, 1999; Greene & Ringwalt, 1996; Molnar, Shade, Kral, Booth, & Watters, 1998; Rotheram-Borus, 1993; Stiffman, 1989; Yoder, 1999). Hwang (1999), in a study conducted in Toronto (Ontario death records 1995–1997), found that homeless males aged 18–24 had a completed suicide rate of 77/100,000. This rate is 10.3 times higher than the national rate for males of that age group. Of the possible explanations for these high rates of suicidal behavior, childhood physical and sexual abuse have received considerable attention. It has been found that street youth who have attempted suicide are more likely to have been physically and/or sexually abused than street youth who have not attempted suicide (Molnar et al., 1998; Yoder, 1999). Other factors that have been linked with suicidal behavior among street youth are being female, having a history of attempting suicide, being a "throwaway," poor self-esteem, depression, having a friend who attempted suicide, lack of food and shelter, fighting with peers, HIV/AIDS, a family history of substance abuse, and substance abuse (Greene & Ringwalt, 1996; Hagan & McCarthy, 1997; Ringwalt, Greene, & Robertson, 1998; Rotheram-Borus, 1993; Rotheram-Borus, Koopman, & Ehrhardt, 1991; Yoder, 1999).

A major stressor in the lives of street youth is finding a source of income. Research has indicated that 16–46% of street youth become involved in prostitution (Kipke, Unger, O'Connor, Palmer, & LaFrance, 1997; McCarthy & Hagan, 1992; Schissel, 1997; Yates, Mackenzie, Pennbridge, & Swofford, 1991), and the majority of those working as prostitutes are street youth (Farley & Barkan, 1998). When compared to other street youth, individuals who engage in prostitution more frequently report histories of childhood abuse, particularly sexual abuse (Adlaf & Zdanowicz, 1999; Schissel, 1997; Yates et al., 1991). Additionally, individuals who enter into prostitution as children/juveniles, especially those with histories of abuse, are more likely to have been forced into the sex trade (over 50%) (Larsen, 2000). The day-to-day experiences of persons who are prostituting themselves are equally bleak. Sexual and physical violence are common, they are an extremely high risk group for AIDS, and are frequently found to be suffering from post-traumatic stress disorder and depression (Earls & David, 1989; Farley & Barkan, 1998). Finally, street youth involved in prostitution have also been found to be more likely to be abusers of crack cocaine, and are more entrenched (heavily identify) with the street lifestyle (Adlaf & Zdanowicz, 1999).

Suicide among street youth working as prostitutes has received relatively little attention.

Yates et al. (1991) found that these youth more often abuse drugs and are more likely to have made a suicide attempt. Seng (1989) found that children who engaged in prostitution were more "potentially suicidal" than children who had been sexually abused but had not been prostitutes. Adlaf and Zdanowicz (1999) did not find a significant difference in the suicide attempt rate for street youth involved in prostitution. This was likely due to the very small number of such youth they used in their cluster analysis ($n = 4$), given that 3 of those 4 youth reported having made a suicide attempt. Such findings, in combination with high rates of recognized risk factors for suicide among this group, highlight the importance of further investigation.

A potential limitation of the research conducted thus far is that very little has been done to access the meanings street youth involved in prostitution give to their experiences. Investigating these meanings is important for determining the variables that might be involved and how these are situated culturally and contextually (Kazdin, 1998). Studying suicide by using narrowly operationalized variables may miss constructs important to the participants. This is especially likely given the differences in the experiences between street youth working as prostitutes and the mainstream populations from which many measures and much of current theory have been developed.

An influential interpretation of the phenomenon of suicide has been put forth by Shneidman (1996), who views suicide as an action taken when a person's threshold for psychological pain has been reached and becomes unbearable. This psychological pain arises from the individual's understanding of his or her past experiences, present circumstances, and potential future. Within this framework, an experience such as a history of sexual abuse is not a binary entry into a linear decision process of whether or not to end one's life. The emotional state of persons as they remember the abuse they suffered, and indeed the memory itself (Schacter, 1996), is strongly influenced by their personal understanding and perception of that experience and the context in which the act of remembering occurs. Further, this understanding changes as a function of context and cultural influence (Shore, 1996). It is from this theoretical stance that the present study was undertaken. The goal was to gain an understanding of what "suicide" means to street youth who have been involved in prostitution—their understanding of the kinds of experiences and feelings that lead up to suicide, what a suicidal act is, and what happens after suicide. Also sought were the participants' perceptions of their strengths and the kinds of experiences that dissuade them from attempting to end their lives (an area too seldom addressed in suicide research). This inductive approach is contrasted with traditional deductive hypothesis testing in which the researcher's understandings of what comprises suicidal distress and risk are applied. It was hoped that the present study would reveal variables and constructs central to sex-trade-involved street youths' understandings of suicide.

METHOD

Participants

Semi-structured interviews focusing on the topic of suicide were conducted with 10 females and 19 males ages 17–24 (mean age = 21.8 years). The criteria for participation were as follows: (1) All participants had to be 24 years of age or younger. This age was chosen as it reflects the age requirement for the social service where the interviews were conducted. (2) Participants must have left the home of their parents or legal guardian, either having run away or been thrown out, which resulted in a significant period of time in which they had no fixed address (i.e., more than a week). The participants were contacted and interviewed at a street outreach agency located in downtown Toronto. This agency offers counseling and a drop-in area for street youth, with a focus on helping youth involved in prostitution. In the agency, clients were directly approached by both the researcher and the staff, and asked if they wished to take part in the study. This method, in combination with a "pyramid effect" by which news of the study spreads among street youth and their friends, was very effective in recruiting participants. A reimbursement of $10 in food coupons was given to each participant. Only one person refused to participate; participants were interested and cooperative.

Interview

Interviews and analysis were done by the first author. An attempt was made to engender a cooperative research relationship with a reduced power differential in the following ways: First, the goals and methods of the study were framed in terms of advocacy and the need to generate material that could help people working with street youth. Many street youth have had painful personal experiences with suicide and were motivated to offer their stories and understandings with a view to helping others in similar situations. Also, my position was negotiated mutually as a "go-between" with mainstream society. My role was to let people "out there" know the difficulties faced by street youth. Assuming this role was extremely important in facilitating the disclosure of participants who could have offered a bare minimum to receive compensation. In other words, they would likely have shared very little if the *only* purpose of the interview was research. An advocacy approach also helped gain access to street youth who might have never participated otherwise (e.g., youth who are extremely angry with members of mainstream society; youth who had a substantial income and for whom the compensation offered for the interview was inconsequential).

Second, the interview was conducted in such a manner that the participant was respected as a self-determining individual. In other words, privacy was respected and areas the person was reluctant to discuss were not aggressively pursued. The participants were not directly asked questions about sensitive or private topics such as abuse or suicide attempts. Rather, they were invited to speak of their experiences in an open-ended manner with the choice being theirs as to level of disclosure.

Interviews typically lasted between 45 minutes and one hour. Before inquiring about suicide, basic demographic information was obtained followed by general questions about their home and street experiences. At that point a series of open-ended questions were used to allow participants to describe their experiences with and understandings of suicide. The following are examples of interview questions: "If it is alright, we will talk about suicide now. You can tell me about a person you know who has committed suicide, and if you want you can tell me about your own experiences with suicide." "Has anyone you have known ever attempted or completed suicide? Can you tell me what happened?" "Do you think that having problems with boy/girlfriends might be related to suicide? How so?"

Analysis

For this analysis the grounded theory coding procedure described by Glaser (1978) and Rennie, Phillips, and Quartaro (1988) was used. Although such a procedure was used, certain methodological differences preclude this study from being considered an example of grounded theory. The major difference was that I did not employ theoretical sampling (see Glaser, 1978, for a detailed description of grounded theory procedures). Stated differently, I have chosen a well-proven and methodologically sound approach to qualitative analysis (Rennie et al.,

1988) and taken from it what best suits this study, as is often necessary in qualitative research (Denzin & Lincoln, 2000). This was the rigorous method of data analysis that is a part of grounded theory.

As the interviews were being conducted, I kept a notebook in which I wrote ideas, impressions, reactions—basically anything that came to mind related to the experience of talking with the participants. This procedure is called "memoing" or fieldnotes, and is an integral part of qualitative analysis (Rennie et al., 1988). It allows researchers to develop ideas about theory and the problem they are studying. Also, and of utmost importance, it provides a means by which researchers document their position in relation to the problem and the lives of the participants. Memoing continues throughout the analysis process.

After the interviews were transcribed, the analysis began by breaking the interviews down into "meaning units"—a few words, phrases or statements that convey a particular meaning. Since finding meaning is the goal of this study, units of meaning form the data rather than units based upon sentences. For example, one participant's comment that drug addiction was a process "like a toboggan slide off a cliff" was considered a meaning unit. In the coding procedure, similar meaning units are extracted and placed together to form categories. This process is referred to as "open coding" because a new category is created for each meaning unit that does not fit any previous category. For example, "incest" might be considered a category. As the categories are developed, they are constantly audited, merging categories that are redundant and breaking into separate categories meaning units within a single category that are better represented separately. The goal is to keep categories as distinct and mutually exclusive as possible while keeping the number of categories manageable and meaningful (i.e., not having hundreds of categories with only one or two meaning units

in each category). During the process of open coding, the analysts keep careful memos documenting their developing ideas about how the categories relate to one another and how they might be arranged conceptually.

There is a movement from coding based primarily on interview content to theoretical coding, in order to determine how categories relate to one another conceptually. Hierarchies of categories are developed, patterns are found, their relationships explored and elucidated, and their conceptual "fit" sought. In theoretical coding, the categories themselves are arranged in an effort to develop a conceptual understanding, as opposed to content-focused coding in which the meaning units are clustered and arranged.

An internal verification process underlies the analysis. The categories and ideas about their relationships are continually brought back to the data for verification and further development. Some categories and ideas are dropped and/or subsumed into new categories as subsequent investigation of interviews results in a more thorough and better developed categorical framework. Furthermore, both theoretical and open coding are always tightly linked to the data with minimal interpretation by the researcher in an effort to reduce the influence of overt biases based upon the researcher's hypotheses.

As the researcher engages in this process of analysis, a category or small number of categories will usually begin to emerge that appear to be most central—core categories around which all others are arrayed and related. Development of core categories and how they are related to the phenomenon studied leads to the final stage of the analysis in which a theoretical model is developed that best fits the categories and their relationships. This step in the process was limited in the present study and forms the main reason why it would not be considered grounded theory. Development of the core category and its conceptual organization was limited since I did not incorporate this task as a part of the interviews.

A number of measures were taken to support validity both during and after the analysis. For a description of validity tests for qualitative research see Maxwell (1998). First, during the analysis, an effort was made to locate evidence that was discrepant or challenged the conclusions. This type of examination can call attention to areas where bias might have occurred and can also add depth to the analysis. Additionally, during the analysis, the amount of inference/interpretation was kept to a minimum by presenting the data close to the way in which the participants presented it. Second, after the initial analysis, an effort was made to obtain feedback from the original participants to determine if they thought the results of the analysis represented their understandings (10 of the original participants were located for this purpose). Third, the presentation of the data was detailed and complete, allowing the reader to directly view the evidence that supports the statements made. This involved providing many excerpts from the transcripts in the results and is known as "rich data." This strategy can serve to identify validity threats, biases, and flaws in the logic of the category developed (i.e., help establish trustworthiness) (Maxwell, 1998; Stiles, 1993). Fourth, "quasi-statistics" were used. This involved using descriptive statistics to illustrate how often a theme, category, or type of participant was present in the analysis. In addition, Fisher's exact test was used on several points of comparison (e.g., males compared with females). This test is appropriate for the analysis of qualitative data with small sample sizes (Hays, 1991). Finally, two research collaborators reviewed the original transcripts, coding, and category structure of six cases chosen at random. This technique of peer debriefing is recommended by Stiles (1993) as a method of offering the assurance that the interpretation has been found convincing by other investigators familiar with the source material.

The researcher worldview is that of a middle-class, white, heterosexual male. Conducting these interviews profoundly challenged many of my stereotypes. The participants trusted me and showed me some of their world with the understanding that this was a means through which their struggle might be heard. This led me to adopt the stance of an advocate along with the original goals of a researcher.

RESULTS

Percentages Given

Throughout the body of the results, percentages are given which indicate the frequency with which various themes and categories arose in the narratives. While these numbers are helpful in forming a picture of the theme structure, their meaning in the context of this study must be made clear. As the interviews were not structured, these percentages only indicate how many people volunteered that piece of information. Thus, a percentage of 25% does not mean that the other 75% disagreed with this view or felt differently. What it does mean is that they did not mention it in their stories, which, while very important, has a different set of implications than what is traditionally indicated with such statistical terms. The only information that was gathered in a structured format was demographic data.

Participant Characteristics

Interviews were conducted with 10 females (mean age = 22.1, range = 20–24) and 19 males (mean age = 21.7, range = 17–24) who were primarily Caucasian (90%). Sixty-nine percent reported that they had been or were currently involved in prostitution (74% of the males and 60% of the females), though this is likely underreported as several chose not to disclose their sources of income. At least one suicide attempt was reported by 76% of the participants (73.6% of the males and 80% of the females), with most attempts involving either slashing of the wrists/arms or overdosing. Of those who reported attempting suicide, 86% reported making more than one attempt. Finally, 17% (11% of the males and 30% of the females) reported a history of self-mutilation, primarily cutting. Fisher's exact test revealed no significant differences between males and females on the variables described above. Generally, these individuals had "prostituted themselves," which refers to activities ranging from working out of escort agencies, to working a "stroll" or street where tricks (customers) picked them up in cars, to trading sex for drugs. Most had a history of drug abuse and, depending on their level of income, lived in places ranging from the street, to hotel rooms, to their own rented apartments.

One Participant's Story

Before the results of the analysis are presented, which are necessarily fragmented in order to elucidate the categories and themes, one participant's larger narrative is presented. It is hoped this will give the reader a sense of the life narratives told by some of the participants.

Home was my dad molesting me and my mom on coke. And my dad leaving and my mom's boyfriends molesting me and my mom on coke. Same trip. I used to get beat a lot when I was a kid. I had a lot of suicidal tendencies, if that's what you're looking for. Home was rough. Home was poor. My mom was bringing tricks home and stuff and shit and fucking up big time. I don't know . . . it was pretty rough so I went to the streets and then I started prostituting. I was eleven and a half when I started selling myself. That was rough. I got raped a couple of times. I got stitches in my pussy, 37 of them to be exact, with a knife. I hung myself when I was thirteen . . . I hung myself three times in a year. I don't know . . . the rest was just junk [heroin]. I used to do heroin and cocaine a lot, but I quit because I overdosed too many times.

Analysis

Qualitative analysis was performed on 23 of the 29 interviews, as 6 of the interviews proved to be of insufficient depth to lend themselves to such analysis (i.e., consisting primarily of very brief answers). Those 6 interviews were used, however, in the compilation of information such as attempt rate, involvement in prostitution, and other demographics. The results are organized according to the chronological order in which they appeared in the narratives of most of the participants. For example, a category such as child abuse is presented before drug abuse which typically arose later in the narratives. Throughout the subcategories and categories certain recurrent/central themes were evident. These themes appear as central (i.e., pervade most categories) in the individual narratives with the following frequencies: Low Self-Worth (74%), Isolation (61%), Rejection/Betrayal (48%), and Lack of Control (30%). These terms arose repeatedly in the accounts of the participants and appear to represent emotional pain for this group. The themes are presented within the contexts that they appeared and the domain areas discussed in the interviews. In other words, rather than presenting a theme such as isolation as a category, its role is highlighted in the presentation of "topic of discussion" categories such as child abuse.

Childhood Experiences

Troubled/abusive family experience was a category in which the central themes appeared with the greatest frequency and intensity. Although not directly questioned in this area, 52% of participants described physical abuse and 44% described sexual abuse in their childhood. Experiences of rejection and betrayal appeared with great intensity in many of the participants' accounts of their lives before they came to the street (44%). The message of rejection and betrayal was perceived in abuse of all kinds, and often led to intense feelings of isolation (35%). This sense of isolation was especially prominent in the narratives of the gay and bisexual participants who revealed their sexual identity to family and friends and experienced rejection and isolation as something that they deserved for having such an identity.

[response to question regarding link between being gay/lesbian/bisexual and suicide] . . . some of us [gay persons] go through a lot of shit. Like me, my parents . . . my dad holding me up by my neck, three inches off the ground when he found out I was gay, saying why are you a fucking faggot. I didn't answer him and then he put a scar on my forehead, beat me to the ground, and then he packed a duffel bag, threw me out on the front step with blood all over me, shot twenty bucks at me and said, "go get yourself a life."

I walked out on Christmas and no one noticed.

[what led up to suicide attempts] I was just feeling abandoned because I was adopted, and then my parents kicked me out of the house after they adopted me and just issues like that, and I just felt worthless . . . .

Closely related to experiences of physical and sexual abuse were the themes of low self-worth (39%) and a lack of control (26%). Most of these participants felt that the abuse and neglect that they suffered were the result of some failing in themselves. Lack of control arose from a combination of abuse and general family instability (e.g., multiple parent figures, deaths).

Getting beat up almost every day sometimes, and . . . you go through so many years of that, especially as a child, and you don't have any self-worth. Nobody has taught you that you have self-worth. You are just taught that you are nothing and anything you do you deserve to be beaten, and you deserve to die.

. . . I really want to kill myself because I came from a really abusive home where my dad used to hit me, and my mother would do the same . . . and I had times when my mother would come into my room and tell me that I'm shit, and in my head I am shit,

and everything around me is shit, and that is why I am falling apart . . . just hearing my mother tell me that I was a street rat and that I was worthless.

Most participants (68%) described their experiences with suicide attempts as beginning while they lived with a legal guardian, with 24% reporting that the only time they attempted suicide was before they came to the street. Of the seven who attempted suicide only before the street, five were gay and reported that the acceptance they found on the street among the gay community reduced their level of distress. The stories of abuse and neglect in childhood, filled with feelings of rejection, isolation, lack of control, and low self-worth, consistently formed a part of their narratives of their experiences with suicide/suicide attempts and understanding of what kinds of experiences resulted in self-destructive actions.

Street Experiences

Prostitution The themes of low self-worth and lack of control were strongly embedded in descriptions of experiences with prostitution. Percentages are not used here because only about one-third of the participants were comfortable with talking in detail about those experiences, thus percentages would likely have little meaning. Of those who did speak about such experiences, many described feelings of being merely an object for someone to "get off on" or "just some hole." Also, the feelings brought on by prostituting were linked with earlier experiences of sexual abuse: "That's what helped me become a prostitute, being abused."

A lot of the suicides come from the cheap prostitutes, because every time you do it, because I do it, every time you do it, it eats a piece of you up. You are sitting there going, some dirty old man wants me to have sex with him, and I don't want to do this, but I need the money, for this and that. Some kids think it is a big joke down there. It is not a big joke, a lot of people do really sick and nasty things to you. You feel so violated, that it eats you away slowly.

I'm a male prostitute . . . nothing but a piece of meat for someone to get off on, right?

In the participants' descriptions of the kinds of experiences that make up a really bad day, or preceded a suicide attempt, a "bad date" was described several times. Experiences which comprised a bad date were incidents such as not getting paid, a trick that takes too long or is too demanding, being beaten up, raped, or tricks who make offensive, demeaning comments. They described how these experiences brought back "all of the old feelings," feelings of anger and rage, and feelings of violation, with some of the participants saying that they had in the past tried to kill themselves immediately after a bad date. In this context the theme of loss of control was pivotal.

I used to be a male prostitute. I really wanted to commit suicide. It was bad; it was only like my second or third time, and I said no, and he [trick] locked both doors, both exits, he said yes. How can I say this [. . .] he was very large. That was the worst night of my life, after the heroin overdose of my girlfriend. I was afraid at the same time, because he was bigger than me too, so I had to stay. But he gave me seven bucks [sarcasm].

Drugs and money Drug use and addiction appeared frequently in the participants' descriptions of the stresses in their lives and in the context of their experiences with, and understandings of, suicide. Drugs were spoken of as a way of forgetting the stresses of street life, forgetting the past, and in general "putting the pain aside" (44%). Another category that arose involved how some people on the street commit what was referred to as a "slow suicide" (22%). This was a phenomenon in which persons become more and more addicted to the drug, not caring about their lives and health, until they end up overdosing. Drugs were seen as being strongly related to suicide, either as a way of killing themselves

(overdose), killing themselves while on the drug or when coming down, or killing themselves because of the addiction and the lifestyle of the addict. The central themes were not prevalent in this category since drug use was viewed as a reaction to those central themes.

It is the crashing, because after the high is gone, you have nothing. The high is gone, you are feeling depressed again, you can't afford any more drugs, you know, problems are back all over again.

I've known people who've had it hard on the street and have tried to kill themselves or killing themselves and prostituting themselves and doing crack and drinking too much. That's killing themselves slowly. And try to ease the pain; it may not be "oh, I'm going to slit my wrist" like I know some people have tried. That is like a slower burn, almost more painful. You just see them waste away. Completely waste away all the time.

Many participants (49%) in describing a "bad day," and the types of experiences that lead up to suicide, mentioned the stress of having little or no money. All other problems appeared to be worse when the person had no money with which to buy drugs, food, or lodging.

The only time I really think about it [suicide] is when everything seems to be caving in like, you know you are not making a lot of money pulling dates, you are pulling like three hundred dollars, four hundred dollars a week which is not a lot of money doing this.

Interpersonal factors The participants, in their descriptions of friendships on the street, often spoke of the superficiality of the contacts made there, with only two participants mentioning being part of a "street family" or close and mutually supportive group of street youth. The central themes of rejection, betrayal, and isolation appeared in descriptions of friends, so-called, who were there when the person had money or drugs but ultimately did not care whether that person lived or died. In contrast, many spoke of having one or two close friends with whom they had been in contact for several years.

[led to a suicide attempt] Nobody cares about what happens to somebody that doesn't have money. Some people call themselves friends and say they are trying to help, but their version of help is using you to control you in some way. Drug dealers are always like, "oh, I'll help you get off the street." It's their way of making more money. And turning you into an addict at the same time because they will feed you tons of drugs in the beginning. [What did people do when you attempted suicide?] Nobody really gave a shit . . . the few people I told, they didn't care.

Most participants (70%) viewed problems with partners as a significant source of emotional pain and stress. All of the central themes of control, rejection/betrayal, self-worth, and especially that of isolation arose in this context. Many felt that intimate relationships were often more "intense" on the street, comprising the majority of that person's support network. The result of this "intensity" was that when there were arguments, abuse, or breakups, a lot of the "old issues" were brought up and in some cases were cited as reasons for a suicide attempt.

Yeah [suicide related to partner problems] because that person becomes your family, it's not totally just boyfriend/girlfriend sort of thing; you are looking for a little bit more sometimes.

. . . and also at the same time I tried it [suicide] my boyfriend at the time, he beat the shit out of me so I said, it's like "okay, I'm worthless," so I just tried ending it all.

Suicide

Feelings Respondents spoke of or were asked what kinds of feelings they were having when they made their suicide attempt(s). Those who had not made a suicide attempt described what feeling "really bad" was like for them. While most participants described having a mixture of feelings at such times, some categories arose from their descriptions. The feeling that dominated the reports was one of "aloneness," or "isolation" (56%). Other feelings that arose

were of "depression" (37%), "emptiness" or "nothingness" (19%), and "anger" (13%).

All my attempts were done by myself. No one was there. So I am all alone. I am by myself, there is nothing there, no one cares.

[re: suicide attempts] A lot of times for me it was just being there and empty, and it is impossible to explain to someone who has never been there. They can't understand. When you have no money, no food, no home, no clothes, no possessions, that's when you feel empty.

Decision Forty-nine percent of the participants identified a definite point when the above-mentioned feelings and negative, stressful experiences could not be tolerated any longer, and they turned to suicide as a way of ending the pain. Additionally, some of the participants analyzed their motivations at the time of their suicide attempts.

. . . all of a sudden it's just all there and you can't escape it . . . your past is there, your present is there, your hopeless future, it's all just in front of you. So at that point, how do I get rid of all these visions in my head, and want to just kill myself.

Sometimes I just think I deserve it [to die/suffer from attempt], and then sometimes . . . I feel guilty for being alive so I kind of try to solve other people's problems . . and then sometimes I just want to put myself through a lot of shit so I do that because I know I am going to be in a lot of shit if I do that kind of thing. [Feel afterwards?] I feel like shit. Which feels good in a way, so you know I got what I deserve kind of thing.

Reducing the Pain: What Helps

Thoughts One thought that several participants (39%) reported as having helped them through bad times was that life was going to improve and that they will not always suffer as they do currently. This was related to self-worth, for though they might not value themselves now, there may come a time when they will be something "more." Other thoughts involved taking strength from their independence and self-reliance (30%), the valuing of oneself (30%), and the thought that they were not meant to die as a result of a suicide attempt after surviving so many (26%).

But then on the other hand I'm thinking to myself, well maybe I'll make it one day. Maybe I'll be famous for my art. Maybe I'll find a love of my life. Just maybe . . . when there is that maybe, why should I give up?

But the thing is, I tell people that I've tried suicide attempts so many times and it has failed. I've got to stop and think to myself: well, I have been put on this earth for one reason, and if I have tried to kill myself and it hasn't worked the first time, or the second time, or the third, fourth, or fifth time, I've got to be here until someone kills me or my time is up.

Actions Most of the participants spoke of talking and spending time with friends as a way of coping with pain (61%). It appeared that while friendships were often perceived as superficial on the street, they still did form a part of the person's (already limited) support network. This action appeared to work against the theme of isolation. Other actions mentioned include sleeping (13%) and crying (9%).

. . . there is not much you can really do about it (emotional pain) . . . the best thing is to have people listen to you. Have people to talk with.

Outside sources of help Very few participants (9%) reported having positive experiences with government-sponsored agencies or authorities. The only time any beneficial assistance was described, it involved street outreach agencies or shelters. They reported positive experiences as utilizing a nonjudgmental approach, with people who listen, and places where they were assured of confidentiality. Many narratives (48%) described negative experiences with agencies and mental health professionals. The central theme of lack of control arose most pervasively in this context; the majority of the reports involved being "locked up" in hospi-

tals, staffed by cold, uncaring professionals who did little but prescribe drugs.

. . . as opposed to a shrink telling me, "oh, it's just a part of your borderline symptoms." Great. "Part of my borderline symptoms" says if that doesn't cure my problems you are going to give me more drugs. Great, yeah, give me more lithium so I can get totally wrecked now.

DISCUSSION

In the present study a qualitative analysis was performed on the narratives of street youth interviewed at an outreach agency in Toronto. The focus of these semi-structured interviews was on suicide and suicidal behavior. The findings were that, for this group, emotional pain was composed of experiences with and feelings of isolation, rejection/betrayal, lack of control, and most pervasively, low self-worth. The participants viewed the origins of their emotional distress in their abusive and neglectful upbringings. These painful experiences at home led to a life on the street, where extremely negative experiences continued, maintaining and in some instances exacerbating this painful self-image of worthlessness. These powerful negative feelings, combined with few options for reducing the pain either due to external factors or internal perceptions, all within an understanding of self-harming/destructive behaviors as a way of reducing pain, appear to lead to an extremely high rate of suicidality.

The incidence of physical/sexual abuse was difficult to assess with this group, as they were not directly questioned on this topic. This point aside, the number of participants who freely described their abusive pasts was consistent with the incidence rates of abuse reported previously (Molnar et al., 1998; Yates et al., 1991). Additionally, the present study supports the street youth literature that suggests that a history of abuse is related to suicidality (Molnar et al. 1998; Schissel, 1997; Yoder,

1999) and prostitution (Yates et al., 1991). This finding is of note because it is the participants who are making this connection rather than having it inferred from correlations between histories of abuse, suicidality, and prostitution. What appears to be absent in the literature is an attempt to discern the meaning street youth give their abusive experiences in terms of their past and current psychological functioning and its relationship to suicidal behavior. The themes that arose from the narratives of the present study in the context of abuse and suicide were feelings of rejection, isolation, low self-worth, and lack of control. These themes represent the participants' experiences of their abusive pasts and their perceptions of a painful experience that necessitated a suicidal action to reduce the pain. As such, interpretations of past abuse involving these themes may indicate a person at risk for suicide among a similar population.

Participants in the present study differ from those commonly found in other studies of street youth in that they are older, and composed mainly of individuals reporting involvement in prostitution. These differences are noteworthy given the present study's finding of a suicide attempt rate of 76%, roughly twice that typically found among the street youth population (e.g., Molnar et al., 1998). Along with demographic considerations, it may also be possible that the semi-structured nature of the qualitative interview facilitated greater disclosure. Of these potential explanations for the high suicide attempt rate reported, involvement in prostitution would appear to be the most salient, given that it has been linked with suicidality among street youth (Yates et al., 1991) and is extremely destructive to both physical and mental health (Farley & Barkan, 1998). The present study expands upon previous findings, noting that for these participants, the elements of prostitution that they felt led to suicide were low self-worth and a loss of control. Also, and described as extremely traumatic by the participants, was the experience of having a "bad date" which means being assaulted during prostituted sex. Exposure to this type of violence was linked to suicidal behavior.

The finding that drug abuse is related to suicidal behavior both as a coping mechanism and a means of suicide supports previous work (Molnar et al., 1998; Rotheram-Borus, 1993). Drug abuse as "slow suicide" may be similar to high-risk behaviors which have been observed at high levels among street youth (Ringwalt et al., 1998), and recent research points to a suicidal element in drug abuse and frequent overdoses (Neale, 2000). The present study's finding that lack of money is related to suicide is found in previous studies, where the stress of poverty has been linked with increased distress, depression, and suicidality (Hagan & McCarthy, 1997). A unique finding of the present study is that a day without food and shelter was often described as the breaking point for the participants, leading to suicidal behavior.

The potentially negative impact of "friends" on the street, a category that arose in this study, has recently been examined by Whitbeck, Hoyt, and Bao (2000). Whitbeck et al. (2000) spoke of how the strong need to quickly form friendships on the street leads street youth into relationships in which they are often coerced and manipulated by street "predators." Even when they are not actively used/manipulated, their association with peers engaged in destructive coping strategies (e.g., drug abuse) leads newcomers to adopt similar behaviors. The somewhat contradictory finding that friends were also spoken of as important for coping has also been noted previously. In the street youth literature, having friends has been inversely correlated with depression (Smart & Walsh, 1993). The importance of partners in the lives of street youth and the distress and suicidality surrounding problems with these relationships have received little attention in the literature.

The central theme of isolation has been observed previously among street youth (McCarthy & Hagan, 1992), with the theme of rejection more often described as an experience (I was rejected) rather than a feeling (I felt rejected) (Savin-Williams, 1994). Neither of these themes has been linked with suicide in this group before. Nor has the central theme of lack of control been found in any previous study on street youth suicide. The most common central theme, low self-worth, is found in the general street youth literature (Hagan & McCarthy, 1997) and has been found to be a risk factor for suicidality (Yoder, 1999). However, its centrality in the construct of suicide has not previously been highlighted. It is difficult to say if the thematic/variable differences described above are due to the inductive methodology employed or are specific to street youth involved in prostitution.

In conclusion, suicidal thoughts and behaviors among these sex-trade-involved street youth appear to be very strongly tied to low self-worth and feelings of isolation, rejection, and lack of control. These are the elements of psychic pain for this population that are linked to suicidality, and need to be addressed by persons working with street youth, by those involved in the design of primary prevention efforts with youth, and by researchers looking closely at the nature of suicide among street youth.

The findings of this study have highlighted the importance of assessing street youth involved in prostitution for strong feelings of worthlessness and lack of control in their descriptions of how prostitution is impacting their lives, and monitoring the outcomes of occurrences such as assault during prostituted sex. There are a few key areas in which suicide intervention/prevention efforts would likely be most useful. A nonjudgmental stance, very important in any such work, is vital when working with street youth. Suicidal street youth often feel worthless as they think about their identity as a drug addict, prostitute or street rat. In such a context, talking to someone who is not judging them can be very powerful. Helping persons find some ability or talent can also be very important in their development of a sense of worth. There is an enormous and largely untapped potential residing in these youth, and helping them find it is a key part of the healing process. Emphasizing their strength at having survived, and the knowledge they have gained through their survival, helps build a sense of control and agency. This can work against the "lack of control" feeling that many associate with suicide. Helping them develop a support system of people who care for them without wanting money, sex or drugs in return will be a part of any such work. This will likely be most effective if it extends beyond mental health workers, who could be perceived as "just doing their job." Addiction work may also play a major role.

The present study had two primary limitations. First, further work must be done to determine if the present findings are applicable to other subgroups of street youth. Second, while the present study had considerable breadth and generated several variables and associations not previously addressed, a more focused and controlled examination of these variables is called for in future studies. While a weakness, this was also this study's strength, as it highlights the utility of inductive, exploratory research in finding new avenues of investigation and in guarding against the researcher's choice of measures that may limit the findings (especially with cultures/subcultures different from previously researched populations). Also, it demonstrates the importance of looking beyond simplistic, linear, risk-factor models to the subjective experiences and contexts of the participants, and the influence these have on their decision to attempt suicide.

STUDY QUESTIONS

1. Do researchers ever do value-free research—that is, without having some kind of vested interest in the outcome?

2. What is the value of researchers being upfront about their interests?

3. What ethical concerns are raised by the researchers' decision to tell potential research subjects that they are planning to use the results of the study to act as advocates for street youth? Suggest concrete ways of limiting these problems. (Students may find the document *Tri-Council Policy Statement: Ethical Conduct for Research Involving Humans, 1998 (with 2000, 2002 updates)*—available at **www .pre.ethics.gc.ca/english/policystatement/ policystatement.cfm**—useful in answering this question).

4. What are the advantages/disadvantages of using qualitative analysis as opposed to quantitative analysis within the context of this study? Explain fully.

5. Explain how the percentages reported in the results section must be interpreted. For example, if 30% of the participants said that they took comfort in their independence and self-reliance, what did the other 70% say?

6. The authors state that they used an "internal verification process." What did they do?

7. Why did the authors do the internal verification process?

REFERENCES

Adlaf, E. M., & Zdanowicz, Y. M. (1999). A cluster-analytic study of substance problems and mental health among street youths. *American Journal of Drug and Alcohol Abuse, 25,* 639–660.

Bruner, J. (1990). *Acts of meaning.* Cambridge: Harvard University Press.

Denzin, N. K., & Lincoln, Y. S. (2000). Introduction: The discipline and practice of qualitative research. In N. K. Denzin & Y. S. Lincoln (Eds.), *Handbook of qualitative research* (pp. 1–29). Thousand Oaks, CA: Sage.

Earls, C. M., & David, H. (1989). A psychosocial study of male prostitution. *Archives of Sexual Behavior, 18,* 401–419.

Farley, M., & Barkan, H. (1998). Prostitution, violence, and posttraumatic stress disorder. *Women & Health, 27,* 37–49.

Glaser, B. J. (1978). *Advances in the methodology of grounded theory: Theoretical sensitivity.* Mill Valley, CA: Sociology Press.

Greene, J. M., & Ringwalt, C. L. (1996). Youth and familial substance use's association with suicide attempts among runaway and homeless youth. *Substance Use & Misuse, 31,* 1041–1058.

Hagan, J., & McCarthy, B. (1997). *Mean streets: Youth crime and homelessness.* Cambridge: Cambridge University Press.

Hays, W. L. (1991). *Statistics.* Orlando, FL: Harcourt Brace.

Hwang, S. (1999). Mortality among homeless men in Toronto, Ontario. Paper presented at the 22nd Annual Meeting of the Society of General Internal Medicine, San Francisco, CA.

Kazdin, A. E. (1998). *Research design in clinical psychology.* Boston: Allyn & Bacon.

Kipke, M. D., Unger, J. B., O'Connor, S., Palmer, R. F., & LaFrance, S. R. (1997). Street youth, their peer group affiliation and differences according to residential status, subsistence patterns, and use of services. *Adolescence, 32,* 655–669.

Langenhove, L. V. (1995). The theoretical foundations of experimental psychology and its alternatives. In J. A. Smith, R. Harre, & L. V. Langenhove (Eds.), *Rethinking psychology* (pp. 10–23). Thousand Oaks, CA: Sage.

Larsen, N. (2000). Prostitution: Deviant activity or legitimate occupation? In L. G. Beaman (Ed.), *New perspectives on deviance: The construction of deviance in everyday life* (pp. 50–66). Scarborough, ON: Prentice Hall Allyn and Bacon Canada.

Maxwell, J. A. (1998). Designing a qualitative study. In L. Bickman & D. S. Rog (Eds.), *Handbook of applied social research methods* (pp. 69–100). Thousand Oaks, CA: Sage.

McCarthy, B., & Hagan, J. (1992). Surviving the street: The experiences of homeless youth. *Journal of Adolescent Research, 7,* 412–430.

Molnar, B. E., Shade, S. B., Kral, A. H., Booth, R. E., & Watters, J. K. (1998). Suicidal behavior and sexual/physical abuse among street youth. *Child Abuse & Neglect, 22,* 213–222.

Much, N. (1995). Cultural psychology. In J. A. Smith, R. Harre, & L. V. Langenhove (Eds.), *Rethinking psychology* (pp. 97–121). Thousand Oaks, CA: Sage.

Neale, J. (2000). Suicidal intent in non-fatal illicit drug use. *Addiction, 95,* 85–93.

Reason, P., & Heron, J. (1995). Co-operative inquiry. In J. A. Smith, R. Harre, & L. V. Langenhove (Eds.), *Rethinking methods in psychology* (pp. 122–142). Thousand Oaks, CA: Sage.

Rennie, D. L., Phillips, J. R., & Quartaro, G. K. (1988). Grounded theory: A promising approach to conceptualization in psychology? *Canadian Psychology, 29,* 139–150.

Ringwalt, C. L., Greene, J. M., & Robertson, M. J. (1998). Familial backgrounds and risk behaviors of youth with throwaway experiences. *Journal of Adolescence, 21,* 241–252.

Rotheram-Borus, M. J. (1993). Suicidal behavior and risk factors among runaway youths. *American Journal of Psychiatry, 150,* 103–107.

Rotheram-Borus, M. J., Koopman, C., & Ehrhardt, A. A. (1991). Homeless youths and HIV infection. *American Psychologist, 46,* 1188–1198.

Savin-Williams, R. C. (1994). Verbal and physical abuse as stressors in the lives of lesbian, gay male, and bisexual youths: Associations with school problems, running away, substance abuse, prostitution, and suicide. *Journal of Consulting and Clinical Psychology, 62(2),* 261–269.

Schacter, D. L. (1996). *Searching for memory.* New York: Basic.

Schissel, B. (1997). *Blaming children.* Halifax, NS: Fernwood.

Seng, M. J. (1989). Child sexual abuse and adolescent prostitution: A comparative analysis. *Adolescence, 24,* 665–675.

Shneidman, E. S. (1996). *The suicidal mind.* New York: Oxford University Press.

Shore, B. (1996). *Culture in mind: Cognition, culture, and the problem of meaning.* New York: Oxford University Press.

Smart, R. G., & Walsh, G. W. (1993). Predictors of depression in street youth. *Adolescence, 28,* 41–53.

Stiffman, A. R. (1989). Suicide attempts in runaway youths. *Suicide and Life Threatening Behavior, 19,* 147–159.

Stiles, W. B. (1993). Quality control in qualitative research. *Clinical Psychology Review, 13,* 593–618.

Whitbeck, L. B., Hoyt, D. R., & Bao, W. (2000). Depressive symptoms and co-occurring depressive symptoms, substance abuse, and conduct problems among runaway and homeless adolescents. *Child Development, 71,* 721–732.

Yates, G. L., Mackenzie, R. G., Pennbridge, J., & Swofford, A. (1991). A risk profile comparison of homeless youth involved in prostitution and homeless youth not involved. *Journal of Adolescent Health, 12,* 545–548.

Yoder, K. A. (1999). Comparing suicide attempters, suicide ideators, and non-suicidal homeless and runaway adolescents. *Suicide and Life Threatening Behavior, 29,* 25–36.

Chapter 11

Gay and Lesbian Physicians in Training: A Qualitative Study

Cathy Risdon, Deborah Cook, and Dennis Willms

Source: Reprinted from *CMAJ* 08-Feb-00; 162 (3), Page(s) 331–334 by permission of the publisher, ©2000 Canadian Medical Association.

ABSTRACT

Background: Gay and lesbian physicians in training face considerable challenges as they become professionalized. Qualitative research is necessary to understand the social and cultural factors that influence their medical training. In this study we explored the significance of gay or lesbian identity on the experiences of medical training using naturalistic methods of inquiry.

Methods: Semi-structured interviews, focus groups and an email listserv were used to explore professional and personal issues of importance to 29 gay and lesbian medical students and residents in 4 Canadian cities. Data, time, method and investigator triangulation were used to identify and corroborate emerging themes. The domains explored included career choice, "coming out," becoming a doctor, the environment and career implications.

Results: Gay or lesbian medical students and residents experienced significant challenges. For all participants, sexual orientation had an effect on their decisions to enter and remain in medicine. Once in training, the safety of a variety of learning environments was of paramount importance, and it affected subsequent decisions about identity disclosure, residency and career path. Respondents' assessment of professional and personal risk was influenced by the presence of identifiable supports, curricula inclusive of gay and lesbian sexuality, and health issues and effective policies censuring discrimination based on sexual orientation. The need for training programs to be proactive in acknowledging and supporting diversity was identified.

Interpretation: Considerable energy and emotion are spent by gay and lesbian medical students and residents navigating training programs, which may be, at best, indifferent and, at worst, hostile.

In 2 national surveys, 40% of general internists[1] and 50% of internal medicine residents[2] reported witnessing homophobic remarks in the workplace directed toward lesbians and gay men. In another study, one-third of psychiatric and family practice residents and psychiatry faculty were found to be homophobic,[3] and an American Association of Physicians for Human Rights survey found that 17% of gay and lesbian physicians reported being refused employment, medical privileges, referrals or educational opportunities because of their sexual orientation.[4]

Less is known about the experiences of lesbians and gay men in medical training. How do people becoming professionalized as doctors[5] deal with the conflict that may arise between a traditionally conservative profession and a minority sexual orientation? What insights can we obtain from physicians in training as they come to terms with the interface between their professional and personal identities? How can their experiences be used to humanize our educational and training cultures?

The objective of this study was to gain an understanding of the experiences of gay and lesbian physicians in training in Canada. Naturalistic methods of inquiry that focused on interpreting the discussions about social and cultural factors that influence the medical training experience[6] were used throughout the study because we were not testing hypotheses experimentally.

METHODS

Critical appraisal of the literature about attitudes toward gay and lesbian persons in the health care setting helped us to determine which experiences would best be understood through qualitative research. Pilot work with 11 participants (6 women and 5 men) involved 3 semi-structured interviews and 2 focus groups. An interview guide was used to sensitively elicit personal and professional issues of importance to gay and lesbian physicians in training, and transcripts of initial meetings were used to formulate 5 domains for further exploration (Table 11.1).

We recruited additional participants through personal contacts and snowball sampling, augmented by an international moderated listserv of gay, lesbian and bisexual physicians. A total of 7 interviews and 5 focus groups involving 29 people (including those in the pilot study) were conducted in Vancouver, Calgary, Toronto and Hamilton. Data were also collected via the Internet by posting messages on the themes relevant to our study to the gay, lesbian and bisexual listserv for 3 months.

At the beginning of each interview and focus group, confidentiality measures, including data security and anonymity, were discussed and tape recorded. We addressed the 5 domains using prompts to initiate dialogue, and discussion about issues relevant to each individual was encouraged. Interviews were continued until no new themes emerged. Audiotapes were transcribed by an individual not involved with training programs. Documents were analysed inductively using a framework that resulted in the identification of emergent themes and abstraction of cultural configurations and meanings.[7] Our findings were member checked by a sample of participants and gay and lesbian physicians.

Bias was minimized through data, method and investigator triangulation; we used multiple data sources (medical students, interns and residents), different qualitative methods (interviews, focus groups and Internet conferencing) and 3 investigators with different perspectives (a family physician with expertise in lesbian and gay health, an internist-epidemiologist with experience in physician-training environ-

Table 11.1 Domains of Inquiry and Questions Asked of Gay and Lesbian Physicians in Training

Domain	Questions Asked*
Career choice	Is sexual orientation a factor when gay and lesbian individuals choose a medical career?
Coming out	What factors determine whether gay and lesbian physicians "come out" during medical school or residency training?
Becoming a doctor	What are the implications of gay or lesbian identity for physician professionalization?
The environment	How do lesbian and gay physicians in training experience their learning and working environments?
Career implications	How does gay or lesbian identity impact on career planning?

* These questions were used to prompt the exploration of experiences (within each domain) of gay and lesbian medical students and residents during their training.

ments, and a medical anthropologist with expertise in ethnographic studies on risk and vulnerability).

This study was approved by St. Joseph's Hospital Ethics Committee.

RESULTS

Of the 16 women and 13 men in the study, ranging between 20 and 42 years of age, 20 (69.0%) were medical students. Postgraduate specialties of the respondents included family medicine, community medicine, psychiatry and internal medicine. The following interpretations and quotations reflect the experiences of the gay and lesbian residents and medical students surveyed in this study.

Career Choice

For those who were aware of their gay or lesbian identity prior to medical school, many found it an important factor in their career choice. The majority of respondents believed that their choice to become a doctor was, in part, to "make up" for their sexual orientation. It took several of them a long time to reconcile their career aspirations and sexual orientation before they could imagine becoming a physician.

I was always worried about disappointing my parents because I was gay, so I really wanted to please them in terms of my educational achievement and career goals. I think that was part of the reason I picked "doctor."

However, one resident reported a transformational experience, turning sexual orientation from a personal liability into an asset:

I could be a good role model as a physician, and gay people need gay physicians.

"Coming Out"

Upon arrival at medical school, lesbian and gay trainees navigated a series of perceived threats based on their sexual orientation. Medical students clearly articulated competing tensions between being honest and true to their selves and risking negative reactions from peers or threats to their future career.

I am really tempted to come out but at the same time am still feeling like I have too much to lose if this doesn't go well.

Becoming a Doctor

The art of medicine is mediated predominantly through human relationships, and learning how to think and act like a physician is a major part of medical training. Within the assumptions and prejudices of human interactions, gay and lesbian trainees found it difficult to integrate "gay" and "physician."

I felt there was really a lot of covert homophobia. . . . I really felt as though I didn't have any place as a gay person in medical school.

The most significant and successful strategy for many struggling with the task of integration was to use professional and peer role models.

I think I was close to suicide, but I was saved by Dr. X who came to my class one day in clerkship and said, "I am a gay doctor myself." I had never met a gay person in my entire life.

The costs of reconciling conflicting identities are considerable.

We extend a lot of energy coping with homophobia that the institution throws at us—a ton of energy that we can turn instead toward making ourselves better doctors.

The Environment

As gay and lesbian students worked toward their medical and specialty degrees, attitudes of colleagues and attendings dominated their training experience. Hateful jokes and remarks targeting gay and lesbian patients were common and usually went unchallenged. One resident was caught in the double jeopardy of feeling uncertain of herself and having her internal struggles mirrored negatively in her professional environment.

I was seeing these patients who were gay and who were really not functioning well with life and choosing a drug overdose as the only option. Then I was having to look after them medically and watch the way they were treated on the ward and listen to comments that were made. All these struggles were inside—a sort of a horrendous turmoil.

A major factor in assessing the safety of the environment related to the assumptions underlying the language used. For example, one student clearly recounted a preceptor's inclusive self-introduction in which she did not specify the sex of her significant other. Inclusivity was assessed in other ways, including observations of heterosexist assumptions embedded within the curriculum.

Whenever a health care problem has a gay person it has to do with AIDS or adolescent sexuality. There aren't any heart attack victims or diabetics who happen to be gay.

The usual anxieties about in-training performance were heightened in those who felt that their sexual orientation increased their risk for a negative evaluation.

Everything here is peer evaluated, and I think that's what scares me. And that is unlike any other program I've ever been in, where your not liking my sexual orientation can't hurt me academically. Here it can, and that scares me.

Career Implications

As with the decision to enter medical school, gay or lesbian identity had an ongoing influence on career decisions.

I made the decision to do HIV primary care. . . . I figured it would be easier to be a gay physician in that area than it would be in many others.

The decision about whether to be "out" on residency applications was a common struggle. Medical students were frightened that their sexual orientation would be disadvantageous.

I don't do anything to let people know. A large part of that is spawned from the fear that I won't get a residency spot in a specialty that I want to be in if people know I'm gay.

A common source of anxiety was the prospect of having to practise in a nonurban centre.

I couldn't imagine setting up shop in a small town and being open about my orientation and having that accepted.

Many respondents reflected on how their gay or lesbian identity informed their practice, including their style of communication and their capacity for empathy.

Being gay has profoundly influenced the kind of physician I am. It has forced me to learn the skill of putting myself in [an] outsider's shoes—whatever [whoever] that outsider is. It has forced me to see the linkages between all the forms of discrimination.

Throughout the interviews and focus groups, participants reflected on the types of changes required to ensure a better experience for gay and lesbian medical students and residents in the future (Table 11.2).

INTERPRETATION

Gay and lesbian medical students and residents reported expending considerable energy constantly assessing their environments, trying to find a balance between self-protection and self-disclosure; this energy represents a net loss to training programs and the profession. We found that those who were coping with their first awareness of themselves as gay or lesbian during their medical training were especially vulnerable. In general, the more comfortable

---

Table 11.2 Recommendations for Medical Schools and Residency Training Programs*

- Clinical and simulated patient problems that include gay or lesbian identity as a normal part of humanity's range
- Enhanced medical school and residency curricula in sexuality
- Institution-sponsored support groups that recognize and allow for the stresses of being gay or lesbian during medical training
- Explicit faculty role models and mentors for gay and lesbian physicians in training
- Written, broadly distributed policies condemning discrimination against gay and lesbian persons with effective reporting and enforcement mechanisms
- Practical institutional measures to address homophobia and heterosexism

* These recommendations were generated by gay and lesbian medical students and residents during interview and focus group discussions of their training experiences.

---

participants were with their sexual orientation, the less stress they experienced.

The decision about whether to be "out" on residency applications is a common struggle that has been documented previously.[8,9] Our findings are consistent with a qualitative study conducted in the United Kingdom[10] that reported most gay practitioners had not openly declared their homosexuality because they thought their career prospects would be jeopardized; reports of gay physicians being turned down for partnerships affirm this fear.[10]

Institutions that are proactive in creating and promoting respectful learning environments are likely to enhance the experiences of students with well-integrated professional and sexual identities.[11] However, a 1991 survey of medical schools in the United States reported that training programs devoted little time to the topic of homosexuality, and it was most commonly discussed in lectures on human sexuality.[12] In our study, trainees who were

"out" and comfortable with their orientation described a duty to better educate their peers and lobby for improved curricula and policies.

Participants also believed that their experiences as an outsider could enrich their capacities to be effective clinicians. Potential benefits cited included an enhanced ability to connect to others from a variety of minority groups, recognition of patients experiencing inner conflict, the use of inclusive language and a heightened understanding of the impact of biases in patient care.

To the best of our knowledge, this is the first qualitative study that explored the experiences of lesbian and gay physicians in training. Respondents were from several Canadian programs and at various stages in their training. We explored the context for coming out and the chronology of professionalization as a physician, focusing on domains such as training environments and career choices. In addition, participants generated concrete recommendations to improve medical training programs. Although there is a body of literature on the "coming-out" process[13] and on the process of becoming a doctor,[5,14] we found no research on the impact of negotiating the 2 concurrently.

Conscious reflection and investigation of "the status quo" as experienced by gay and lesbian physicians in training is one step toward improving the training system, and this may benefit those learning, those teaching and, ultimately, those receiving care. Our study has several limitations, however. We could not capture the experiences of people who were unable to talk with us, and we had no strategy for identifying gay and lesbian people who discounted a career in medicine or had dropped out of medical school. Future investigations could target these additional experiences. The design of this study was cross-sectional; additional longitudinal studies might examine how the careers of gay and lesbian physicians evolve over time.

STUDY QUESTIONS

1. How did the authors argue that there was a need for their study (i.e., what gaps in the literature did it address)?

2. What do the authors do to argue for the objectivity of their analysis?

3. Why would the ethical procedures around confidentiality be so important in this study?

4. The authors stated that "gay and lesbian medical students and residents reported expending considerable energy constantly assessing their environment." Did the authors directly measure energy expenditure? On what basis are they making this inference?

5. How was the literature review used to identify themes for the interviews? What are the potential strengths and weaknesses of this procedure?

6. The authors don't identify a clear theoretical model for their study. What practical and methodological implications does this pose?

REFERENCES

1. Cook DJ, Griffith LE, Cohen M, Guyatt GH, O'Brien B. Discrimination and abuse experienced by general internists in Canada. *J Gen Intern Med* 1995;10(10): 565–72.

2. vanIneveld CH, Cook DJ, Kane SL, King D. Discrimination and abuse in internal medicine residency. The Internal Medicine Program Directors of Canada. *J Gen Intern Med* 1996;11:401–5.

3. Chaimowitz GA. Homophobia among psychiatric residents, family practice residents and psychiatric faculty. *Can J Psychiatry* 1991;36:206–9.

4. Schatz B, O'Hanlan KA. *Anti-gay discrimination in medicine: results of a national survey of lesbian, gay and bisexual physicians.* San Francisco: Gay and Lesbian Medical Association; 1994. Available: www.glma.org (accessed 1999 Dec 29).

5. Haas J, Shaffir W. Taking on the role of doctor: a dramaturgic analysis of professionalization. *Symbolic Interact* 1982;5(20):187–203.

6. Lincoln YS, Guba EG. *Naturalistic inquiry.* London: Sage Publications; 1985.

7. Willms D, Best A, Taylor D. A systematic approach to qualitative methods in primary prevention research. *Med Anthropol Q* 1990;4(4):391–409.

8. Tinmouth J. The experience of gay and lesbian students in medical school. *JAMA* 1994;271(9):714–5.

9. Vaias L. Normal white female. *JAMA* 1994;271(9): 716–7.

10. Rose L. Homophobia among doctors. *BMJ* 1994;308:586–7.

11. Townsend MH, Wallick MM, Cambre KM. Follow-up survey of support services for lesbian, gay and bisexual medical students. *Acad Med* 1996;71(9): 1012–4.

12. Wallick MM, Cambre KM, Townsend MH. How the topic of homosexuality is taught at U.S. medical schools. *Acad Med* 1992;67:601–3.

13. Martin HP. The coming out process for homosexuals. *Hosp Community Psychiatry* 1991;42(2):158–62.

14. Konner M. *Becoming a doctor.* New York: Penguin; 1988.

PART 3

Quantitative

Chapter 12

Public Opinion on the Health Benefits of Moderate Drinking: Results from a Canadian National Population Health Survey

Alan C. Ogborne and Reginald G. Smart

Source: From A.C. Ogborne and R.G. Smart (2001). *Addiction*, 96: pp. 641–649. Reprinted with kind permission of Blackwell Publishing Ltd.

INTRODUCTION

Interest in the possible health benefits of moderate alcohol consumption has greatly increased in the past decade as scientific and media reports have suggested that light to moderate drinking may reduce the risk of coronary heart disease (Klatsky, Friedman & Siegelaub, 1981; Rimm *et al.*, 1991; Maclure, 1993; Serdula, 1995), ischaemic stroke (Van Gign *et al.*, 1993; Hansagi *et al.*, 1995) and other diseases (Shaper, 1990; Doll *et al.*, 1994). The alcohol industry has, of course, welcomed and promoted this view of moderate drinking. In the United States, wine growers have persuaded the Federal government to allow the use of labels on bottle labels that describe the health benefits of moderate consumption. Some health agencies have also endorsed moderate drinking as having health benefits. For example, the American Council on Science and Health (1999) now 'encourages individuals to take advantage of the potential health benefits of moderate drinking without endangering either themselves or others'. In the United Kingdom, the Department of Health and Social Security (1995) recommended that abstainers consider drinking small amounts to counter their greater risk of cardiovascular problems. In Canada, the Centre for Addiction and Mental Health, the Canadian Centre on Substance Abuse and the College of Family Physicians endorsed a booklet that was distributed in liquor stores and that clearly associated moderate drinking and healthy living. However, this booklet also advised against the use of alcohol for those with health problems, when taking medication, during pregnancy and when operating machinery.

Only one survey has considered the extent to which the general public have come to view moderate drinking as having health benefits (Hall, 1996). This was carried out in Australia and it showed that 39% of the population believed in the cardiovascular benefits of alcohol compared to 0% 5 years earlier. Also, 54% of those surveyed believed that alcohol promoted relaxation. Belief in the benefits of alcohol was greatest among males, younger people, the better-educated and more frequent drinkers. This high level of belief in the health benefits of moderate drinking has significant implications for health education and for attempts to reduce alcohol abuse by reducing per capita alcohol consumption. This paper uses data from a Canadian National Survey to explore beliefs about the health benefits of drinking alcohol in the general population.

METHODS

Data for this paper come from the second National Population Health Survey (NPHS) conducted in 1996/97 by Statistics Canada. This is a household telephone survey that collects cross-sectional and longitudinal information about health status and health determinants. The results considered here are those obtained from a sample of the general population of household residents. This excluded people living on Indian reserves, on Canadian Forces bases and in some remote areas of Ontario and Quebec. The overall response rate for the survey was 85%. Further details are provided in the survey users guide (Statistics Canada, 1999). The present report focuses on respondents aged 12 years or over living in any province except Alberta. Those from Alberta were excluded because they were not asked questions about the health benefits of alcohol.

In addition to questions about respondents' socio-demographic characteristics, the survey instrument included 22 questions about chronic health problems, three questions about drinking behaviours (frequency of drinking in last year, frequency of drinking five or more drinks a day in last year, number of drinks in the seven days prior to interview) and seven questions from the short form of the WHO Composite International Diagnostic Interview (http://www.who.int/msa/cidi) designed to produce a diagnoses of alcohol dependence in accordance with the DSM-III-R criteria (American Psychiatric Association, 1987). These questions concerned role interference as a result of alcohol use, alcohol use in hazardous situations, emotional or psychological problems as a result of alcohol use, strong desire or urge to drink, a great amount of time drinking or recovering, drinking more or for a longer period than intended, and drinking more to get the same effects. The computer file obtained from Statistics Canada included a variable derived from responses to these questions that represented the probability that a respondent qualified for a DSM-III-R

diagnosis of alcohol dependence. This variable was used in the present analysis. The algorithm used to compute this variable was derived using information from the US National Comorbidity Study (Kessler *et al.*, 1997; http://www.who.int/msa/cidi/cidisf.htm).

The survey instrument also included two questions concerning moderate drinking: (1) how would you define moderate drinking? (2) Please tell me whether or not you agree or disagree with the following—moderate drinking can be good for your health? The following response options were read by interviewers after they asked the first question: (1) no drinks; (2) less than one drink per week; (3) one to three drinks per week; (4) four to six drinks per week; (5) one or two drinks per day; and (6) three or more drinks per day. The 'no drinks' response option resulted in some ambiguities in the data. For the present purposes, those who chose this option and who also said that moderate drinking has health benefits (1.5% of all respondents) were assumed to mean that *abstinence* has health benefits. However, those who chose this 'no drinks' definition of moderate drinking and who also said that moderate drinking has no health benefits (2.6%) were assumed to mean that *alcohol use* has no health benefits. The results reported below were not substantially changed in analyses based on different assumptions.

All analyses were performed using SPSS for Windows. In accordance with recommendations from Statistics Canada, responses were weighted such that the average weight was one. This was accomplished by using a weight that was equal to the original weight provided in the user file divided by the average of this weight. This weighting procedure partially adjusts for estimates of variance associated with the complexities of the survey design. The original sample size was 59 199 and the weighted sample size was 72 375. Because SPSS does not adjust for the survey's clustering and stratification features and thus underestimates population variances, a very conservative level of statistical significance was used ($p < 0.0001$) in the interpretation of results.

RESULTS

Ten per cent of cases in the weighted sample had no responses to the questions about moderate drinking and health and these were excluded from all subsequent analyses. The majority

Table 12.1 Beliefs about the Health Benefits of Moderate Drinking According to Respondents' Demographic Characteristics, Drinking Behaviour and Health Status

	Believes Moderate Drinking Has Health Benefits	Does Not Believe Moderate Drinking Has Health Benefits	Says Not Sure If Moderate Drinking Has Health Benefits
Total sample	57.6	30.4	11.9
Sex			
Male	62.5	26.7	10.8
Female	53.0	34.0	13.0
Age (years)			
12–24	44.4	45.1	10.8
25–44	57.3	30.3	12.4
45–64	66.6	22.1	11.3
65 or over	62.2	24.3	13.5
Province			
NFLD	49.5	41.6	9.0
PEI	45.8	38.2	16.0
NS	47.4	36.1	16.5
NB	44.7	46.6	8.8
QUE	63.8	25.3	10.9
ONT	58.4	29.0	12.7
MB	53.8	35.3	11.0
SASK	47.6	39.6	12.8
BC	54.4	33.8	11.8
Frequency of drinking			
Abstainer	35.0	52.0	13.0
1/month or less	53.5	33.9	12.6
2–12 times/month	69.0	19.1	11.9
4 + times/week	85.4	8.5	6.0
Mean number of drinks last 7 days[1]	3.5	1.7	1.7
Frequency has 5 + drinks/day			
Never	53.5	33.7	12.7
< than weekly	64.5	24.7	10.8
< once/week or more often	76.0	17.5	6.5
Probability of alcohol dependence[2]			
0.0	56.6	31.2	12.2
0.05	71.5	19.7	8.8
0.40	73.2	20.1	6.7
0.85	66.0	27.7	6.3
1.00	71.3	22.0	6.7
Chronic health condition			
No	57.0	31.4	11.6
Ischaemic heart disease	67.8	20.2	12.1
Other	57.9	29.9	12.2

[1] Sum of drinks reported for each of last 7 days.
[2] Based on items from the Composite International Diagnostic Interview (CIDI).

(57.7%) of others accepted one of the offered definitions of moderate drinking and agreed that this can have health benefits, while 29.1% disagreed that moderate drinking (by any definition) can have health benefits. Others (13.2%) said that they did not know if moderate drinking could have health benefits.

Table 12.1 shows the relationships between opinions about the health benefits of moderate drinking as defined by respondents, gender, age, province of residence, drinking behaviour, alcohol dependence and self-reported ischaemic heart disease or other chronic condition. For all variables in this table the difference between those holding different views on the health benefits of moderate drinking were statistically significant ($p < 0.0001$ based on chi-square tests). However, this is not unexpected given the large sample size.

The greatest differences among subgroups in Table 12.1 were with respect to age, drinking behaviours and the probability of alcohol dependence. Over 60% of those over 45 believed that moderate drinking has health benefits compared with 44.4% of those aged 12–24. Of those who reported drinking four or more times a week, 85.4% indicated that they believed moderate drinking has health benefits compared with only 35% of abstainers. Those who reported drinking five or more drinks at least once a week were more likely to indicate that they believed in the health benefits of moderate drinking than those who said that they never drank at this level (76% vs. 53.5%). Those whose responses to questions about drinking problems indicated a high probability of alcohol dependence were more likely to believe in the health benefits of moderate drinking than those with who reported no symptoms of alcohol dependence (71.3% vs. 56.6%).

A logistic regression analysis was performed to explore the unique effects of variables in Table 12.1 on beliefs about drinking and health. The results are summarized in Table 12.2. The largest effects (odds > 2) were for age

and frequency of drinking. The effects for number of drinks, gender, ischaemic heart disease and living in Quebec or Ontario (reference province was Newfoundland) were also highly significant. A few other differences were also statistically significant at $p < 0.05$ or $p < 0.01$. However, these have not been highlighted

Table 12.2 Results of a Logistic Regression Predicting Belief That Moderate Drinking Has Health Benefits (Yes vs. No or Uncertain)

Independent Variables	Odds Ratios	Confidence Limits
Gender		
Male	1.0	—
Female	0.83***	0.78–0.90
Age (years)		
12–24	1.00	—
25–44	1.38***	1.22–1.55
45–64	2.23***	1.96–2.52
65 +	2.33***	2.01–2.71
Province		
NFLD	1.00	—
PEI	0.86	0.67–1.11
NS	0.87	0.69–1.11
NB	0.84	0.66–1.05
QUE	1.67***	1.36–2.04
ONT	1.35***	1.14–1.61
MB	1.05	0.87–1.08
SASK	0.85	0.67–1.08
BC	1.06	0.85–1.31
Frequency of drinking		
Abstainer	1.00	—
1/month or less often	2.24***	2.01–2.49
1–12 times/month	3.97***	3.51–4.49
4 + times/week	7.76***	6.21–9.73
Frequency of drinking 5 + drinks		
Never	1.00	—
< weekly	0.97	0.87–1.01
Once/week or more	1.14	0.87–1.48
Probability of alcohol dependence		
0.00	1.00	—
0.05	1.17	0.92–1.14
0.40	1.32	0.96–1.81
0.85	0.83	0.53–1.28
1.00	1.02	0.63–1.66
Chronic health condition		
No	1.00	—
Ischaemic heart disease	1.33***	0.96–1.84
Other	0.95	0.87–1.03
Mean number of drinks in last week	1.01***	1.00–1.02

*** $p < 0.0001$.

because, as noted in the introduction, the SPSS software does not compensate for the survey's clustering and stratification features and thus underestimates population variances.

The percentages in the weighted sample accepting each definition of moderate drinking (not tabled) were as follows: no drinking (5.8%), less than one drink/week (17.6%), one to three drinks/week (46.1%), four to six drinks/week (15.3%), one to two drinks/day (14.0%), three + drinks/day (1.2%). Table 12.3 shows the relationship between these different definitions of moderate drinking and the respondents' beliefs about its health benefits. The relationship was statistically significant (χ^2 = 6424; 8 df, p < 0.0001). Those who accepted higher levels of drinking as defining moderate drinking were more likely to believe that moderate drinking had health benefits.

In order to explore the relationships between different definitions of moderate drinking, beliefs about moderate drinking and other variables, three mutually exclusive groups were created:

1. Those who defined moderate drinking as 'no drinking', plus those who disagreed that moderate drinking (by any definition) was good for health and those who indicated that they did not know if moderate drinking (by any definition) was good for health.

2. Those who defined moderate drinking as involving less than one drink per day and

who agreed that moderate drinking was good for health.

3. Those who defined moderate drinking as drinking at least one drink per day and agreed that this was good for health.

Table 12.4 shows the percentage of all respondents in each group and relationships between group membership and the variables considered in Table 12.1. There were substantial subgroup differences with respect to most variables, and all relationships were statistically significant (p < 0.0001 based on chi-square tests). The belief that there are health benefits associated with drinking at least one drink a day was most common among males, those over 45 years of age, those living in Quebec or Ontario, frequent drinkers, frequent heavy drinkers, those with a higher probability of alcohol dependence and those with ischaemic heart disease.

Logistic regression analysis was used to determine which variables in Table 12.4 best discriminated those who believed in the health benefits of daily drinking and those who believed that drinking less than daily had health benefits (groups 2 and 3 in Table 12.4). The results are summarized in Table 12.5. As expected, the results were very similar to those for the previous regression analysis. The largest effects (odds > 2) were found between some categories for age and frequency of drinking. The effects for number of drinks, gender,

Table 12.3 Respondents' Definitions of Moderate Drinking and Beliefs about Its Health Benefits

Respondents' Definition of Moderate Drinking	Belief about the Health Benefits of Moderate Drinking		
	Believes in Health Benefits[1]	Does Not Believe in Health Benefits	Not Sure
Abstinence or less than 1 drink/week	34.3%	54.0%	11.2%
1–3 drinks/week	60.5%	26.0%	13.4%
4–6 drinks/week	66.6%	24.2%	12.1%
1–2 drinks/day	76.4%	15.0%	8.6%
3 or more drinks/day	67.8%	26.8%	4.8%

χ^2 = 6424; df = 8, p < 0.0001.

[1] See introduction for interpretation of the beliefs of those who defined moderate drinking as no drinking.

Table 12.4 Definitions of Moderate Drinking, Beliefs about the Health Benefits of Moderate Drinking and Other Characteristics

	Does Not Believe That Any or Moderate Drinking[1] Is Good for Health	Defines Moderate Drinking as Less than 1 Drink/Day and Believes This Is Good for Health	Defines Moderate Drinking as 1 or More Drinks/Day and Believes This Is Good for Health
Total sample	40.8%	47.7%	11.5%
Sex			
Male	36.0%	49.2%	14.7%
Female	45.4%	46.3%	8.3%
Age (years)			
12–24	54.4%	41.7%	3.9%
25–44	41.6%	49.7%	8.7%
45–64	31.6%	50.9%	17.4%
65 or over	34.8%	44.8%	20.4%
Province			
NFLD	50.0%	40.1%	9.8%
PEI	53.8%	40.4%	5.8%
NS	51.3%	41.5%	7.2%
NB	53.7%	38.8%	7.5%
QUE	34.2%	54.7%	11.1%
ONT	39.9%	46.0%	14.1%
MB	45.2%	45.2%	9.6%
SASK	50.9%	42.4%	6.7%
BC	44.6%	46.1%	9.2%
Frequency of drinking			
Abstainer	60.3%	33.7%	6.3%
1/month or less	45.3%	49.0%	5.7%
2–12 times/month	30.8%	58.4%	10.8%
4 + times/week	14.3%	31.7%	54.0%
Mean number of drinks last 7 days[2]	1.7	2.8	6.9
Frequency has 5 + drinks/day			
Never	44.3%	49.3%	9.8%
< than weekly	35.2%	52.1%	12.7%
> once/week or more often	23.9%	45.9%	26.7%
Probability of alcohol dependence[3]			
0.0	41.8%	47.4%	10.9%
0.05	28.2%	53.4%	18.4%
0.40	26.3%	55.0%	18.8%
0.85	34.0%	47.4%	18.6%
1.00	28.7%	50.4%	20.8%
Chronic health condition			
No	41.5%	48.0%	9.7%
Ischaemic heart disease	30.9%	45.1%	24.1%
Other	40.5%	47.0%	12.5%

[1] However defined.
[2] Sum of drinks reported for each last 7 days.
[3] Based on items from the Composite International Diagnostic Interview (CIDI).

ischaemic heart disease, other chronic diseases and for some provinces (reference province was Newfoundland) were also highly significant. However, in this case the greatest differences were for Saskatchewan and British Columbia and not for Quebec and Ontario as was the case in Table 12.2.

Table 12.5 Results of a Logistic Regression Analysis Predicting Belief in the Health Benefits of Drinking at Least Once a Day vs. Drinking Less than One Drink a Day

Independent Variables	Odds Ratios	Confidence Limits
Gender		
Male	1.0	—
Female	0.76***	0.67–0.88
Age (years)		
12–24	1.00	—
25–44	1.51***	1.16–1.96
45–64	2.93***	2.24–3.84
65 +	4.04***	3.00–5.43
Province		
NFLD	1.00	—
PEI	0.58	0.36–0.92
NS	0.57	0.37–0.87
NB	0.76	0.51–1.20
QUE	0.74	0.53–1.04
ONT	1.14	0.86–1.51
MB	0.74	0.54–1.01
SASK	0.55***	0.37–0.84
BC	0.55***	0.38–0.79
Frequency of drinking		
Abstainer	1.00	—
1/month or less often	0.61***	0.48–0.76
1–12 times/month	0.84***	0.69–1.04
4 + times/week	5.48***	4.14–7.25
Frequency of drinking 5 + drinks		
Never	1.00	—
< weekly	1.07	0.90–1.28
Once/week or more often	1.31	0.93–1.86
Probability of alcohol dependence		
0.00	1.00	—
0.05	1.15	0.77–1.71
0.40	1.15	0.66–2.00
0.85	1.07	0.57–2.03
1.00	1.09	0.59–2.01
Chronic health condition		
No	1.00	—
Ischaemic heart disease	1.65***	1.01–2.69
Other	1.17***	1.01–1.35
Mean number of drinks in last week	1.02***	1.00–1.03

*** $p < 0.0001$.

DISCUSSION

This study shows that a majority of Canadian adults believe that moderate alcohol consumption has health benefits. This belief is most common among older people, men, those living in Quebec and Ontario, frequent and heavy drinkers, those with higher probabilities for alcohol dependence and those who report having ischaemic heart disease. Those who accepted higher levels of drinking as defining moderate drinking were more likely to believe that moderate drinking has health benefits.

It is of note that most respondents who believed that moderate drinking has health benefits defined this as drinking less than one drink per day. This is a conservative view of moderate drinking but consistent with the evidence that any cardiovascular benefits of drinking can be achieved at low levels of consumption (1–4 drinks per week) (Ashley *et al.*, 1997). The Centre for Addiction and Mental Health (1999) has also indicated that drinking up to two drinks per day would pose few risks to healthy adults except during pregnancy. Thus, the majority of those who believe drinking to be healthy would not be at risk for alcohol-related problems if they actually drank at their self-defined moderate levels.

It is also of note that the majority of those who reported frequent heavy drinking (5 + drinks/day) and those with the highest probability of alcohol dependence also believed that the health benefits of drinking could be achieved by drinking less than one drink per day. It thus seems unlikely that alcohol consumption among these heavy or dependent drinkers has been much affected by their beliefs in the health benefits of drinking.

This study does not show if respondents actually drank alcohol for health reasons or changed their drinking habits when they learned that drinking could be healthy; thus the implications for the effectiveness of population-based health policies are unclear. There are concerns that reports of the health benefits of moderate drinking could lead to increased per capita consumption and reduce the chances for effective population-based health policies that aim to reduce per capita consumption

(Casswell, 1993; Harrison, 1998). This could be a concern in societies where consumption is very low or uncommon. However, where moderate drinking already is common, as in most western countries, overall consumption may not be much affected if there is a dominant belief that alcohol can have health benefits when consumed at a low level. It is, however, possible that some heavy or dependent drinkers believe that high levels of consumption are healthy and use this as an excuse to maintain high-risk consumption levels. This concern is supported by the finding that belief in the health value of drinking was most common among heavy and dependent drinkers. These were also the most likely to define moderate drinking as one or more drinks per day. Some efforts to change the health beliefs of heavy drinkers may therefore be needed to reduce the chances that they will increase their problems by continuing to drink for their health reasons.

A substantial minority of respondents did not believe that drinking has health benefits. However, many of these did drink at least occasionally and could thus gain health benefits from drinking in some cases. Attempts to actively promote drinking for health thus seem unwarranted and could be misconstrued. However, it would be of interest to know why some people do not believe that alcohol can be healthy. It seems likely that religious beliefs and bad family or personal experiences with alcohol would be important but many other factors, including a sophisticated understanding of the scientific literature, could also play a role.

It is not known if these findings would be replicated in other countries, and there is a need to explore relationships between health beliefs about alcohol consumption in a variety of countries with different drinking habits and traditions. In this regard it is of note that there were some significant inter-provincial differences with respect to the belief that moderate drinking can have health benefits and the belief in the health benefits of daily drinking.

However, there is no obvious explanation for these differences and further research is needed to determine if they reflect provincial differences in drinking patterns, other beliefs, or ways in which research on the health benefits of drinking have been presented in the local media.

STUDY QUESTIONS

1. How do the authors indicate when they are drawing conclusions that go beyond their data? (Hint: see page 153.)

2. What is the theoretical/practical value of this study? Explain.

3. Why are the probabilities reported as < or >, rather than = ?

4. The authors state that participants were asked to either agree or disagree that moderate drinking was healthy. What problems might this pose for interpreting the results?

5. Could the limited options available to participants for this question have accounted for the apparent inconsistencies discussed by the authors?

6. What kind of statistics do the authors use? What is the advantage of using logistic regression over other types of regression?

REFERENCES

American Council on Science and Health (1999) *New Report Clarifies Health Effects of Moderate Alcohol Consumption*, press release, New York, February, 1999.

American Psychiatric Association (1987) *Diagnostic and Statistical Manual of Mental Disorders*, 3rd edn, revised (Washington, DC, American Psychiatric Association).

Ashley, M. J., Ferrence, R., Room, R., Bondy, S., Rehm, J. & Single, E. (1997) Moderate drinking and health, *Canadian Family Physician*, 43, 687–694.

Casswells, S. (1993) Public discourse on the benefits of moderation: implications for alcohol policy development, *Addiction*, *88*, 459–465.

Centre for Addiction and Mental Health (1999) *Alcohol and Your Health* (Toronto, Canada).

Doll, R., Peto, R., Hall, E., Wheatley, K. & Gray, R. (1994) Mortality in relation to consumption of alcohol: 13 years' observation on male British doctors, *British Medical Journal*, *309*, 911–918.

Hall, W. (1996) Changes in the public perceptions of the health benefits of alcohol use, 1989 to 1994, *Australia and New Zealand Journal of Public Health*, *20*, 93–95.

Hansagi, H., Romelsjo, A., Gerhardsson de Verdier, M., Andreasson, S. & Leifman, A. (1995) Alcohol consumption and stroke mortality: 20-year follow-up of 15,077 men and women, *Stroke*, *26*, 1768–1773.

Harrison, P. (1998) Royal College debates whether MDs should promote moderate consumption of alcohol, *Canadian Medical Association Journal*, *159*, 1289–1290.

Kessler, R. C., Crum, R. M., Warner, L. A., Nelson, C. B., Schulenberg, J. & Anthony, J. C. (1997) Lifetime co-occurrence of DSM-III-R alcohol abuse and dependence with other psychiatric disorders in the National Comorbidity Survey, *Archives of General Psychiatry*, *54*, 313–321.

Klatsky, A. L., Freidman, G. D. & Siegelaub, A. B. (1981) Alcohol and mortality: a 10-year Kaiser-Permanente experience, *Annals of Internal Medicine*, *95*, 139–145.

Maclure, M. (1993) Demonstration of deductive meta-analysis: ethanol intake and risk of myocardial infarction, *Epidemiologic Reviews*, *15*, 328–352.

Rimm, E. B., Giovannucci, E. L., Willett, W. C., Colditz, G. A., Ascherio, A., Rosner, B. *et al.* (1991) Prospective study of alcohol consumption and risk of coronary disease in men, *Lancet*, *338*, 464–468.

Serdula, M. K. (1995) Alcohol intake and mortality findings from the NHANES 1 follow-up study, *Journal of Studies on Alcohol*, *56*, 233–239.

Shaper, A. G. (1990) Alcohol and mortality: a review of prospective studies, *British Journal of Addiction*, *85*, 837–847.

Statistics Canada (1999) *1996–97 NPHS Public Use Microdata Documentation* (Ottawa, Statistics Canada).

UK Department of Health and Social Security (1995) *Sensible Drinking: The report of an Interdepartmental Working Group* (London, HMSO).

Van Gign, J., Stampfer, M. J., Wolfe, C. & Algra, A. (1993) The association between alcohol and stroke, in: Verschuren, P. M. (Ed.) *Health Issues Related to Alcohol Consumption* (Washington, DC, ILSI).

Chapter 13

Mock Juror Ratings of Guilt in Canada: Modern Racism and Ethnic Heritage

Jeffrey E. Pfeifer and James R. P. Ogloff

Source: From "Mock Juror Ratings of Guilt in Canada: Modern racism and ethnic heritage" by J.E. Pfeifer and J.R.P. Ogloff, *Social Behavior and Personality: An International Journal*, Vol. 31(3), pp. 301–12 (2003). Reprinted with kind permission from Scientific Journal Publishers.

The study of discrimination has long been a topic of interest for researchers in both the United States (see e.g., Allport, 1958; Kinder & Sears, 1981; McConahay, 1982; Pfeifer, 1988, 1999; Tomkins & Pfeifer, 1991) and Canada (see e.g., Berry, Kalin, & Taylor, 1977; Dutta, Norman, & Kanungo, 1972; Frideres, 1973; Gardner, LaLonde, Nero, & Young, 1988; Henry, 1969; Henry & Ginzberg, 1985; Taylor & Gardner, 1969). One area that has become especially salient in recent years is the study of prejudicial attitudes and juror perceptions of guilt and criminal sentencing in the United States (for a review of these studies see Pfeifer, 1990). A number of these laboratory studies have found that participants either: (1) rate black defendants guilty significantly more often than white defendants in both rape and murder cases, or (2) assign lengthier sentences to black defendants, especially when the rape or murder victim is white (see e.g., Bernard, 1979; Bullock, 1961; Field, 1979; Foley & Chamblin, 1982; Gleason & Harris, 1975; Gray & Ashmore, 1976; Johnson, 1985; Klein & Creech, 1982; Scroggs, 1976; Ugwuegbu, 1979). These disparate dispositional findings have been further supported by evaluations of legal and archival data indicating that black Americans are more likely than are white Americans to receive the death penalty in the United States (see e.g., Baldus, Pulaski, & Woodworth, 1986; Baldus, Woodworth, & Pulaski, 1985; Gerard & Terry, 1970; Howard, 1975; Paternoster, 1984; Wolfgang & Reidel, 1975; Zeisal, 1981).

The importance of the issues raised in these studies is illustrated by the fact that the United States Supreme Court discussed the data noted above in *McCleskey v. Kemp* (1987). Mr. McCleskey, a black defendant, claimed that the imposition of the death sentence violated his constitutional right to equal protection because his sentence was racially based. His argument relied, in part, upon an archival study conducted by Baldus and his colleagues (1986) indicating that black defendants were significantly more likely to receive the death penalty than were white defendants when the victim was white. The Court, however, rejected McCleskey's argument, holding that while these data might reflect a "general" prejudice in sentencing, there was no direct proof to suggest that the defendant had been subject to "personal" sentencing prejudice (for a discussion of this distinction see Pfeifer, 1990). Despite the Court's opinion in the McCleskey case, social scientific data on prejudicial decision making has continued to be employed as part of defense claims in several cases in the United States (*People v. Girvies*, 1988; *People v. Stewart*, 1988) as well as in Canada (see e.g., *Regina v. Parks*, 1993; *Regina v. Williams*, 1998).

Recently, however, a number of studies have begun to question the applicability of the laboratory and archival studies noted above. Specifically, it has been argued that although archival data indicate that black defendants are more likely to receive the death penalty than are white defendants, the data do not indicate that the jury is solely responsible for this discrepancy (Pfeifer, 1990). In addition, it has been suggested that the majority of the laboratory studies on mock juror racism lack a number of major elements of the actual trial situation and, as such, their findings may not be directly generalized to the legal arena (Pfeifer, 1996).

Pfeifer and Ogloff (1991), for example, found that although white American mock jurors tend to rate a black defendant more guilty than a white defendant, this effect dissipates when jurors are supplied with specific instructions to guide their decision making. According to the authors, this finding may be explained by theories of "modern racism" which suggest that white Americans will express their racist tendencies only in situations that they perceive to be ambiguous enough to allow for nonracist interpretation (Gaertner & Dovidio, 1986; McConahay & Hough, 1976). Accordingly, when supplied with specific instructions to guide their decision making, white mock jurors are not able to express their prejudicial attitudes due to the lack of situational ambiguity. The vitiating effect of instructions on juror decision making has been replicated in a number of recent studies dealing with sexism and racism (see e.g., Campbell et al., 1992; Hill & Pfeifer, 1992; Pfeifer & Bernstein, in review; Wolbaum & Pfeifer, in review).

In comparison to American investigators, however, researchers in Canada have invested very little effort in examining the potential influence of prejudice on courtroom interactions (see e.g., Avio, 1987, 1988; Bagby & Rector, 1992; Palys & Divorski, 1984). One exception is Avio (1987; 1988) who, like Baldus et al., has also employed archival data to demonstrate that certain groups in Canada were more likely to receive the death penalty based on their ethnicity. According to Avio, from 1926 to 1957 the odds of having been executed in Canada increased significantly for defendants who were not English Canadian. Specifically, the data suggest French Canadian defendants were 2.4 times more likely to be executed than were English Canadian defendants and that Native Canadian defendants were 6.1 times more likely to be executed than were English Canadians.

These data, combined with earlier work on Canadian ethnic relations (see e.g., Esses, Haddock, & Zanna, 1993; Hiller, 1976; Zieglar, 1980), appear to suggest that English Canadians may hold prejudicial attitudes toward both French and Native Canadians similar to those that white Americans hold toward black Americans in the United States. As such, if prejudicial attitudes of English Canadians toward French and Native Canadians do indeed exist, it may be that they are playing a role in the Canadian judicial system similar to that reported in the American. Specifically, it may be that—like the U.S.-based research cited above—English Canadians harbor negative prejudicial attitudes toward their French and Native Canadian counterparts and that these attitudes can be illustrated through their guilt ratings in a mock juror experimental paradigm. Further, it may also be that these prejudicial attitudes can be constrained by the inclusion of standard judicial instructions.

In order to investigate whether the prejudicial sentencing trends in the United States and Canada are similar, at least four hypotheses must be confirmed. First, it must be shown that the prejudicial attitudes held by English Canadians toward their French and Native Canadian counterparts can be replicated in a legal setting, such as a sexual assault trial. Second, it must be established that these prejudicial attitudes are affecting subjective perceptions of both the victim and defendant in the trial. Third, it must be shown that participants' perceptions of the defendant are being affected to such an extent that their sentencing decisions are being prejudiced to the same degree that they seem to be in U.S. studies. Finally, in order to support our theory regarding modern racism, it must be demonstrated that these ethnic-based differential guilt ratings may be overridden by the inclusion of jury instructions that specify the elements of the crime. This mock juror study was designed to determine whether or not these hypotheses are supported.

METHOD

Participants

In this study, 213 English Canadian undergraduate students from a mid-western university volunteered to act as participants. The sample was composed of 81 men and 132 women ranging in age from 18 to 45, with a mean age of 20.61.

Procedure

Participants were randomly assigned to one of nine conditions and asked to assume the role of a juror and read a transcript depicting a sexual assault trial. In the trial, the ethnicity of both the victim and the defendant was varied in order to produce a 3 (English, French or Native victim) × 3 (English, French or Native defendant) factorial design. After reading the transcript, participants were asked to rate how guilty they believed the defendant to be in two ways. First, participants were asked to indicate how guilty they personally felt the defendant was on a 7-point bipolar scale (Subjective Guilt Rating) ranging from 1 (*not guilty*) to 7 (*extremely guilty*). Second, participants were asked whether the defendant was legally guilty or not guilty on a dichotomous

scale according to the judge's instructions to the jury (Legal Standard Guilt Rating). These instructions specified the elements of the crime of sexual assault and noted that in order to find the defendant guilty each element had to be proven beyond a reasonable doubt. It is important to note that the presentation of the guilt questions was counter-balanced in such a way that one-half of the participants were presented with the bipolar scale first, while the other half of the participants were presented with the dichotomous scale.

Participants were also instructed to complete a questionnaire probing their attitudes toward the defendant and the victim along a number of personality traits (e.g., dishonest-honest, unattractive-attractive). As a manipulation check, all participants were asked to identify the ethnic background of both the victim and the defendant.

RESULTS

Subjective Guilt Ratings

A two-way analysis of variance (ANOVA) on subjective guilt ratings of the defendant produced a main effect for defendant ethnicity [$F(2,204) = 10.98, p < .01$] and a main effect for victim ethnicity [$F(2,204) = 4.22, p < .05$], but did yield an interaction effect [$F(4,204) = 1.50$, (ns)]. Specifically, participants rated the Native Canadian defendant significantly more guilty than the English or French Canadian defendant if the victim was portrayed as English Canadian or French Canadian. In addition, participants rated the English Canadian defendant as significantly less guilty if the victim was portrayed as Native Canadian rather than French or English Canadian (see Table 13.1).

Subsequent simple effect analyses on defendant and victim ethnicity confirmed this trend with regard to guilt ratings. Specifically, when the race of the victim was held constant, participants rated the Native Canadian defendant

Table 13.1 Mean Subjective Guilt Ratings Based on Defendant and Victim Ethnicity

	Defendant Ethnicity		
	English	**French**	**Native**
Victim Ethnicity			
English Canadian	3.90_a	4.00_a	5.06_b
French Canadian	3.72_a	3.91_a	5.30_b
Native Canadian	2.52_c	4.09_a	4.04_a

Note: Ratings are based on 7-point bipolar scales with 1 representing *not guilty* and 7 representing *extremely guilty*. Means that do not share a common subscript differ significantly at the .05 level of significance.

significantly more guilty ($M = 4.80$) than the French Canadian defendant ($M = 4.00$), and rated the English Canadian defendant least guilty ($M = 3.38$). Similarly, when the race of the defendant was held constant, participants were significantly more likely to rate the defendant as more guilty if the victim was portrayed as English ($M = 4.32$) or French Canadian ($M = 4.31$) as opposed to Native Canadian ($M = 3.55$).

Legal Standard Guilt Ratings

In contrast to the Subjective Guilt Ratings discussed above, examination of the Legal Standard Guilt Ratings indicated no significant difference between subject responses [$x^2(8, N=213) = 4.22, p< .05$ (ns)]. Specifically, results suggest that, when supplied with standard judicial instructions and asked to adhere to them, participants did not rate the defendant significantly more guilty in any condition, regardless of the ethnicity of either the victim or the defendant (see Table 13.2). As hypothesized, these results indicate that participants are more likely to rate defendants differentially if not provided with information to guide their decisions. These differences, however, seem to disappear when participants are asked to make their decisions using a dichotomous scale based on jury instructions that emphasize the elements of the crime of sexual assault and specify that each ele-

Table 13.2 Legal Standard Guilt Ratings Based on Defendant and Victim Ethnicity

	Verdict	
Ethnicity (Defendant/Victim)	**Guilty**	**Not Guilty**
English/English	9(45%)	11(55%)
English/French	10(56%)	8(44%)
English/Native	10(43%)	13(57%)
French/English	10(48%)	11(52%)
French/French	12(52%)	11(48%)
French/Native	10(43%)	13(57%)
Native/English	16(44%)	20(56%)
Native/French	11(48%)	12(52%)
Native/Native	15(58%)	11(42%)

ment must be proven beyond a reasonable doubt in order to find the defendant guilty.

Defendant Ratings

A series of ANOVAs performed on ratings of the defendant indicated significant main effects for intelligence [$F(2,210) = 16.27, p< .01$], attractiveness [$F(2,210) = 31.77, p< .01$], wealth [$F(2,210) = 36.30, p< .01$], and laziness [$F(2,210) = 16.69, p< .01$]. Specifically, participants rated the English Canadian defendant significantly more positively than the French and Native Canadian defendants on all four personality traits. Interestingly, the trend of rating the English Canadian defendant most positively, followed by the French and Native Canadian defendants, was found for all traits (see Table 13.3).

Victim Ratings

A series of ANOVAs performed on ratings of the victim indicated significant main effects for attractiveness [$F(2,210) = 15.28, p< .01$], honesty [$F(2,210) = 17.50, p< .01$], and responsibility [$F(2,210) = 13.45, p< .01$]. Specifically, participants rated the French Canadian victim as significantly more attractive, honest and responsible than the English and Native Canadian victims. Interestingly, the trend of rat-

Table 13.3 Mean Ratings of Defendant

	Defendant Ethnicity			
	Native	French	English	
Trait				
Unattractive	2.96$_a$	3.88$_b$	4.38$_c$	Attractive
Unintelligent	3.44$_a$	4.10$_b$	4.57$_c$	Intelligent
Poor	3.04$_a$	3.97$_b$	4.57$_c$	Rich
Lazy	3.73$_a$	4.37$_b$	4.90$_c$	Hard-Working

Note: Ratings are based on 7-point bipolar scales with 1 representing the trait on the left and 7 representing the trait on the right. Means within the same row that do not share a common subscript differ significantly at the .01 level of significance.

ing the French Canadian victim most positively followed by the English and Native Canadian victim was found for all attributes (see Table 13.4).

DISCUSSION

Taken as a whole, these results seem to provide evidence for the proposition that ethnic stereotypes are playing a role in simulated juror ratings of guilt in Canada that is similar to that documented in the United States. To begin with, support for our first and second hypotheses comes from the fact that participants, within the context of a sexual assault trial, consistently rated French Canadian victims more positively than either English or Native Canadians. This finding suggests that the prejudicial attitudes of

Table 13.4 Mean Ratings of Victim

	Victim Ethnicity			
	Native	English	French	
Trait				
Unattractive	3.90$_a$	4.47$_b$	4.94$_c$	Attractive
Dishonest	3.88$_a$	4.68$_b$	5.30$_c$	Honest
Irresponsible	3.71$_a$	4.40$_b$	5.02$_c$	Responsible

Note: Ratings are based on 7-point bipolar scales with 1 representing the trait on the left and 7 representing the trait on the right. Means within the same row that do not share a common subscript differ significantly at the .01 level of significance.

English Canadians can in fact be replicated in a legal setting, and are affecting subjective perceptions of the victim. These results also confirm previous research by Lambert (1967) and Larimer (1972) which suggest that English Canadians consistently rate French Canadian women more positively (e.g., more ambitious, intelligent, and self-confident) than English Canadian women.

Similarly, support for the third hypothesis comes from the fact that guilt ratings were also impacted by the ethnic background of the victim. In effect, participants rated the defendant less favorably if he was accused of raping a French Canadian woman. Again, these results are consistent with previous U.S. research that suggests that juror ratings in a rape trial are highly reflective of attitudes towards the victim as well as the defendant (Field, 1979).

It seems, therefore, that simulated jurors in Canada do indeed hold prejudicial attitudes similar to those found in the U.S. studies and that these attitudes can be replicated in a legal setting (i.e., a sexual assault trial). The issue of major importance, however, arises from the fourth hypothesis that tests whether these prejudicial attitudes are affecting participants to such an extent that the attitudes are overriding other aspects of the trial process.

In order to investigate this hypothesis we may look at the two sets of results concerned with guilt ratings. First, when participants were simply asked to give their subjective perceptions of guilt (i.e., Subjective Guilt Rating) they rated the Native Canadian defendant significantly more guilty than the English or French Canadian defendant if the victim was portrayed as English Canadian or French Canadian. In addition, participants rated the English Canadian defendant as significantly less guilty if the victim was portrayed as Native Canadian rather than French or English Canadian. These results would seem to indicate that the ethnic backgrounds of both the victim and defendant are playing a significant role in encouraging differential dispositional evaluations. In contrast, when participants were asked to rate the guilt of the defendant according to the legal standard on a dichotomous scale (i.e., Legal Standard Guilt Rating), there was no significant difference found based on either defendant or victim ethnicity.

It seems, therefore, that participants place less emphasis on their prejudicial attitudes when faced with deciding the fate of a defendant in accordance with standard judicial instructions. It may, of course, be argued that this differential in guilt ratings may be attributed to the incorporation of a dichotomous scale (as opposed to a bipolar scale) rather than to the addition of instructions. However, research by Pfeifer and Ogloff (1991) suggests that it is the addition of instructions, as opposed to the response scale employed, which plays a major role in subjective perceptions of guilt. Specifically, these authors found that the addition of standard judicial instructions neutralized the prejudicial responses of white mock jurors toward a black defendant regardless of the type of scale employed to measure guilt ratings.

In light of these findings, it may be hypothesized that Canadian participants, like their U.S. counterparts, were unable (or unwilling) to express their prejudicial attitudes when specifically asked to evaluate the defendant's guilt based on the legal standard because of the lack of situational ambiguity. Conversely, when simply asked whether they believed the defendant to be guilty (i.e., Subjective Guilt Rating), participants had no specific standard to guide them in their determination of the defendant's guilt and consequently may have been guided by their prejudices. Like white American mock jurors then, the expression of prejudicial tendencies may have been restricted when English Canadian mock jurors were provided with legal standards for determining the guilt of the defendant. This possibility is perhaps best illustrated by the response of one subject who

wrote, "He [the defendant] is Indian therefore I am 99% sure he is a liar and is guilty—but I can't find him legally guilty according to the judge's instructions."

The results of this study also underline the caution that must be taken when one attempts to draw direct legal conclusions from psychological research (Loh, 1981; Melton, 1986, 1987; Monahan & Loftus, 1982; Pfeifer, 1990). Specifically, this study indicates the importance that standard jury instructions may play in the guilt determinations of jurors—an aspect that was apparently not incorporated in much of the early research in this area. Although this study investigated the effect of incorporating a legal standard into studies of juror decision making, there still exist a number of other limitations to the external validity of this study, particularly related to the legal context used to explore this issue.

First, it must be recognized that participants were asked to rate the guilt of the defendant without deliberating with other "jurors." Whether this deliberation process serves to exacerbate or minimize prejudicial attitudes has yet to be discovered. In addition, these results were obtained with regard to a sexual assault trial and as such cannot be readily generalized to other types of trials, especially due to the complex issues involved in sexual assault trials (Field, 1979; Hans & Vidmar, 1986).

Although this study may not be directly generalized to the legal system, the findings do contain important social scientific, as well as psycholegal, information concerning aspects of racism. As a social scientific study concerned with prejudice, this research seems to provide internally valid evidence for the fact that prejudicial attitudes, based on ethnicity, do indeed exist in Canada today. Further, it appears that, like our American counterparts, English Canadians are affected by the tenets of modern racism—at least within the confines of a jury simulation study. Given these findings, it may be suggested that future research on racism in Canada take into account the effect of perceived situational ambiguity on cross-racial evaluations. In addition, the results of this study also attest to the importance of judicial instruction on juror decisions and as such suggest that future psycholegal investigation of courtroom racism examine the possible further use of instructions to constrain prejudicial tendencies.

STUDY QUESTIONS

1. Why would the mean age of the subjects in this study possibly be important to the interpretation of the study results?

2. Why do the authors question the applicability of the laboratory and archival studies? Do you agree with their argument? Explain fully.

3. The authors were not able to strongly conclude that the addition of jury instructions neutralized the use of prejudicial attitudes in assessing defendant guilt. What other methodological factors and/or sampling issues might the authors have considered to enable them to draw more definitive conclusions?

4. What are the possible limitations of the sampling technique they employed?

5. Suggest further studies that would strengthen the authors' interpretation of the results.

REFERENCES

Allport, G. (1958). *The nature of prejudice.* Garden City, New York: Doubleday.

Avio, K. (1987). The quality of mercy: Exercise of the royal prerogative in Canada. *Canadian Public Policy, 13,* 366–379.

Avio, K. (1988). Capital punishment in Canada: Statistical evidence and constitutional issues. *Canadian Journal of Criminology,* October, 331–349.

Bagby, M., & Rector, N. (1992). Prejudice in a simulated legal context: A further application of social identity theory. *European Journal of Social Psychology, 22,* 397–406.

Baldus, D. C., Pulaski, C. A., & Woodworth, G. (1986). Arbitrariness and discrimination of the death penalty: A challenge to state supreme courts. *Stetson Law Review, 15,* 133–261.

Baldus, D. C., Woodworth, G., & Pulaski, C. A. (1985). Monitoring and evaluating contemporary death sentencing systems: Lessons from Georgia. *University of California Davis Law Review, 18,* 1327–1407.

Bernard, J. L. (1979). Interaction between the race of the defendant and that of the jurors in determining verdicts. *Law and Psychological Review, 5,* 103–111.

Berry, J. W., Kalin, R., & Taylor, D. (1977). *Multiculturalism and ethnic attitudes in Canada.* Ottawa: Supply and Services Canada.

Bullock, H. A. (1961). Significance of the racial factor in the length of prison sentences. *Journal of Criminal Law, Criminology and Police Science, 52,* 411–417.

Campbell, E., Pierre-Trettel, D., Koenig, H., Pfeifer, J., Wolfe, D., & Gabriel-Harper, K. (1992). Gender and presentational style: When the verdict of a trial is unaffected by an attorney's personal characteristics and behavior, justice is served. *Washburn Law Review, 31,* 415–454.

Dutta, S., Norman, L., & Kanungo, R. N. (1972). A scale for the measurement of attitudes toward French Canadians. In J. W. Berry & G. J. S. Wilde (Eds.), *The Canadian Context* (pp.69–82). Toronto: McClelland and Stewart.

Esses, V. M., Haddock, G., & Zanna, M. P. (1993). Values, stereotypes, and emotions as determinants of intergroup attitudes. In D. M. Mackie & D. L. Hamilton (Eds.), *Affect, cognition and stereotyping* (pp.137–166). Toronto: Academic Press.

Field, H. S. (1979). Rape trials and jurors' decisions: A psycholegal analysis of the effects of victim, defendant, and case characteristics. *Law and Human Behavior, 3,* 261–284.

Foley, L. A., & Chamblin, M. H. (1982). The effect of race and personality on mock jurors' decisions. *Journal of Psychology, 112,* 47–51.

Frideres, J. S. (1973). Discrimination in western Canada. *Race, 15,* 213–222.

Gaertner, S. L., & Dovidio, J. F. (1986). The aversive form of racism. In J. F. Dovidio & S. L. Gaertner (Eds.), *Prejudice, discrimination, and racism* (pp.61–90). Toronto: Academic Press.

Gardner, R. C., LaLonde, R. N., Nero, A. M., & Young, M. Y. (1988). Ethnic stereotypes: Implications of measurement strategy. *Social Cognition, 6,* 40–60.

Gerard, J. B., & Terry, T. R. (1970). Discrimination against negroes in the administration of criminal law in Missouri. *Washington State University Law Quarterly,* 415–437.

Gleason, J., & Harris, V. (1975). Race, socioeconomic status and perceived similarity as determinants of judgments by simulated jurors. *Social Behavior and Personality, 3,* 175–180.

Gray, D. B., & Ashmore, R. D. (1976). Biasing influence on defendants' characteristics on simulated sentencing. *Psychological Reports, 38,* 727–738.

Hans, V., & Vidmar, N. (1986). *Judging the jury.* New York: Plenum Press.

Henry, F. J. (1969). The measurement of perceived discrimination: A Canadian case study. *Race, 10,* 449–461.

Henry, F. J., & Ginzberg, E. (1985). *Who gets the work: A test of racial discrimination in employment in Toronto.* Toronto: The Urban Alliance on Race Relations and the Social Planning Council of Metropolitan Toronto.

Hill, E., & Pfeifer, J. (1992). Nullification instructions and juror guilt ratings: An examination of modern racism. *Contemporary Social Psychology, 16,* 6–10.

Hiller, H. H. (1976). *Canadian society: A sociological analysis.* Scarborough, Ontario: Prentice-Hall.

Howard, J. (1975). Racial discrimination in sentencing. *Judicature, 59,* 121–125.

Johnson, S. L. (1985). Black innocence and the white jury. *Michigan Law Review, 83,* 1611–1708.

Kinder, D. R., & Sears, D. O. (1981). Prejudice and politics: Symbolic racism versus racial threats to the good life. *Journal of Personality and Social Psychology, 40,* 414–431.

Klein, K., & Creech, B. (1982). Race, rape, and bias: Distortion of prior odds and meaning changes. *Basic and Applied Social Psychology, 3,* 21–33.

Lambert, W. E. (1967). A social psychology of bilingualism. *Journal of Social Issues, 23,* 91–109.

Larimer, G. S. (1972). Indirect assessment of intercultural prejudices. In J. W. Berry & G. J. S. Wilde (Eds.),

The Canadian context (pp.59–69). Toronto: McClelland and Stewart.

Loh, W. (1981). Psycholegal research: Past and present. *Michigan Law Review, 79,* 659–707.

McCleskey v. Kemp, 107 S.Ct. 1756 (1987).

McConahay, J. B. (1982). Self-interest versus racial attitudes as correlates of anti-busing attitudes in Louisville: Is it the buses or the blacks? *Journal of Politics, 44,* 692–720.

McConahay, J. B., & Hough, J. C. (1976). Symbolic racism. *Journal of Social Issues, 32,* 23–45.

Melton, G. (1986). Introduction: The law and motivation. In G. B. Melton (Ed.), *Nebraska symposium on motivation: The law as a behavioral instrument* (pp.xiii–xxvii). Lincoln: University of Nebraska Press.

Melton, G. (1987). Bringing psychology to the legal system: Opportunities, obstacles, and efficiency. *American Psychologist, 42,* 488–495.

Monahan, J., & Loftus, E. F. (1982). The psychology of law. *Annual Review of Psychology, 33,* 441–475.

Palys, T. S., & Divorski, S. (1984). Judicial decision-making: An examination of sentencing disparity among Canadian provincial court judges. In D. J. Muller, D. E. Blackman & A. J. Chapman (Eds.), *Psychology and Law* (pp.333–344). Toronto: Wiley.

Paternoster, R. (1984). Prosecutorial discretion in requesting the death penalty: A case of victim biased racial discrimination. *Law and Society Review, 18,* 437–445.

People v. Girvies, 119 Ill.2d 61, 518 N.E.2d 78 (1988).

People v. Stewart, 121 Ill.2d 93, 520 N.E.2d 348 (1988).

Pfeifer, J. (1988). Courtroom prejudice: An application of symbolic sexism. *Contemporary Social Psychology, 13,* 1–8.

Pfeifer, J. (1990). Reviewing the evidence on jury racism: Findings of discrimination or discriminatory findings? *Nebraska Law Review, 69,* 230–250.

Pfeifer, J. E. (1996). Social psychology in the courtroom. In S. W. Sadava & D. R. McCreary (Eds.), *Applied Social Psychology* (pp.157–184). New York: Prentice-Hall.

Pfeifer, J. (1999). Perceptual biases and mock juror decision making: Minority religions in court. *Social Justice Research, 12,* 409–419.

Pfeifer, J., & Bernstein, D. (in review). Mock juror decision making and modern racism: Examining the role of task and target specificity on judgmental evaluations.

Pfeifer, J., & Ogloff, J. (1991). Ambiguity and guilt determinations: A modern racism perspective. *Journal of Applied Social Psychology, 21,* 1713–1725.

Regina v. Parks, 84 C.C.C. (3d), 353 (1993).

Regina v. Williams, 124 C.C.C. (3d), 481 (S.C.C) (1998).

Scroggs, J. R. (1976). Penalties for rape as a function of victim provocativeness, damage, and resistance. *Journal of Applied Social Psychology, 6,* 360–368.

Taylor, D., & Gardner, R. C. (1969). Ethnic stereotypes: Their effects on the perception of communicators of varying credibility. *Canadian Journal of Psychology, 23,* 161–173.

Tomkins, A., & Pfeifer, J. E. (1991). Modern social scientific theories and data concerning discrimination: Implications for using social science evidence in the courts. In D. K. Kagehiro & W. S. Laufer (Eds.), *Handbook of psychology and law* (pp.385–407). New York: Springer-Verlag.

Ugwuegbu, D. C. E. (1979). Racial and evidential factors in juror attribution of legal responsibility. *Journal of Experimental Social Psychology, 15,* 133–146.

Wolbaum, J., & Pfeifer, J. E. (in review). Aboriginal and white juvenile defendants: Examining the role of race and task specificity on mock juror decision making.

Wolfgang, M. E., & Reidel, M. (1975). Rape, race and the death penalty in Georgia. *American Journal of Orthopsychiatry, 45,* 658–668.

Zeisal, H. (1981). Race bias in the administration of the death penalty: The Florida experience. *Harvard Law Review, 95,* 456–468.

Zieglar, S. (1980). Measuring inter-ethnic attitudes in a multi-ethnic context. *Canadian Ethnic Studies, 12,* 45–55.

Chapter 14

Public Attitudes towards Conditional Sentencing: Results of a National Survey

Trevor Sanders and Julian V. Roberts

Source: From T. Sanders and J. Roberts (2000). *Canadian J. of Behavioral Science,* 32(4), 199–207. Copyright © 2000 Canadian Psychological Association. Reprinted with permission.

Public attitudes towards crime and criminal justice have become the object of considerable research by scholars in Canada (e.g., Doob & Roberts, 1988; Higginbottom & Zamble, 1988; Roberts, 1992; Roberts & Stalans, 2000; Tremblay, Cordeau, & Ouimet, 1994; Zamble & Annesley, 1987; Zamble & Kalm, 1990). A major focus of this research has been on the issue of sentencing, which attracts widespread public attention and criticism. Much of this criticism reflects the perception of leniency: Most Canadians (as well as residents of other Western nations—see Roberts & Stalans, 2000) hold the view that judges are too lenient towards convicted offenders. Researchers have attempted to explain the perception of leniency and to explore the relationship between judicial practice and the opinions of the public.

In 1996, Parliament took a significant step towards reducing the use of incarceration as a sanction. Bill C-41, the sentencing reform bill proclaimed in that year, contained a number of important provisions, including one that created a new sentence (see Daubney & Parry, 1999; Roberts & Cole, 1999 for a review and discussion of the sentencing reforms). The new disposition is called a "conditional term of imprisonment," and although such a sentence has been a sentencing option in most Western nations for decades, it is the first time that Canada has adopted such an innovation. In the over three years since the passage of sentencing reform legislation, conditional sentencing has emerged as the most important (and controversial issue) in the area of sentencing in Canada. In January 2000, the Supreme Court of Canada issued several guideline judgements with respect to conditional sentencing. The lead decision (*R. v. Proulx*) underlined the importance of public opinion to the conditional sentence.[1]

Definition of a Conditional Sentence

A conditional sentence of imprisonment is in many respects a legal paradox: a term of imprisonment that the offender nevertheless serves in the community, under supervision. According to Section 742 of the *Criminal Code,* a judge has the discretion to impose such a sentence if certain prerequisite conditions are fulfilled. First, the offence of which the offender has been convicted must not carry a minimum term of imprisonment (This includes a small number of offences, including first- and second-degree murder). Second, the judge must have already decided to sentence the offender to a prison term of less than two years' duration. Third, the court must be satisfied that the presence of the offender in the community would not endanger the community. Finally, the judge must also be satisfied that the imposition of a conditional sentence would be consistent with the purposes and principles of sentencing contained in sections 718–718.2 of the *Criminal Code.*

All offenders who receive a conditional sentence must observe a number of conditions. The compulsory conditions include requirements such as keeping the peace and reporting to a probation officer. The optional conditions are crafted to respond to the needs of the particular offender, and may include following a drug treatment program or performing some community service. If these conditions are observed, the offender can remain at home, without having to go to prison. However, if the conditions are violated, a hearing will be held (unless the breach occurs relatively late in the sentence, in which case proceeding with a hearing may be perceived by the Crown as a waste of time). An offender who violates the compulsory or optional conditions of a conditional sentence order runs the risk of being imprisoned for the balance of the sentence, or some portion of the balance of the sentence.

The conditional sentence has proved both popular with judges and controversial. Over 40,000 conditional sentences had been imposed within three years of creation of the new sanction (La Prairie, 1999). As for criticism, it has come from victims' rights groups, victims themselves, from political parties, as well as from academics (e.g., Paciocco, 1999; Roberts, 1997). A private member's bill (C-302) has also been introduced in Parliament which, if passed, will greatly restrict the kinds of crimes that could result in a conditional sentence. Some critics have argued that the conditional sentence should not be imposed in cases involving violence, particularly crimes of sexual aggression. At the same time, others have praised the new sanction as providing a new sentencing option that will help judges reduce the number of offenders sent to prison every year (see Gemmell, 1997; Healy, 1999; Manson, 1997).

Importance of Public Attitudes to Conditional Sentencing

There are several reasons why the views of the public are critical to the issue of conditional sentencing. First, section 718 of the *Criminal Code* specifies that the fundamental purpose of sentencing is to contribute "to respect for the law." If the public are opposed to conditional sentencing, the widespread use of the new sanction is likely to further undermine public respect for the law and confidence in the courts. Second, there is evidence that, when sentencing offenders, judges are sensitive to the issue of public perception. A recent national survey of the judiciary found that 80% of judges acknowledged considering public reaction before they imposed a conditional sentence (Roberts, Doob, & Marinos, 1999). Thus if the public are, or become, implacably opposed to the new sanction, it is likely to fall into disfavour with the judiciary as well.

Third, adverse public opinion has been cited by critics of conditional sentencing as justifying amendments to, or even repeal of, the conditional sentencing provisions in the *Criminal Code.* Some critics have suggested that the public are willing to support the use of conditional sentencing only in cases of minor property crimes such as theft or small-scale frauds. While researchers in psychology have explored many issues in the area of sentencing and parole (c.f. Cumberland & Zamble, 1992; Doob & Roberts, 1988; Zamble & Kahn, 1990), we know little about public reaction to this new disposition. Finally, the recent (January 2000) Supreme Court guideline judgement with respect to conditional sentencing (*R. v. Proulx*) identified the leniency of conditional sentences as a potential weakness of the new sanction which might not "be accepted by the public" (*R. v. Proulx*, p. 19). The court also noted that: "Inadequate sanctions undermine respect for the law" (*R. v. Proulx*, p. 19). It is therefore important to know the extent to which conditional sentences are supported by the public.

We do not even know the degree to which the public are aware of the nature of the sanction. Misperceptions abound with regard to crime and the criminal justice system (see Roberts, 1994, for a review). It is possible that the public are opposed to conditional sentencing without knowing much about the nature and purpose of the new sanction. Clearly, it is necessary to gauge the level of public knowledge before evaluating the nature of public attitudes to conditional sentencing.

It is also important to know about the relationship between public knowledge of, and attitudes towards, the new sanction. One issue that emerges clearly from the literature on public attitudes to sentencing is the importance of the level of information available to members of the public. It has been convincingly demonstrated that when the public are provided with an adequate amount of information about a sentencing decision, they respond less punitively. Zamble and Kalm (1990), for example, found that when participants were asked to sentence offenders described in some detail in crime scenarios rather than simply asked a broad question such as, "Are sentences too lenient or too harsh?" responses were significantly less punitive (see also Covell & Howe, 1996; Doob & Roberts, 1988). It is not clear whether public attitudes towards conditional sentencing are equally sensitive to the amount of information available to the participant.

The only survey to date of public attitudes to conditional sentencing was a preliminary examination of 500 Ontario residents conducted shortly after the new sentence was created (see Marinos & Doob, 1997,[2] p.1). That study uncovered some important findings about public reaction to conditional sentences. However, since then several developments have taken place that may well have affected the tenor of public opinion with respect to conditional sentences of imprisonment. A significant number of conditional sentences involving very serious cases of homicide have been imposed. For example, in 1998, an Ottawa woman who shot her husband while he was asleep was sentenced to a term of imprisonment to be served in the community (*R. v. Getkate*). Such well-publicized cases may well have provoked widespread opposition to conditional sentencing. As well, the conditional sentence attracted intense media attention when six cases were argued before the Supreme Court of Canada in 1999. Much of this press coverage was negative; for example, one national newspaper described the appeals in an article headlined "Law lets convicts serve time in style" (National Post, 1999).

Purpose of Study

The purpose of the present nation-wide survey was therefore four-fold: First, to evaluate the extent of public knowledge of a major penal reform three years after the law was passed; second, to explore, using crimes representing a range of seriousness, the degree of public support for the new conditional sentence of imprisonment; third, to test an experimental hypothesis relating to public opinion with respect to alternatives to imprisonment. The hypothesis being tested was that public support for the conditional sentence would increase if the specific conditions attached to the sanction were made salient to respondents. Finally, in order to see whether public views had changed, an attempt was made to replicate one of the principal findings emerging from the only previous study of public opinion conducted two years earlier by Marinos and Doob (1997). The method employed consisted of a survey using a representative, national sample of Canadians.

METHOD

Materials

A questionnaire was developed and pretested. The survey included a number of dependent measures, including general questions about the sentencing process. For example, respondents were asked to identify the most important purpose of sentencing. As well, they were asked whether sentences were too harsh, too lenient or about right. Another question tested their knowledge of conditional sentencing, using a multiple-choice format. Several crime scenarios were employed to explore respondents' reactions to conditional sentencing in specific cases. Participants were read brief descriptions of crimes and were then asked to choose between imposing a term of imprisonment or a conditional sentence of imprisonment (to be served in the community). Prior to being asked to make this choice, participants were provided with a clear definition of a conditional sentence. The specific offence descriptions were summaries of actual cases in which a conditional sentence had been imposed. As well, the offences included four of the five cases which were the object of the Supreme Court of Canada decisions released in January 2000. The offences used were the following:

1. Sexual assault: A man was convicted of several sexual assaults against his five-year-old stepdaughter. The crimes were committed over a period of several years.

2. Impaired driving causing bodily harm: After drinking heavily, the offender stole a car and drove at a high rate of speed through the city. He eventually lost control of the car and crashed. Two people were seriously injured. One person suffered permanent injuries that have had a devastating impact on her life.

3. Fraud (by an employee): The offender was convicted of fraud. He defrauded his employer of over a quarter of a million dollars. The fraud contributed to the company going out of business with the resulting loss of employment for many people.

4. Fraud (breach of trust by a lawyer): A lawyer was convicted of stealing $90,000 from his clients. His victims were in another country

and the fraud was only discovered as a result of a routine check of their bank accounts.

5. Common assault: A man has been convicted of assaulting his wife. She received medical treatment for minor injuries. The man has no prior criminal record.

6. Assault causing bodily harm: A 23-year-old man has been convicted of assault causing bodily harm. He hit and broke the nose of a man that he had a disagreement with in a local bar.

Finally, respondents were randomly assigned to one of three versions of a question in which the nature of information about the conditional sentence was manipulated, to see if this affected the level of public support for the conditional sentence. In one condition, participants were asked to make a choice between imposing a term of custody and a conditional sentence of equal duration. In the second condition, the same choice was provided, but the conditions of the conditional sentence order (e.g., to perform community service) were specified. In the third condition, respondents were asked to impose either a 6-month prison term or a 12-month conditional sentence. The purpose of the third condition was to see whether making the conditional sentence longer than the alternative of imprisonment would generate more public support.

Participants and Procedure

The survey employed a representative national sample and was conducted over the telephone between June 26 and July 3, 1999, by the Angus Reid Group, a national polling firm. Interviews were conducted with 1,501 respondents. A sample size of this nature has a margin of error of +/–2.5%, 19 times out of 20. The survey used a multistage sampling frame and computerized random digit dialling. This methodology ensures that every household has an equal probability of inclusion, regardless of whether the household's telephone number is listed or unlisted. (Interviewers are required to make up to six attempts before disqualifying an otherwise eligible respondent.) The data were weighted to reflect regional age and gender distributions according to the 1996 census data provided by Statistics Canada. All respondents were asked the general questions. Each respondent then was asked about two of the six scenarios (selection of scenarios was randomly determined) and received one of three versions of the experimental question. The refusal rate was 20%, which is comparable with the industry standard for telephone surveys. The survey required 20 minutes on average to administer.

RESULTS

Attitudes towards Sentencing Severity

Respondents were asked the following question which has been used repeatedly over the past 20 years: "In general, would you say that sentences handed down by the courts are too severe, about right or not severe enough?" Consistent with the results of previous research, the majority of respondents (69%) endorsed the view that sentences were too lenient. Only 1% of respondents were of the opinion that sentences were too harsh, while 28% responded that sentences were about right. (One percent chose "don't know" as a response.) The perception of leniency in sentencing that has been documented for a generation (see Roberts & Stalans, 2000, for a review) is therefore still prevalent. In fact, the percentage of the public expressing this view has fluctuated little over the past 15 years: In 1983, 80% of the public felt that sentences were too lenient (Doob & Roberts, 1983). However, the statistic emerging from the present survey does suggest some attenuation in the level of public dissatisfaction with sentence severity. Five years earlier, a comparable poll conducted by the same company found that 82% of the polled public felt that sentences were too lenient (Angus Reid Group, 1994). The widespread perception of leniency in sentencing helps to explain why public confidence ratings of judges are typically very low. A recent survey of the public found that only 6% expressed confidence in the courts (Environics Canada, 1998).

Support for Different Purposes of Sentencing

Respondents were next asked to identify the most important purpose of sentencing offenders. They were given four options and were asked to select one. The options included: (a) to discourage the offender or other potential offenders from committing further crimes (specific and general deterrence); (b) to impose a punishment that reflects the seriousness of the crime (just deserts); (c) to rehabilitate the offender (rehabilitation); and (d) to protect the public. No single sentencing purpose attracted the support of a majority of the respondents. In fact, support was fairly evenly distributed among the four sentencing purposes: protection of the public was chosen by 27%, just deserts by 26%, deterrence 24%, and rehabilitation 16%. Six percent endorsed the position that all four goals were of equal importance (1% responded "don't know"). These results are also consistent with previous research (e.g., Canadian Sentencing Commission, 1987) which found that, as with judges, no clear consensus exists among members of the public with respect to the most important purpose of sentencing.

Knowledge of Conditional Sentencing

It is important to know whether the public have a clear idea of the nature of conditional sentencing. Attitudes towards the new sanction can only be evaluated in light of public awareness. In order to evaluate the extent of public knowledge of the conditional sentence, respondents were provided with three descriptions and asked to identify the correct one. The two incorrect definitions described judicial interim release (bail) and conditional release from prison (full parole). Since only three options were offered, on the basis of chance alone we would expect that one-third of the sample would choose the correct definition.

Results demonstrated poor levels of public knowledge: fewer than half the respondents (43%) chose the correct definition. This statistic is not significantly different from chance ($\chi^{(1)} = 1.6$, $p < .05$). Almost as many (38%) chose the definition of parole, while 13% selected the definition of bail, and 6% responded "don't know." Clearly then, the intense media coverage of conditional sentencing since 1996 has not resulted in widespread awareness of the nature of the new sanction. A forward-entry multiple regression was conducted using the knowledge question as the dependent variable and the demographic variables as predictors. Respondent age, sex, and educational level emerged as significant predictors, but these variables accounted for relatively small amounts of variance: the adjusted r-square for the multiple regression model containing these variables was .027.

Support for Conditional Sentencing in Specific Cases

In order to explore the extent of public support for conditional sentencing as an alternative to imprisonment, a series of crime scenarios was used. The six cases were: sexual assault; impaired driving causing bodily harm; fraud by an employee; fraud by a lawyer; spousal assault; and assault. Prior to being asked to make a choice between the imposition of a prison term or a conditional sentence, participants were provided with a description of a conditional sentence, as follows:

"Since the conditional sentence is a new sentence, let me tell you how it works. Let's take the example of a 12-month conditional sentence. An offender

who receives a 12-month conditional sentence does not have to go to prison, provided that he or she follows certain conditions, such as staying out of trouble and reporting regularly to authorities. Other conditions imposed on the offender may include performing community service or attending an alcohol treatment program. If the offender violates these conditions, he or she may be sent to prison for part of the sentence. For example, an offender who violates their conditions after 9 months may be required to spend the last 3 months in prison. However, offenders who follow their conditions imposed will not have to go to prison."

In order to ensure that the definition was legally accurate, and captured the essence of the sentence, it was developed in conjunction with a provincial court judge with considerable experience with the new sanction. As well, respondents were given a clear description of a term of imprisonment, including the effect of release on parole. The description of imprisonment was as follows: "An offender who goes to prison will serve much of the sentence in custody. For example, an offender sent to prison for 12 months will probably serve six months in prison and the remainder of the sentence under supervision in the community." In this way, respondents were able to make an informed choice between a conditional sentence and a conventional term of imprisonment.

Having been provided with a description of the conditional sentence (and a term of imprisonment), respondents were given (at random) two of the six crime scenarios, and were asked to choose between the imposition of a term of imprisonment or a conditional sentence of imprisonment. Figure 14.1 summarizes the results for the six offences.

As can be seen, support for conditional sentencing (over imprisonment) varied from a low of 3% in the sexual assault case to a high of 76% in the case of assault causing bodily harm. It is perhaps not surprising that there was so little support for conditional sentencing in the

---

Figure 14.1   Public Support for Conditional Sentencing for Six Crimes

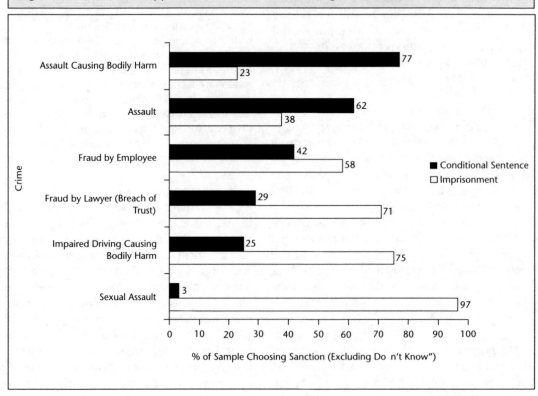

---

sexual assault scenario, as crimes of sexual aggression are generally regarded by the public as among the most serious (e.g., Roberts, 1988). In addition, this particular sexual assault involved several aggravating factors: the offender was related to the victim (and therefore was guilty of breach of trust); the victim was young (and therefore particularly vulnerable); and the offences occurred over a sustained period of time. Having used only a single case of sexual assault, it is unclear whether less serious cases of sexual assault would attract more public support for the imposition of a conditional sentence.

It is noteworthy that the majority of respondents who were asked to sentence the offender convicted of spousal assault favoured the impo-

sition of a conditional sentence rather than a term of imprisonment. Domestic violence is also an offence that attracts considerable public condemnation, yet almost two-thirds of the sample rejected sending the offender to prison, and favoured the imposition of a conditional sentence. This result suggests that the public see conditional sentencing as applying to more than just offenders convicted of crimes involving property.

Effects of Manipulating Information about the Conditional Sentence

The experimental hypothesis tested was that public support for the imposition of a conditional sentence would be greater if respondents were made aware of the specific conditions imposed on the offender. Respondents were provided with a description of a typical case of break and enter committed by an offender with several previous convictions for the same crime. The most recent court statistics reveal that an offender convicted of this offence with this criminal record would almost certainly be imprisoned (see Roberts & Grimes, 2000).

Respondents were randomly assigned to one of three experimental conditions. In one condition participants were given a choice between imposing six months in prison or six months conditional imprisonment in the community. Specifically, they were told that "The judge is trying to decide between a 6-month prison sentence or 6 months to be served in the community as a conditional sentence. Which do you think is appropriate, a 6-month prison sentence or a 6-month conditional sentence?"

Participants assigned to the second condition were given the same choice, except that the specific conditions attached to the conditional sentence were identified. Respondents were informed that if the offender received the conditional sentence, he would have to report to authorities, obey a curfew, make restitution, and perform some work for the community. (These are typical conditions imposed in conditional sentence orders.) Participants assigned to the third condition were given the expanded description of the conditional sentence but in this version were also told that the choice was between 6 months in prison or 12 months in the community.

Figure 14.2 summarizes respondents' reactions to the three versions. As can be seen, given the minimal amount of information about the conditional sentence, almost three-quarters (73%) of the sample favoured the

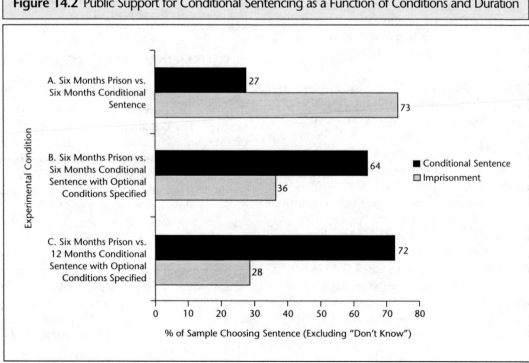

Figure 14.2 Public Support for Conditional Sentencing as a Function of Conditions and Duration

imposition of a conventional term of custody. This percentage is consistent with previous research in which members of the public were asked to sentence an offender convicted of this offence (Canadian Sentencing Commission, 1987). *However, the trend is almost completely reversed in responses from the participants in the second condition (where the conditions imposed on the offender were made salient): support for the conditional sentence rose from 27% to almost two-thirds of the sample (64%).* The difference between conditions is statistically significant ($\chi^{(1)} = 26.6$, $p < .001$). Only one respondent chose "don't know" as a response.

This finding sheds some important light on the source of public opposition to conditional sentencing. It suggests that it is not the presence of the offender in the community to which members of the public object, but rather the perception that the offender is merely spending the time at home, without being expected to do more than refrain from further offending. Simply making the conditions explicit to participants resulted in an almost complete reversal of support for the two sanctions (conditional and conventional imprisonment).[3]

Support for the conditional sentence was also significantly higher in the third condition, although the difference was much smaller than the difference between the first two conditions. When information about the conditions was added, support rose by 37%. Doubling the length of the conditional sentence increased support by only an additional 8%. This suggests that public support for the conditional sentence rests not so much upon merely making the sentence more punitive, but rather simply ensuring that conditions imposed on the offender are appropriate. If the public simply wanted to visit a greater degree of punishment on the offender, it would be reasonable to expect doubling the duration of the length of the sentence to result in much greater public support.

Replicating Previous Findings

Finally, we compared the results from one question on this survey with responses to the same question in the one previous survey of public attitudes towards conditional sentencing. In 1997, Marinos and Doob provided respondents in a survey of Ontario residents with the offence description described here as an assault involving two individuals in a bar. In the present survey, 77% of participants endorsed the imposition of a conditional sentence in this case. This is very close to the percentage of the sample endorsing a conditional sentence (71%) reported by Marinos and Doob in their study. The two surveys were conducted over two years apart, used different sample populations of the public (one provincial, the other national), and slightly different definitions of a conditional sentence. The fact that public support for the conditional sentence was nevertheless so similar suggests that there is considerable public support for the conditional sentence, for this profile of offender at least.

DISCUSSION AND CONCLUSIONS

This study has demonstrated both the limitations and the possibilities of Canada's newest sanction. The limitations on public acceptance of the conditional sentence clearly relate to crimes of sexual aggression. The public appear to be almost unanimous in their rejection of a conditional sentence for the more serious forms of sexual violence. What is not clear from this research is whether this public opposition is founded upon a perception that offenders convicted of such crimes should be excluded on grounds related to deservedness or dangerousness. Is the conditional sentence unjustifiable for crimes of sexual aggression because these offenders represent a threat to the community (in terms of re-offending) or because they simply deserve to be imprisoned?

Importance of Conditions Imposed on Offenders Serving Conditional Sentences

Although public awareness of the new sanction is limited and support is restricted to certain offences, the survey reveals a clear direction for trial court judges wishing to use the new sanction without provoking negative public reaction. In order to make a community-based sanction like the conditional sentence of imprisonment acceptable to the public, the court must ensure that significant conditions are imposed which have a real impact on the offender's life. In this way the sentence is not simply a "warning" to the offender. If this can be accomplished, the public will support the imposition of a conditional sentence over a term of imprisonment, even for a serious personal injury offence. Of course, if the news media do not accurately convey the conditional sentence to members of the public, then the most well-crafted conditional sentence will still attract public disapproval. To date, news media coverage of conditional sentencing has been poor, focussing upon its potential for leniency in sentencing and overlooking the restrictions imposed on the offender's lifestyle.

These findings also provide strong support for the position of the Supreme Court of Canada in its recent guideline judgement (*R. v. Proulx*) with regard to conditional sentencing. In that unanimous decision, the Court argued that it was important to add punitive conditions to a conditional sentence in order to (a) distinguish the new sanction from a term of probation, and (b) to prevent the public from perceiving the sentence as being too lenient, and therefore inappropriate for all but the least serious offences. The reactions of participants in this experimental survey provide empirical support for the Court's position, and show that it is not the notion of the offender's presence in the community (rather than prison) to which people object, but rather the imposition

of a community sentence which carries insufficient conditions to have an impact on the offender. Once these conditions are added, a conditional sentence can be a preferable alternative to a term of custody.

There is a more general lesson for other community-based sanctions, such as probation. The public clearly accept the principle that offenders can be adequately punished while remaining in the community. However, public support turns upon the presence of conditions that have an impact on the offender's lifestyle. If community sanctions are ever to achieve general acceptance as a legitimate alternative to prison (see Doob, 1990) these penalties must impose significant restrictions on offenders. This is particularly true for the conditional sentence, which, unlike a term of probation, is supposed to carry the same penal "value" as a term of custody.

Implications for Critics and Advocates of Conditional Sentencing

The survey generated support for both critics and advocates of community-based imprisonment. Advocates can take comfort from the fact that public support for conditional sentencing was not restricted to nonviolent crimes (as critics have contended). Also, when the conditions were made salient, most people preferred to impose the conditional sentence rather than a term of custody in a correctional institution. On the other hand, critics of the new sanction can derive support for their position that the public are nearly unanimous in their opposition to the imposition of a conditional sentence in cases of serious sexual aggression. This finding may be of interest to trial judges: in the three years since its creation, approximately 2,000 conditional sentences were imposed for sexual offences (Roberts & La Prairie, 2000).

The results of this survey suggest that there is a considerable lag between passage of a criminal justice reform and public awareness of the legislation. Three years after the creation of the conditional sentence, during which time the sentence was frequently in the news, most people are still unaware of the nature of the new disposition. Moreover, the test of public knowledge in this survey was a relatively easy one: respondents had one chance in three of guessing correctly, and the wrong options did not include a definition of probation. Since a term of probation is quite similar to a conditional term of imprisonment, had we included probation as a response alternative the percentage of respondents with the correct answer would have diminished considerably. An important challenge for the criminal justice system is therefore to improve the extent of public knowledge with respect to the new sanction. If this is accomplished, conditional sentencing will attract greater support from the community, and judges will feel more confident in imposing such sentences. Only then is there a chance that the purpose underlying the conditional sentence—reducing the number of admissions to provincial correctional institutions—will be fulfilled.[4]

STUDY QUESTIONS

1. On pages 167–168, the authors stated that their sampling method "[ensured] that every household [had] an equal probability of inclusion, regardless of whether the household's telephone number is listed or unlisted." To what extent can we have absolute confidence in this claim? Which households would be excluded by the sampling method chosen? Are there any social groups who would have been more likely to be excluded?

2. How might the method of sampling be related to results about public perceptions of conditional sentencing?

3. Why did the research design that was used allow the authors to support conclusions about changes in public attitudes relating to conditional sentencing?

4. Why was it important for the authors to report the two nonsignificant findings from the experiment?

NOTES

1. Five of the six conditional sentence judgements issued by the Supreme Court in January 2000 (including the unanimous leading decision in *R. v. Proulx*) are published in the April 2000 issue of the *Criminal Reports*.

2. A summary of this survey's results can also be found in Marinos and Doob, 1999.

3. It is important to note that participants in the first condition (no description of specific conditions) were nevertheless aware that conditions would be imposed on the offender. As noted, all participants in the survey had received a description of the conditional sentence that included the information that conditions would be imposed on the offender (they just were not specified in detail).

4. Preliminary research on the impact of conditional sentencing suggests that although a significant number of such sentences have been imposed, the incarceration rate has not declined (see Reed and Roberts, 1999).

REFERENCES

Angus Reid Group (1994). News Release. *Attitudes towards sentencing.* Ottawa, ON: Angus Reid Group.

Canadian Sentencing Commission (1987). *Sentencing Reform: A Canadian approach.* Ottawa, ON: Supply and Services Canada.

Covell, K., & Howe, B. (1996). Public attitudes and juvenile justice in Canada. *The International Journal of Children's Rights, 4,* 345–355.

Cumberland, J., & Zamble, E. (1992). General and specific measures of attitudes toward early release of criminal offenders. *Canadian Journal of Behavioural Science, 24,* 442–455.

Daubney, D., & Parry, G. (1999). An overview of Bill C-41 (The Sentencing Reform Act). In J.V. Roberts & D.P. Cole (Eds.), *Making sense of sentencing.* Toronto, ON: University of Toronto Press.

Doob, A.N. (1990). Community sanctions and imprisonment: Hoping for a miracle but not even bothering to pray for it. *Canadian Journal of Criminology, 32*, 415–428.

Doob, A.N., & Roberts, J.V. (1983). *Sentencing: An analysis of the public's view.* Ottawa, ON: Department of Justice Canada.

Doob, A.N., & Roberts, J.V. (1988). Public punitiveness and public knowledge of the facts: Some Canadian surveys. In N. Walker & M. Hough (Eds.), *Public attitudes to sentencing. Cambridge Studies in Criminology.* Aldershot, UK: Gower.

Environics Canada (1998). Survey of public confidence in the justice system. Ottawa, ON: Environics Canada.

Healy, P. (1999). Questions and answers on conditional sentencing. *Criminal Law Quarterly, 42,* 12–37.

Higginbottom, S., & Zamble, E. (1988). Categorizations of homicide cases: Agreement, accuracy and confidence of public assignments. *Canadian Journal of Criminology, 30,* 351–366.

La Prairie, C. (1999). *Conditional sentencing: Final report.* Ottawa, ON: Department of Justice Canada.

Manson, A. (1997). Finding a place for conditional sentences. *Criminal Reports, 19,* 283–300.

Marinos, V., & Doob, A.N. (1997). *A Preliminary examination of public views of conditional sentences of imprisonment.* Ottawa, ON: Department of Justice Canada.

Marinos, V., & Doob, A.N. (1999). Understanding public attitudes toward conditional sentences of imprisonment. *Criminal Reports, 21,* 31–41.

National Post (1999, May 15). Law lets convicts serve time in style. p. A2.

Paciocco, D. (1999). *Getting away with murder.* Toronto, ON: Irwin Law.

R. v. Getkate, Ontario Court (General Division) November 10, 1998.

R. v. Proulx, (2000). (S.C.C.) *Criminal Reports, (5th) 30*: 1–49.

Reed, M., & Roberts, J.V. (1999). Adult correctional trends in Canada, 1997–1998. *Juristat,* Vol. 19, No.4.

Roberts, J.V. (1988). *Public opinion and sentencing: the surveys of the Canadian Sentencing Commission.* Ottawa, ON: Department of Justice Canada.

Roberts, J.V. (1992). Public opinion, crime and criminal justice. In M. Tonry (Ed.), *Crime and justice: A review of research.* Chicago, IL: University of Chicago Press.

Roberts, J.V. (1994). *Public knowledge of crime and criminal justice.* Ottawa, ON: Department of Justice Canada.

Roberts, J.V. (1997). The sword of Damocles: Conditional sentencing in Canada. *Canadian Criminal Law Review, 2,* 183–206.

Roberts, J.V., & Cole, D.P. (1999). *Making sense of sentencing.* Toronto, ON: University of Toronto Press.

Roberts. J.V., Doob, A.N., & Marinos, V. (1999). *Judicial attitudes to conditional terms of imprisonment: Results of a national survey.* Ottawa, ON: Department of Justice Canada.

Roberts, J.V., & Grimes, C. (2000). Adult criminal court statistics, 1998/99. *Juristat,* Vol. 20, No. 1.

Roberts, J.V., & La Prairie, C. (2000). *Research on conditional sentencing, 1996–1999.* Ottawa, ON: Department of Justice Canada.

Roberts, J.V., & Stalans, L.S. (2000). *Public opinion, crime and criminal justice.* Boulder, CO: Westview Press.

Tremblay. P., Cordeau, G., & Ouimet, M. (1994). Underpunishing offenders: Towards a theory of legal tolerance. *Canadian Journal of Criminology, 25,* 407–434.

Zamble, E., & Annesley, P. (1987). Some determinants of public attitudes toward the police. *Journal of Police Science and Police Administration, 15,* 285–290.

Zamble, E., & Kalm, K. (1990). General and specific measures of public attitudes toward sentencing. *Canadian Journal of Behavioural Science, 22,* 327–337.

Chapter 15

Breaking Up Is Hard to Do: The Heartbreak of Dichotomizing Continuous Data

David L. Streiner

Source: From "Breaking up is hard to do: the heartbreak of dichotomizing continuous data." By D.L. Streiner, *The Canadian Journal of Psychiatry*, 47(3): pp. 262–6 (2002).

Those of you who are old enough may remember Neil Sedaka singing "Breaking Up Is Hard to Do." If only that were true when it comes to the variables we use in research! Many times (I would say far too many), a researcher uses a continuous measure, such as a depression inventory, as an outcome variable and then dichotomizes it— above or below some cut-point, for example, or the number of people who did and did not show a 50% reduction in their scores from baseline to follow-up.[1] Less often, but again far too frequently, researchers may assign patients to different groups by dichotomizing or trichotomizing scores from a continuous scale.

Over the years, several arguments have tried to justify this practice. Perhaps the most common one runs something like this: "Clinicians have to make dichotomous decisions to treat or not to treat, so it makes sense to have a binary outcome." Another rationale that is offered is, "Physicians find it easier to understand the results when they're expressed as proportions or odds ratios. They have difficulty grasping the meaning of beta weights and other indices that emerge when we use continuous variables." In this article, I'll try to show that you pay a very stiff penalty in terms of power or sample size when continuous variables are broken up, with the consequent risk of a Type II error (that is, failing to detect real differences). But before we begin, let me assume the role of a marriage counsellor and see whether the arguments in favour of splitting up are really viable.

The rationale for dichotomizing outcomes because clinical decisions are binary fails on 3 grounds. The primary one is that it confuses measurement with decision making. The purpose of most research is to discover relations— relations between or among variables or between treatment interventions and outcomes. The more accurate the findings, the better the decisions that we can make; that is, the findings come first and the decision making follows. As we will see, findings come more readily and more accurately when we retain the scaling of continuous variables. The second reason is that all the research using the old dichotomy becomes useless if the cut-point changes. For example, the definition of hypertension used to be 160/95.[2] If we defined the outcome of intervention trials dichotomously—with above 160/95 being hypertensive and below being normotensive—then those findings would become useless after the definition changed to 140/90.[3] If we expressed the outcome as a continuum, however, the values of beta coefficients and similar indices showing the effects of various risk and protective factors would not change at all: if we wanted to use statistics such as odds ratios (ORs) or the percentage of patients who improved, it would be a trivial matter to recalculate the results. We have a similar situation in psychiatry. The diagnosis of antisocial personality disorder (ASP), for example, is a binary one: the person either does or does not satisfy the diagnostic criteria (that is, a certain number of symptoms are present). However, Livesley and others maintain that ASP and many other disorders should actually be seen as a continuum: the more symptoms that are checked off, the more of the trait the person has.[4] If the number of symptoms necessary to meet the criteria were to change, as occurred when DSM-IV replaced DSM-III-R, then much previous research using a dichotomous diagnosis would have to be discarded. If the diagnosis were expressed as the number of symptoms present, though, it would be relatively easy to reinterpret the findings using the new criteria.

Finally, whether to hospitalize a patient with suicidal ideation or to discharge a patient with symptoms of schizophrenia may be binary decisions, but many treatments—perhaps most—fall along a continuum involving the dosage or strength of a medication and the number and frequency of therapy sessions.

As for the argument that physicians are more comfortable with statistics based on categorical measures, we are likely dealing with both a base canard that they, like old dogs, cannot learn new tricks and a vicious circle. As long as the belief persists, studies will be designed, analyzed, and reported using proportions and ORs, meaning that physicians will not have the opportunity to become more comfortable with other approaches.

First, I'll give some examples of how dichotomizing can lead us astray, and then I'll use these examples to discuss why this is the case.

EXAMPLE 1

Let's look at the data in Table 15.1, which shows scores on a scale for 2 groups, each with 10 subjects. Let's assume that, if we were to dichotomize the scale, we would use a criterion for "caseness" of 15/16: people with scores from 1 to 15 would be considered normal, and those with scores of 16 and over would be defined as cases. The mean for Group 1 is 11.70, and the mean for Group 2 is 16.80. There is slightly more than a 5-point difference between the groups, and the average of the first group is well below the cut-off of 15/16, while the average of the second group is above the cut-point. If we used a *t*-test to compare the groups, we'd find that $t(18) = 2.16$, $P = 0.045$. That is, there is a statistically significant difference between the means. Now, let's dichotomize the results and count the number of people above and below the cut-point in each group. What we'd find is shown in Table 15.2. Because 2 of the cells have frequencies below 5, we'd use a Fisher's exact test, rather than a chi-square test, and we'd find that the *P* level is 0.057. In other words, the difference is not statistically significant.

Table 15.1 Data on an Outcome Measure for 2 Groups

Group 1	Group 2
9	16
14	12
13	25
12	14
5	16
5	9
12	10
22	23
13	22
12	21

Table 15.2 The Number of People in Each Group above and below a Cut-Point of 15/16

	Group 1	Group 2
15 and below	9	4
16 and below	1	6

EXAMPLE 2

In the second example, we have 40 subjects, measured on 4 variables, A through D. If we were to correlate these variables, we'd find the results shown in the upper triangle of Table 15.3. Of the 6 correlations, 5 are significant at the $P < 0.01$ level. Now, we'll do a median split on each of these variables, so that roughly one-half of the subjects fall above, and one-half below, the cut-point. If we reran the correlations, we would find the results in the lower triangle of the same table. In every case, the correlations are lower—sometimes substantively so—and only 2 of the 6 correlations are significant at the $P < 0.01$ level.

Taking this example a bit further, we can run a regression equation, with A as the dependent variable (DV) and B through D as the predictors. Keeping the variables as continua, we'd find the multiple R is 0.767 and $R^2 = 0.588$, which would lead to thoughts of publication and promotion for most people. If we dichotomized the variables, however, we'd find that the multiple R is 0.460, with an associated R^2 of 0.211, which might jeopardize that promotion by at least a year. (Purists might say that we should really use a logistic regression with a dichotomous DV. If we did, we'd find the Cox and Snell pseudo-R^2 to be an even more disappointing 0.20.)

Table 15.3 Correlations among 4 Variables[a]				
	A	**B**	**C**	**D**
A		0.59[b]	0.56[b]	0.70[b]
B	0.3		0.28	0.84[b]
C	0.16	0.25		0.39
D	0.45[b]	0.55[b]	0.2	

[a] Correlations above the diagonal are for the variables as continual; below the diagonal as dichotomized
[b] $P < 0.01$

WHY THIS OCCURS

These examples illustrate 2 points. First, the magnitude of the effects (for example, the differences between groups, the correlations between variables, and the amount of variance explained by the regression) were lower—sometimes dramatically lower—when we took continuous variables and treated them as dichotomies. Second, findings that were significant using continuous variables were sometimes not significant when we dichotomized those variables. Let's examine each of these issues separately.

Dichotomizing variables results in a tremendous loss of information. If the values in example 1 were scores on a Beck Depression Inventory (BDI), the possible range would be between 0 and 69. When we dichotomize this scale, we are saying, in essence, that there is no difference between a score of 0 and one of 15 (both would be coded as 1), nor between scores of 16 and 69 (both coded as 2). At the same time, we are making a qualitative difference between scores of 15 and 16. This doesn't seem conceptually logical and ignores the problem of measurement error. As we discussed in previous articles in this series,[5,6] every observed score (for example, a numerical value on a questionnaire, a blood level, or the number of diagnostic criteria that are satisfied) is made up of 2 parts: a "true" score, which is never seen, plus some error. The more reliable the scale, the smaller the error and the closer the observed score to the true score. But, since no measurement has a reliability of 1.00 (and this includes lab tests as well as paper-and-pencil ones), every score has some degree of error associated with it. We also assume that the errors are random and have a mean of 0; that is, over a large number of people or over many observations on the same person (or both), the errors will tend to cancel each other out. This means that, if we treat the scores as numbers along a continuum, we may misplace a person to some degree, and this will be reflected in, for example, a lower correlation between the scale score and some other variable. However, because the errors are random with a mean of 0, there will not be any bias in the relation.

But the situation is different when we dichotomize the scale. Now, for people near the cut-point, the measurement error may result not just in a score that's slightly off but in their being misclassified into the wrong group. A person suffering from depression, with a true score of 16 and a relatively small error of –1 point, would end up in the group without depression. Thus, we can see that using a scale as a continuum will present us with some degree of random error (which is inevitable), but dichotomization can easily result in misclassification error.

Another reason dichotomizing variables puts us behind the eight ball is a function of the statistical tests themselves. All statistical procedures can be seen as a ratio between a signal and noise.[6] The "signal" is the information that we've captured in the measurement—the difference between group means, the relation between 2 variables, and so forth. The "noise" is the error, usually captured by the differences among the subjects within the same group (when we're comparing means), deviations from a linear relation (in correlational tests), or misclassifications (in procedures such as chi-squared, ORs, and relative risks). As we mentioned, dichotomization results in a loss of information, so that the "signal" is weaker than when we use continua. Not surprisingly, tests based on dichotomous variables are generally less powerful than those based on continuous variables. Suissa[7] determined that a dichotomized outcome is at best only 67% as efficient as a continuous one; that is, if you need 50 subjects in each group to demonstrate statistical significance with a continuous scale, you would need 75 subjects per group to show the same effect after dichotomizing. In fact, though, most clinical scales are split at a clinically important point that doesn't usually correspond to the best place from a statistical point of view, with the result that the efficiency rarely approaches even 67% and may drop to as low as 10% (that is, the required sample size is 10 times as large). Similarly, if the dichotomy is statistically ideal, resulting in one-half the people being in one group and one-half in the other, the correlation of that variable with another one is reduced by about 20%. The more the split deviates from 50–50, the more the correlation is reduced. By the time the division is 90–10, the correlation is reduced by 41%.[8]

IT'S NOT ALL BAD

Up to now, we've treated categorization of a continuum as an unmitigated disaster with no redeeming features. At the risk of appearing to be a Pollyanna who can find positive things to say about the worst situations, there are in fact a few situations wherein we actually should divide a continuous variable into a dichotomy or an ordinal variable. These, though, are based on statistical considerations; they are not based on clinical considerations or on what is convenient.

Most parametric statistical tests assume that the variables are normally distributed. While we can often get away with variables that deviate from normality to some degree (and, as Micceri has shown, almost all do[9]), there are limits. One of these is found when a variable resembles a J-shaped distribution; that is, most of the subjects clump at one end, and the rest trail off in the opposite direction. This occurs most frequently if there is a "wall," or limit, at one end but not at the other. For example, a population survey may find that most people have had no psychiatric admissions, and a small proportion have had a single admission. Then the numbers trickle off, with a few people having a large number of admissions. There's a lower limit, in that you can't have fewer than 0 admissions, but no upper limit. We can try to transform the variable, but if it's very highly skewed even this won't help. The only solution is to dichotomize (none versus any) or trichotomize it (none, 1 to 2, 3 or more, for example), and treat it as an ordinal variable.

Similarly, we may feel that the relation between 2 variables is not linear. For example, we may suspect that, within the range of low income (say up to $10 000 a year), the actual dollar amount is unimportant, insofar as it buffers against stress, while above a certain amount ($60 000, for example), more money doesn't provide more protection. Within the middle range, however, we may suspect that there is a linear relation. In other words, the relation between income and buffering looks like an elongated S. We can try to model this with a complicated, higher-order equation, but it's often easier to divide income into 3 categories, and again, treat it as if it were an ordinal variable.

CONCLUSIONS

Except when the variable deviates considerably from normal, splitting a variable into categories results in lost information, the requirement to use less powerful nonparametric tests, and increased probability of a Type II error. We are most often much further ahead to retain the continuous nature of the variable and analyze the data using the appropriate statistics.

This discussion has focused primarily on taking data that were gathered as continua and then splitting them into categories. The other side of this is that we should gather the data as continua whenever possible. For example, an item on a questionnaire might look like the following:

How old were you on your last birthday?

- ❏ 15–19
- ❏ 20–29
- ❏ 30–39
- ❏ 40–49
- ❏ 50–59
- ❏ 60–65
- ❏ Over 65

It would be better, however, to ask the question, "How old were you on your last birthday?": _____ years.

If you use the first format, you lose fine-grained information, and you're forced to use those categories in all subsequent analyses. With the second format, you can later split age any way you want (although I don't know why you would want to, after all that's been said), and you have all the advantages of a continuous variable. The only possible exception may be income: people may feel more comfortable reporting it within a range, rather than reporting the exact amount, but the jury is still out on this.

So, in conclusion, the one word of advice about turning continuous variables into dichotomies is—don't!

STUDY QUESTIONS

1. Why is the concept of measurement so important when conducting research?

2. What is a Type II error? What does the concept relate to and what are the implications of having a Type II error in your study?

3. Why is it important to understand the type of variables you use in a study?

4. What rationales does the author offer for categorizing continuous data?

REFERENCES

1. Keller M.B., McCullough J.P., Klein D.N., Arnow B., Dunner D.L., Gelenberg A.J., and others. A comparison of nefazodone, the cognitive behavioral-analysis system of psychotherapy, and their combination for the treatment of chronic depression. *New England J Medicine,* 2000;342:1462–70.

2. Arterial Hypertension. Report of WHO Expert Committee. Technical Report Series, No. 628. Geneva: WHO; 1978.

3. Zanchetti A. Guidelines for the management of hypertension: the World Health Organization/ International Society of Hypertension view. *J Hypertension Supplements,* 1995;13:S119–S122.

4. Livesley W.J., Schroeder M.L., Jackson D.L., Jang K.L. Categorical distinctions in the study of personality disorder: implications for classification. *J Abnormal Psychology,* 1994;103:6–17.

5. Streiner D.L. A checklist for evaluating the usefulness of rating scales. *Can J Psychiatry,* 1993;38:140–8.

6. Norman G.R., Streiner D.L. *Biostatistics: the bare essentials* (2nd ed.). Toronto: BC Decker; 2000.

7. Suissa S. Binary methods for continuous outcomes: a parametric alternative. *J Clin Epidemiology,* 1991;44:241–8.

8. Hunter J.E., Schmidt F.L. Dichotomization of continuous variables: the implications for meta-analysis. *J Applied Psychology,* 1990;75:334–49.

9. Micceri T. The unicorn, the normal curve, and other improbable creatures. *Psychological Bulletin,* 1989;105:156–66.

Chapter 16

Gender Differences in Survey Respondents' Written Definitions of Date Rape

Norine Verberg, Serge Desmarais, Eileen Wood, and Charlene Senn

Source: Reprinted from *The Canadian Journal of Human Sexuality*, 2000, Vol. 9, Issue 3, pp. 181–191.

INTRODUCTION

The feminist anti-rape movement has had a dramatic impact on public awareness of rape and other forms of sexual violence, and feminist perspectives have shaped much of the discourse surrounding these issues (Begin, 1989; Boyle, 1984; Donat & D'Emilio, 1992; Hinch, 1988; McNickle-Rose, 1977; Osborne, 1984; Pride, 1981; Roberts & Mohr, 1994; Sorenson & White, 1992). In the 1970s and early 1980s, Canadian feminists were leaders in lobbying the federal government to address the sexism inherent in the prevailing rape legislation, a campaign that led eventually to the new sexual assault law (Bill C-127) and to subsequent legislative amendments, such as Bill C-49, which set guidelines regarding the definition of consent and the admissibility of a woman's sexual history during a trial (Roberts & Mohr, 1994). The new sexual assault law thus eliminated the term "rape" from the criminal code in favour of emphasizing the assaultive, non-consensual, and non-gendered nature of the offence. Yet the term "date rape" is still used to denote and educate about one aspect of this area of social concern. We therefore ask here whether the perspectives that shaped the new legislation are now embodied in public thinking about the topic. The study examines women's and men's written definitions of date rape with a view to determining the extent to which their understandings of date rape/sexual assault are influenced by gender and age and by traditional versus non-gendered understandings of rape.

Background

The process of drafting the new sexual assault legislation involved considerable debate (Begin, 1989; Kasinsky, 1978; National Association of Women and the Law, 1979, 1981; Osborne, 1984). One key issue was whether the word rape should remain in the legislation or be replaced by the term sexual assault. In the early 1980s, rape (R.S.C. 1970, c. C-34, section 143) was defined as an act of sexual intercourse (i.e., vaginal penetration) committed by a man against a woman without her consent or with her consent if it was extorted by means of threats or fear of physical assault, by impersonating a woman's husband, or by false representation of the act (e.g., proposal of marriage) when the act did not occur between husband and wife (Department of Justice, 1990). In addition, the offence of rape was situated in Part IV of the Criminal Code under the heading "Sexual Offences, Public Morals and Disorderly Conduct."

Many feminists and others believed that the legal emphasis on rape reinforced a rape myth—that rape is a type of moral or personality offence (i.e., a "sex crime"). In addition, the social construction of rape law mirrored unequal gender relations, such as patriarchal power and privilege in marriage (Roberts & Mohr, 1994). Some proponents of legislative change thus argued that use of the term sexual assault, because it encompassed rape and other acts of sexual violence and provided legal recourse to female and male victims, was the best way to establish that rape and other forms of sexual violence are, in fact, types of assault (i.e., a "power crime") (Clarke & Lewis, 1977; Hinch, 1988; Osborne, 1994). This view was not universal and some feminists who wanted new legislation lobbied to keep the term rape because it reflected the gendered nature of sexual violence (see Los, 1994; Roberts & Mohr, 1994). In the end, rape law reform resulted in the so-called "degendering" of the offences subsumed under the term sexual assault. In addition, the new sexual assault laws were relocated in Part VI of the code under the heading "Offences Against the Person and Reputation". Bill C-127 thus represented an attempt to eliminate sex discrimination in the law in keeping with the equality clause in the Charter of Rights and Freedoms (Roberts & Mohr, 1994).

Although current discourse about rape reiterates the key points made during the debate about Bill C-127, other related issues have emerged as well. The first of these issues is a dual and contradictory understanding of the role of gender in shaping perspectives on rape/sexual assault. On the one hand, rape is now defined as gender-neutral. It is any assaultive act of a sexual nature perpetrated or experienced by either a man or a woman. On the other hand, concern persists that the gender-neutral term detracts from the fact that rape is a gendered act of violence (Roberts & Mohr, 1994), a view expressed by Los (1994) who wrote that the "systematic de-sexualization of rape might actually obscure the relationship between male power, violence, and sex" (p. 33). From this perspective it seems inappropriate to remove "rape" from the law given that it is such a serious crime rooted in gender inequality. The

expression of this dual understanding of rape is evident in courses on sexual assault awareness and prevention. A common practice in these courses is to teach students that *anyone* can be a victim of sexual violence (Sorenson & White, 1992). Yet these courses also report statistics indicating that women are far more likely to experience victimization, most often by a man known to them (Sorenson & White, 1992). Moreover, feminist-based education programs specifically teach that sexual violence is gendered (Gauthier, 1992; Lenskyj, 1992). Thus, the current discourse would suggest that rape is gender-neutral in theory and, for the most part, gender-specific in practice.

A second key point concerning the discourse about rape/sexual assault is the claim that we lack a clear, concrete definition of sexual assault (Hinch, 1988; Osborne, 1994). Sexual assault is currently defined as any act of sexual contact that takes place by force and without consent, ranging from sexual touching to oral, anal, or genital contact (Gauthier, 1992; Lenskyj, 1992; Sorenson & White, 1992). There is little agreement on what constitutes consent and/or force. For example, definitions of consent can range from verbal to physical behaviours, and such definitions can include or omit the ability of participants to provide consent (i.e., whether influenced by intoxication, unconsciousness). The much-publicized Antioch College case serves as one of the best exemplars of how challenging it is to develop an agreed upon understanding of consent. In this case, the school administration clearly articulated the expectations for consent, yet received criticism for expectations that were seen as unrealistic and inappropriate (see Hickman & Muehlenhard, 1999; Muehlenhard, 1995/1996; Muehlenhard, Powch, Phelps & Giusti, 1992, for a discussion). The point is clear that even when the guidelines for consent are made explicit, agreement is not universal (see also Humphreys, 2000). Interestingly, education programs continue to emphasize consensual contact as a critical component of their programs (Sorensen & White, 1992) despite the fact "that consent is complex and can take many forms" (Muehlenhard, 1999, p. 270), and that a common understanding of what constitutes consent is difficult to find.

A third key point is that a similar lack of agreement prevails on what constitutes force. The breadth of definitions for force in feminist-based educational programs ranges from the use of psychological or emotional pressure to the use of physical force or violence (Gauthier, 1992; Lenskyj, 1992; Sorenson & White, 1992). Again, despite the lack of agreement in definition, force remains an important point in educational programs.

Since the new sexual assault legislation has been in place for some time and debate and discussion about it was so widely publicized (Roberts & Mohr, 1994), one might expect to find some uniformity in the perspectives of women and men on the topic of date rape. Yet there are a number of reasons to think that women may be more likely than men to hold gender-specific understandings of date rape. First, the feminist perspective on rape that helped to shape the new legislation has been discussed in the media, particularly in women's magazines and feminist magazines (Verberg, 1998), as well as in women's studies and gender relations courses, which, based on the first author's personal correspondence with Women's Studies Program Coordinators at three Canadian Universities, tend to have extremely high female and low male enrolment. In addition, prevalence research indicates that women are far more likely to experience sexual assault than men (DeKeseredy, Schwartz & Tait, 1993; Koss, Gidycz & Wisniewski, 1987). With respect to possible age differences in perspectives on date rape, one might expect younger cohorts to have greater exposure to and familiarity with recent conceptualizations of date rape because educational institutions are now playing a

greater role in providing date rape awareness and prevention programs.

Given the importance of identifying factors that influence how individuals perceive sexual assault in general and date rape in particular, the present study examines current characterizations of date rape through a qualitative and quantitative analysis of written definitions provided by a sample of single (i.e., unmarried) women and men of various ages. Four issues were assessed in relation to respondents' understanding: Was date rape perceived as gendered or gender neutral?; was it identified with specific types of sexual acts or behaviours?; how were the issues of consent and use of force understood in relation to date rape?; how did the context of the situation influence perceptions of date rape?

We also sought to determine whether age of respondent had an impact on these perceptions and to assess, albeit indirectly, whether the feminist perspectives that shaped the current Canadian sexual assault legislation have been absorbed into contemporary perceptions of date rape.

METHOD

Participants

Participants included 102 women and 68 men ranging in age from 18 to 85 years, all of whom lived in the same mid-sized Canadian city and indicated that they were single and available to date. Participants were recruited from a number of recreational and leisure groups/centres (e.g., gyms, retirement centres, social clubs) as well as through advertisements posted in public areas (e.g., libraries, grocery stores). The age distribution of the sample was: 18–21 years (25%); 22–29 years (24%); 30–39 years (23%); 40–59 years (19%); and 60 or older (9%). A sizeable majority of participants was thus under 40 years of age (72%) and 91% were under 60 years of age.

Procedure

Participants were recruited for a larger study of positive and negative dating experiences across the life cycle that also included an assessment of participants' definitions of date rape. Individuals who agreed to participate were either given or sent a survey package containing a letter of introduction, the survey and a stamped return envelope. Participants completed the information independently and mailed their information to the researchers. All responses were anonymous, and 100% of those who agreed to participate and received surveys returned them. The analyses presented here are based on written responses to the open-ended question that asked, "How would you define date rape?"

Qualitative Analyses

Analytic qualitative analysis followed Strauss's (1987) and Glaser and Strauss's (1967) constant comparative method. The first stage of the analysis involved open (or substantive) coding of the data. Open coding involved reading the definitions for specific words and/or themes that emerged from the respondents' definitions. Two of the authors did the open coding independently, and then compared the themes that emerged from their reading of the respondents' definitions. Both coders identified five key themes that emerged from the data. The themes were: (1) gender, (2) consent, (3) force, (4) context, and (5) type of sex act.

The second stage of the analysis involved axial coding. In this stage, the coders did more intensive coding around each theme to discern whether further distinctions could be drawn. For instance, in the case of consent, the coders observed that most participants mentioned its relevance to the behaviour being classified as date rape; however, some participants explained which types of verbal and/or non-verbal behaviours they believed were indicative of consent or a lack of consent. The two coders, working independently, agreed on the categories within each theme (axial coding). To assess the reliability of the coding scheme, 18% of the data were scored by both coders with over 95% agreement. The few differences that were noted actually provided clarification of the coding system. Coding thus proved to be reliable. Note that the coders did not have information on participant gender during the stages of open and axial coding.

Selective coding, which assesses links among categories, was also used (Glaser & Strauss, 1987). The selective coding indicated that variations in the written definitions were influenced by gender. Finally, quantitative procedures were used to determine associations among the 5 themes and whether differences emerged as a function of gender or age.

RESULTS

Qualitative Findings

Explanations and examples of the five themes that emerged from open coding of participants' written perspectives on date rape process are presented below along with a categorization of the responses within each of the themes.

Theme 1: Type of Sexual Act or Acts Referred to in the Definition Respondents differed in terms of how they defined the sex act in their definition of "date rape". The three main groups that emerged for defining date rape based on the type of sexual act or acts involved were: (1) date rape involves sexual intercourse (i.e., "had sex"," intercourse", "rape", or "had sexual relations"); (2) date rape involves forced sexual contact (e.g., "Date rape is when two people who have decided to go out on a date, either in public or private, become sexually active. It doesn't necessarily have to be sexual intercourse; any petting or fondling against one's will is also date rape" (18-year-old woman); and (3) no reference was made to a sex act in the written text.

Theme 2: Understanding of Consent Most respondents mentioned consent in their definition. In addition, many respondents listed behaviours that were indicative of consent or lack of consent. Responses were divided into 2 groups, those that simply mentioned lack of consent as an aspect of rape (such as "against one's will", "without prior consent", "does not want to", or "unwanted"), and those that both mentioned the issue of consent and defined the behaviour that indicated the lack of consent. For example:

Any intercourse that is not mutually agreed upon by two, coherent people, that is, clearly understood. If one partner is drunk and cannot get "no" across, the other partner is guilty of rape. (44-year-old woman)

Where a woman is forced against her will to do something. The man feels she must want it, and though she says no, or struggles, he has sex with her. (22-year-old man)

When sex is forced upon a person by their date, despite the fact that the "rapist" has been told to stop. It could also be considered date rape if a person is rendered incapable of granting consent (example: extremely drunk) and sexual intercourse is carried out while this person is incapacitated. (36-year-old woman)

Theme 3: Understanding of the Use of Force
Three groups of responses were noted. Most respondents mentioned the use of force in their definition of date rape, and usually the relevance of force was indicated by the terms "force" or "forced". As in the case of consent, some respondents specified what behaviour was indicative of force, using phrases such as "persisting and pushing", "physical assertion" or "proceeds without consent". Consider the following examples:

When your date tries to convince, coerce, or force you to have sex with him when it's really NOT what you want when you say "NO!" and he keeps on trying—keeps trying to convince you to "give in"—or keeps fondling hoping you'll get turned on. Problem:

you may not be strong enough to MAKE your no mean NO! He may persist, cajole, and convince you to do what he wants. (44-year-old woman)

Date rape occurs when one partner does not respect the wishes of the other not to engage in sexual intercourse and instead forces them either forcibly or by perseverance to submit to intercourse although it is against their wishes. (22-year-old woman)

A small proportion of definitions did not mention or define force.

Theme 4: Context: Dating versus Any Acquaintance The term "date rape" implies that the sexual assault took place between dating partners. Nonetheless, we noted that a number of respondents emphasized "acquaintance rape". Sexual assault educators use both the terms date and acquaintance rape, with the latter term emphasizing the fact that the victims of sexual assault typically *know* the assailant. Date rape has a specific dynamic—it occurs on a date. Three types of responses emerged: definitions referring to dating partners only, those referring to acquaintances, and those referring to neither dating partners nor acquaintances.

Theme 5: Relevance of Gender in the Understanding of Date Rape Respondents differed in whether they provided a gender-neutral or gender-specific understanding of date rape. A response was coded *gender-neutral* if the respondent indicated that either a man or woman could be either the perpetrator or the victim of rape or sexual assault. For example:

Date rape is when one person has sex with another person who has not given consent. (male participant)

Date rape occurs when a person who is a friend or acquaintance forces sexual vaginal intercourse on another person where this victim has not been given consent and has said no. It can be a date rape for either male or female. For the males, the female forces him to perform vaginal intercourse on her without his consent. (female participant)

Date rape occurs at ANY time when either a male or a female is doing or being forced to do something that they do not want to do and have expressed this by saying "NO" or something equivalent. (male participant)

Two respondents explained that rape could occur in heterosexual or homosexual contexts. For example: "Date rape is forcible sexual contact or sexual intercourse. It could be man-man, or man-woman, or woman-woman on a date" (male participant).

A definition was coded *gender-specific* if its author indicated that the gender of the perpetrator was male and the gender of the victim was female. If the respondent implied that date rape was gendered, the definition was coded as *gender-implied*. Consider the following examples:

Date rape is when a female is forced to have sexual intercourse without her consent. Even if she is in bed with her date and changes her mind to say no and he still proceeds, that is date rape too. (female participant)

Where a woman is forced against her will. The man feels she must want it, and though she says no, or struggles, he has sex with her. (male participant)

A male and female go out socially or are at home socially and the male physically forces his body on the female's body and has sex with her knowing fully that she does not want him to have sex with her. She is making physical movements away from him. (female participant)

The category *gender-implied* was included after we noted that several respondents provided definitions using personal pronouns that, when read from the first-person perspective, indicated a gendered understanding of date rape. In other words, when the definition is read, one can guess whether the respondent was a male or a female if one acknowledges the fact that females are more often the victims and males the perpetrators of rape. For instance, a male respondent said, "Date rape is when your date says no to your come-on but you continue because you want to have sex". Another respondent wrote,

"Date rape is when you say NO and they don't understand NO and force unwanted sex with you. [It's] forced sex or anything you don't want to do against your own will." This respondent was a woman. And finally, "It's when you want to get laid, but the other person doesn't want to, but is forced into sex" (male respondent). Because a gendered understanding is evident, these definitions were recoded for the subsequent statistical analysis as gender-specific.

Quantitative Analysis

The issues identified in the qualitative analyses were analysed with respect to their occurrence as a function of gender and age. Specifically, the definition of rape was assessed in terms of the sex act identified, the understanding of consent and force, and the context in which the rape occurred (see Table 16.1).

The responses were also analysed to determine the percentage of respondents who provided gender-neutral, gender-specific, and gender-implied understandings of date rape. This analysis was done for the overall sample, and for males and females and age cohorts (see Table 16.2 and Table 16.3).

Theme 1: Type of Sexual Act or Acts Referred to in the Definition
Traditionally, the social and legal definition of *rape* refers to vaginal penetration. Consistent with this understanding, 50% of the sample defined date rape in this way. Interestingly, 46.5% of respondents indicated that the term referred to any unwanted sexual contact (this approach is consistent with the more inclusive notion implied by the current legal definition of sexual assault). Only 3.5% of the sample did not mention the type of sexual act, perhaps because they assume it to refer to the traditional understanding of sexual intercourse. Using a Chi-square analysis, we found a significant gender difference, with far more women (57.8%) identifying sexual intercourse as the sex act than men (38.2%), $\chi^2 (2, n = 170) = 9.37$, $p < .001$

Table 16.1 Participants' Definitions of "Date Rape" in Relation to the Themes of Sexual Act, Consent, Use of Force, and Context

| | Number and % of Responses in Each Category | | | | | | |
| | Overall | | Female | | Male | | |
Coding	n	%	n	%	n	%	χ^2
Which sex act definition refers to:							
Forced Intercourse	85	50.0	59	57.8	26	38.2	
Any Forced Sexual Contact	79	46.5	42	41.2	37	54.4	
No Mention of Sex Act	6	3.5	1	1.0	5	7.4	9.37[a]
Reference made to consent:							
Referred to lack of consent	74	43.5	34	33.3	40	58.8	
Defined consent behaviour	79	46.5	59	57.8	20	29.4	
Did not mention consent	17	10.0	9	8.8	8	11.8	13.54[a]
Reference made to use of force:							
Referred to use of force	64	37.6	38	37.3	26	38.2	
Defined forceful behaviour	56	32.9	38	37.3	18	26.5	
Did not mention use of force	50	29.4	26	25.5	24	35.3	2.78[ns]
Reference made to context:							
Refers only to dating partner	87	51.2	53	52.0	34	50.0	
Refers to any acquaintance	26	15.3	16	15.7	10	14.7	
No mention of context	57	33.5	33	32.3	24	35.3	0.16[ns]

[a] $p < .01$;
ns = non-significant

Table 16.2 Number and Percentage of Respondents Who Provided Gender-Neutral versus Gender-Specific Definitions of Date Rape

| | Gender of Respondent | | | | | | |
| | Overall | | Female | | Male | | |
Definition Type	n	%	n	%	n	%	χ^2
Gender-neutral	109	64.1	57	55.9	52	76.5	
Gender-specific	23	13.5	17	16.7	6	8.8	
Gender-implied	38	22.4	28	27.5	10	14.7	7.517[a]
(Gender-specific & gender-implied)	(61)	35.9	(45)	(44.2)	(16)	(23.5)	7.517[a]
Total	170	100%	102	100%	68	100%	

[a] $p < .05$

(see Table 16.1). Age was not a significant predictor of type of sex act identified, χ^2 (8, $n = 170) = 11.31$, $p > .05$.

Theme 2: Understanding of Consent The overwhelming majority of respondents (90%) identified consent as an issue, and about half of them (46.5%) described what consent entailed. More women (57.8%) than men (29.4%) explained the kind of behaviour that would indicate consent or lack of consent whereas men were more likely than women to identify

Table 16.3 Number and Percentage of Females and Males in Each Age Category Who Provided Gender-Neutral, Gender-Specific, or Gender-Implied Definitions of Date Rape

Age	Definition Type	Female n	Female %	Male n	Male %	χ^2
18–21	Gender-Neutral	12	63.2	22	84.6	
(n=45)	Gender-Specific	3	15.8	1	3.8	
	Gender-Implied	4	21.1	3	11.5	
22–29	Gender-Neutral	9	47.4	16	69.9	
(n=46)	Gender-Specific	5	26.3	4	17.4	
	Gender-Implied	5	26.3	3	13.0	
30–39	Gender-Neutral	15	53.6	10	83.3	
(n=40)	Gender-Specific	5	17.9	—	—	
	Gender-Implied	8	28.6	2	16.7	
40–59	Gender-Neutral	17	60.7	4	66.7	
(n=34)	Gender-Specific	3	10.7	—	—	
	Gender-Implied	8	28.6	2	33.3	
60+	Gender-Neutral	4	50.0	—	—	
(n=8)	Gender-Specific	1	12.5	—	—	
	Gender-Implied	3	37.5	—	—	7.502[ns]
	Total	102		68		

ns = non-significant

lack of consent, χ^2 (2, $n = 170$) = 13.54, $p < .001$ (see Table 16.1). Age did not predict understanding of consent, χ^2 (8, $n = 170$) = 8.05, $p > .05$.

Theme 3: Understanding of the Use of Force
Overall, 70.5% of participants referred to force as an aspect of date rape. However, only about one third of the sample (32.9%) explained what behaviour constituted force. Although more women (37.3%) than men (26.5%) provided definitions of what behaviour constituted the use of force, this difference was not statistically significant, χ^2 (2, $n = 170$) = 2.78, $p > .05$ (see Table 16.1). Age did not predict understanding of force, χ^2 (8, $n = 170$) = 4.92, $p > .05$.

Theme 4: Context: Dating versus Any Acquaintance The majority (51.2%) of the respondents referred to the rape as occurring between dating partners. Approximately one third of the participants (33.5%) did not refer to the context (dating versus acquaintance situations), probably because to them the term date rape implied that the context was a date. Another 15.3% of respondents extended the definition to specify that these rapes could occur between acquaintances. There were no significant differences as a function of gender or age of respondents with respect to the context of the date rape, largest χ^2 (8, $n = 170$) = 4.66, $p > .05$ (see Table 16.1).

Theme 5: Relevance of Gender in the Understanding of Date Rape The majority of respondents (64.1%) provided gender-neutral definitions of date rape. When broken down by gender, men (76.5%) were significantly more likely than women (55.9%) to provide gender-neutral definitions of date rape, χ^2 (2, $n = 170$) = 7.52, $p < .05$ (see Table 16.2). Age was not a significant factor in explaining the participants' understanding of the role of gender, χ^2 (8, $n = 170$) = 7.50, $p > .05$ (see Table 16.3).

DISCUSSION

The definition of rape for the participants in this study corresponds with many elements of the feminist discourse on sexual violence. The majority of participants incorporated the concepts of consent and force in their definitions. In fact, significant proportions of the sample further defined what behaviours constituted consent (and refusal) and the use of force, perhaps reflecting the feminist lobbying efforts around consent issues, which resulted in legislative amendments such as Bill C-49 (which set guidelines regarding the definition of consent and the admissibility of a woman's sexual history during a trial) (Roberts & Mohr, 1994).

Feminists have actively sought to shift the construction of rape from a crime of passion to a physical assault on the person (Clarke & Lewis, 1977; Hinch, 1988; Osborne, 1994). This shift is certainly reflected in the fact that nearly half the sample extended the term rape to include all sexual acts imposed by force. It is also noteworthy that the majority of respondents provided gender-neutral definitions of date rape. This finding reflects the so-called "degendering" of the sexual assault law, which sought to eliminate the sex discrimination in the old rape law through the use of the gender-neutral term sexual assault. It appears, then, that much of the feminist discourse on rape and sexual assault has had an impact on the current social construction of rape.

The findings suggest that while feminist-based lobbying has been successful in certain ways, far more effort is needed to convey that rape and sexual assault is a gendered act of violence. Some feminists argued that the term sexual assault would lead to a degendering of rape (Los, 1994; Roberts & Mohr, 1994). Among our sample, awareness that rape was a gendered phenomenon was more evident among women than men. Even among women, however, only about half of the sample provided a gendered understanding of date rape. Women and men also differed on other elements of the definition. Women were more likely to emphasize rape and to mention and/or define consent. Our findings corroborate other research indicating a gender difference in men's and women's accounts of violence against women (Dobash, Dobash, Cavanagh & Lewis, 1998), and men's and women's adherence to date rape myth (Lonsway & Fitzgerald, 1994).

Why women and men hold different understandings of date rape is unclear. It may be that the campaigns associated with the feminist anti-rape movement have engaged women more than men. Women's magazines have written feature articles on rape and sexual assault and documented the feminist critique of rape and sexual assault law and prosecutions (Hinch, 1988; Verberg, 1998). Women may also be more sensitive to the gendered nature of rape because they are most likely to be the victims (Koss, Gidycz & Wisniewski, 1987; DeKeseredy, Schwartz & Tait, 1993), and because most women fear rape (Statistics Canada, 1993) along with the social humiliation that accompanies the "status" of being a rape victim (Gardner, 1990; Riger & Gordon, 1981) and the experience of being put "on trial" if they were involved in legal proceedings (Department of Justice, Canada, 1990).

On the other hand, all changes in the law pertaining to rape (sexual assault) have been widely publicized in the mainstream press. Moreover, sexual assault awareness and prevention courses target both women and men. In addition, these courses have been introduced recently in male domains such as the military (Sorenson et al., 1992). Perhaps then, we should not be surprised that both men and women perceive being a victim of rape as a possible event in their lives.

The tendency of the present sample to ascribe rape as gender-neutral may be a direct reflection of the media's emphasis on the gender neutrality of sexual coercion, even if this emphasis contradicts what we know about sexual coercion and gender relations. Observers of the media coverage of feminist antiviolence lobbies have remarked on the way that the media will mainstream certain feminist messages while obfuscating others (Croft, 1981; Stone, 1993). Others have argued that in the process of law reform, only the most conservative of the feminists' recommendations for change were adopted, such as adopting the term sexual assault (see Boyle, 1984; Hinch, 1988; Osborne, 1984).

We are left with the question raised by feminists a decade ago. What is to be gained and what is lost by the emphasis on a gender-neutral definition of sexual assault? Maybe we can take this question further and ask, "What does it mean for the prospects of real and enduring social change if men are less likely to appreciate that rape and sexual assault are typically gendered in this society?" For sexual assault awareness and prevention educators, the concern is how to convey the understanding that although either men or women can experience sexual coercion, the fact remains that rape and sexual assault remain gendered acts of violence.

STUDY QUESTIONS

1. What is the advantage of using both qualitative and quantitative analysis in the context of this study?

2. To what extent was the authors' claim that "much of the feminist discourse on rape and sexual assault has had an impact on the current social construction of rape" directly supported by the data?

3. What would have been a stronger research design to measure change from pre-1980s to today?

4. In the section on Theme 3, the authors give the percentage of subjects that explained what constituted force. Did the authors state whether the participants were asked to explain force? How does this affect the reader's interpretation of the frequencies reported?

5. Are there errors in the numbers and percentages reported in Table 16.1? Explain.

REFERENCES

Begin, P. (1989). Rape law reform in Canada: Evaluating Impact. In E. Viano (Ed.), *Crime and Its Victims: International and Public Policy Issues*. New York: Hemisphere Publishing.

Boyle, C. (1984). *Sexual Assault*. Toronto: Carswell.

Brownmiller, S. (1970). *Against Our Will: Men, Women and Rape*. New York: Bantam.

Clark, L., & Lewis, D. (1977). *Rape: The Price of Coercive Sexuality*. Toronto: The Women's Press.

Croft, N. (1981). Drifting from the mainstream: Anti-rape organization. In F. Delacoste & F. Newman (Eds.), *Fight Back: Feminist Resistance to Male Violence*. Minneapolis: Cleis Press.

DeKeseredy, W., Schwartz, M., & Tait, K. (1993). Sexual assault and stranger aggression on a Canadian university campus. *Sex Roles, 28,* 263–277.

Department of Justice. (1990). *Sexual Assault Legislation in Canada: An Evaluation*. Ottawa: Research Section, Department of Justice, Canada.

Dobash, R., Dobash, R., Cavanagh, K., & Lewis, R. (1998). Separate and intersecting realities: A comparison of men's and women's accounts of violence against women. *Violence Against Women, 4,* 382–414.

Donat, P., & D'Emilio, P. (1992). A feminist re-definition of rape and sexual assault: Historical foundations and change. *Journal of Social Issues, 48,* 9–22.

Gardner, C. (1990). Safe conduct: Women, crime, and self in public place. *Social Problems, 37,* 311–328.

Glaser, B., & Strauss, A. (1967). *The Discovery of Grounded Theory: Strategies for Qualitative Research*. New York: Aldine.

Hickman, S., & Muehlenhard, C. (1999). By the semi-mystical appearance of a condom: How young women and men communicate sexual consent in heterosexual situations. *The Journal of Sex Research, 36,* 258–272.

Hinch, R. (1988). Inconsistencies and contradictions in Canada's sexual assault law. *Canadian Public Policy, 14,* 282–294.

Humphreys, T.P. (2000). Sexual consent in heterosexual dating relationships: attitudes and behaviours of university students. Unpublished Ph.D. dissertation. University of Guelph.

Kasinsky, R. (1978). The anti-rape movement in Canada. In M. Beyer-Gammon (Ed.), *Violence in Canada*. Toronto: Methuen.

Koss, M., Gidycz, C., & Wisniewski, N. (1987). The scope of rape: Incidence and prevalence of sexual aggression and victimization in a national sample of higher educated students. *Journal of Consulting and Clinical Psychology, 55,* 162–170.

Lonsway, K.A., & Fitzgerald, L. (1994). Rape myth: In Review. *Psychology of Women Quarterly, 18,* 133–164.

Los, M. (1994). The struggle to redefine rape in the early 1980s. In J. Roberts & J. Mohr (Eds.), *Confronting Sexual Assault: A Decade of Legal and Social Change.* Toronto: University of Toronto Press.

McNickle-Rose, V. (1977). Rape as a social problem: A byproduct of the feminist movement. *Social Problems, 25,* 75–89.

Muehlenhard, C. (1995/1996). The complexities of sexual consent. *Siecus Report, 24,* 5–7.

Muehlenhard, C., Powich, I., Phelps, J., & Giusti, L. (1992). Definitions of rape: Scientific and political implications. *Journal of Social Issues, 48,* 23–44.

National Association of Women and the Law. (1979). *Recommendations on Sexual Assault Offences.* Ottawa.

National Association of Women and the Law. (1981). *A New Image for Sexual Offences in the Criminal Code: A Brief in Response to Bill C-53.* Ottawa.

Osborne, J. (1984). Rape law reform: The new cosmetic for Canadian women. *Women and Politics, 4,* 49–64.

Pride, A. (1981). To respectibility and back: A ten year review of the anti-rape movement. In F. Delacoste & F. Newman (Eds.), *Fight Back: Feminist Resistance to Male Violence.* Minneapolis: Cleis Press.

Riger, S., & Gordon. M. (1981). The fear of rape: A study in social control. *Journal Of Social Issues, 37,* 71–90.

Roberts, J., & Mohr, R. (1994). *Confronting Sexual Assault: A Decade of Legal and Social Change.* Toronto: University of Toronto Press.

Sorenson, S., & White, J. (1992). Adult sexual assault: Overview of research. *Journal of Social Issues, 48,* 18.

Statistics Canada. (1993, Nov.). The violence against women survey. *The Daily.*

Stone, S. (1993). Getting the message out: Feminists, the press, and violence against women. *Canadian Review of Sociology and Anthropology, 30,* 377–400.

Strauss, A. (1987). *Qualitative Analysis for Social Scientists.* New York: Cambridge.

Verberg, N. (1998). Feminism and the media: What the women's magazines teach women about sexual assault. Paper presented at the Canadian Sociology and Anthropology Association, Ottawa, Canada.

NOTES

NOTES

0 1341 1387530 3

NOTES